Computer Supported Cooperative Work

Springer

London
Berlin
Heidelberg
New York
Barcelona
Hong Kong
Milan
Paris
Singapore
Tokyo

A list of out of print titles is available at the end of the book

Elayne Coakes, Dianne Willis and
Steve Clarke (Eds)

Knowledge Management in the SocioTechnical World

The Graffiti Continues

With 46 Figures

Springer

Elayne Coakes, BA, MSc, MIDP, AMBCS
Westminster Business School, University of Westminister,
35 Marylebone Road, London NW1 5LS, UK

Dianne Willis, BA, MA, AMBCS
School of Information Management, Leeds Metropolitan University,
Beckett Park Campus, Leeds LS6 3QS, UK

Steve Clarke, BSc, MBA, PhD
Department of Finance, Systems and Operations, University of Luton,
Park Square, Luton LU1 3JU, UK

Series Editors
Dan Diaper, PhD, MBCS
Head, Department of Computing, School of Design, Engineering and Computing,
Bournemouth University, Talbot Campus, Fern Barrow, Poole, Dorset BH12 5BB, UK
Colston Sanger
Shottersley Research Limited, Little Shottersley, Farnham Lane,
Haslemere, Surrey GU27 1HA, UK

British Library Cataloguing in Publication Data
A catalogue record for this book is available from the British Library

Library of Congress Cataloging-in-Publication Data
Knowledge management in the sociotechnical world: the grafitti continues/Elayne Coakes,
Dianne Willis, and Steve Clarke (eds.)
       p. cm. – (Computer supported cooperative work)
   Includes bibliographical references and index.
   ISBN 1-85233-441-X (alk. paper)
   1. Knowledge management. I. Coakes, Elayne, 1950– II. Willis, Dianne, 1952–
   III. Clarke Steve, 1950– IV. Series
   HD30.2.K6374 2001
   658.4′038–dc21   200145965

ISBN 1-85233-441-X Springer-Verlag London Berlin Heidelberg
a member of BertelsmannSpringer Science+Business Media GmbH
http://www.springer.co.uk

© Springer-Verlag London Limited 2002
Printed in Great Britain

Typesetting: Gray Publishing, Tunbridge Wells
Printed and bound at the Athenæum Press Ltd., Gateshead, Tyne & Wear
34/3830-543210 Printed on acid-free paper SPIN 10792887

Contents

List of Contributors

W. Al-Karaghouli
Westminster Business School, University of Westminster, 35 Marylebone Road, London NW1 8LS, UK
Email: Alkarawy@wmin.ac.uk

S. Alshawi
Brunel University, Uxbridge Road, Middlesex UB8 3PH, UK
Email: Sarmad.AlShawi@brunel.ac.uk

Anders Avdic
Department of Informatics, Örebro University, SE-701 82 Örebro, Sweden
Email: anders.avdic@esa.oru.se

Derek Binney
Chief Knowledge Officer, Global Knowledge Management Services, (GKMS), Asia & Australia, CSC, 6th Flr, Christie Street, St Leonards, NSW Australia 2065
Email: dbinney@csc.com.au

Anton Bradburn
Westminster Business School, University of Westminster, 35 Marylebone Road, London NW1 8LS, UK
E-mail: bradbua@wmin.ac.uk

Ewa Braf
Jönköping International Business School, PO 1026, S-551 11 Jönköping, Sweden
Email: ewa.braf@ihh.hj.se

Jason-Phillip Camilleri
McKinsey & Co., 55 East 52nd Street, New York NY 10055, USA
Email: jason_camilleri@mckinsey.com

Steve Clarke
Department of Finance, Systems and Operations, University of Luton, Park Square, Luton LU1 3JU, UK
Email: Steve.Clarke@Luton.ac.uk

Elayne Coakes
Westminster Business School, University of Westminster, 35 Marylebone Road, London NW1 8LS, UK
Email: coakese@wmin.ac.uk

Christine Cuthbertson
Oxford Institute of Retail Management, Templeton College, University of Oxford, Oxford OX1 5NY, UK
Email: Christine.Cuthbertson@templeton.oxford.ac.uk

Fredrik Ericsson
Department of Informatics, Örebro University, SE-701 82 Örebro, Sweden
Email: fredrik.ericsson@esa.oru.se

John Farrington
Royal Navy, UK, c/o MOD, Whitehall, London

G. Fitzgerald
Brunel University, Uxbridge Road, Middlesex UB8 3PH, UK
Email: Guy.Fitzgerald@brunel.ac.uk

Göran Goldkuhl
CMTO, Linköping University, SE-581 83 Linkoping, Sweden
Email: Ggo@ida.liu.se

Matti Hannus
VTT – Technical Research Centre of Finland, P.O. Box 1801, FIN-02044 VTT, Finland
Email: Matti.Hannus@vtt.fi

Jimmy C. Huang
University of Aberdeen, Department of Management Studies, Dunbar Street, Aberdeen AB24 3QY, UK
Email: j.huang@abdn.ac.uk

Christian Ifvarsson
Department of Business Administration and Social Science, Luleå University of Technology, SE-971 87 Luleå, Sweden
Email: Christian.ifvarsson@ies.luth.se

Abdul Samad (Sami) Kazi
VTT – Technical Research Centre of Finland, P.O. Box 1801, FI-02044 VTT, Finland
Email: Sami.Kazi@vtt.fi

Shan Ling Pan

Assistant Professor of Information Systems, Department of Information Systems, School of Computing, National University of Singapore, Block S17 04-23, 3 Science Drive 2, Singapore 117543
Email: PANSL@comp.nus.edu.sg

Keith Patrick

School of Computing Information Systems and Mathematics, South Bank University, 103 Borough Road, Southwark, London SE1 0AA, UK
Email: patrick@sbu.ac.uk

Jonathan D. Pemberton

Newcastle Business School, Northumberland Building, University of Northumbria, Newcastle upon Tyne NE1 8ST, UK
Email: jon.pemberton@unn.ac.uk

Nigel Phillips

School of Computing Information Systems and Mathematics, South Bank University, 103 Borough Road, Southwark, London SE1 0AA, UK
Email: phillinp@sbu.ac.uk

Jari Puttonen

Fortum Engineering Ltd, P.O. Box 10, FIN-00048 FORTUM, Finland
Email: jari.puttonen@fortum.com

Steve Russell

Email: steverus_uk@hotmail.com

Vicki Scholtz

IT Manager, Humanities Faculty, University of Cape Town, Rondebosch 7701, South Africa
Email: vicki@humanities.uct.ac.za

George H. Stonehouse

Newcastle Business School, Northumberland Building, University of Northumbria, Newcastle upon Tyne NE1 8ST, UK
Email: george.stonehouse@unn.ac.uk

Gill Sugden

Westminster Business School, University of Westminster, 35 Marylebone Road, London NW1 5LS, UK
Email: gill@wmin.ac.uk

Mika Sulkusalmi

Fortum Engineering Ltd, P.O. Box 10, FIN-00048 FORTUM, Finland

Pekka Välikangas
Fortum Engineering Ltd, P.O. Box 10, FIN-00048 FORTUM, Finland
Email: pekka.valikangas@fortum.com

Dianne Willis
School of Information Management, Leeds Metropolitan University, Beckett
Park Campus, Leeds LS6 3QS, UK
Email: d.willis@lmu.ac.uk

Jessi Qing Yi
Personal Communications Sector, Motorola, 600 North US Highway 45,
Libertyville, IL 60048, USA
Email: Jessi.Yi@motorola.com

Yougjin Yoo
Weatherhead School of Management, Case Western Reserve University,
10900 Euclid Avenue, Cleveland, OH 44106-7135, USA
Email: Yxy23@po.cwru.edu

Chapter 1
Introduction

Elayne Coakes, Dianne Willis and Steve Clarke

The effective use of knowledge management in organisations is an essential factor in their successful operation, but knowledge management is a many faceted domain, in which there is a danger of emphasising only a limited view.

The purpose of this book is therefore to present for discussion those issues which practitioners and researchers have found to be critical to understanding and progress within the knowledge management domain. This seems to have led quite naturally to the study of knowledge management from three perspectives: technology, organisations and people, which in turn makes this the first text to present a sociotechnical view of knowledge management.

Knowledge management has been a major topic for management academics and practitioners alike in the 1990s. It may be seen as the extraction and conversion of tacit knowledge on an individual and organisational level into explicit knowledge, the latter often taking the form of specific electronic tools or assets which can be manipulated for competitive gain (e.g. intranets, groupware and knowledge repositories).

> Tacit knowledge is often described as the "hunches, intuition and know-how" of people; or "skills, routines, competencies".

There is some scepticism about the extent to which this often highly subjective knowledge and learning can actually be made explicit, and a feeling that knowledge management is no more than a new form of technology. But knowledge is much more than technology: it is personal, often dormant or unconscious and closely bound up with learning and organisation theory. Learning, in turn, has been described as the way in which an organisation enhances its knowledge. If so, how is this done and what is the role of information technology (IT) and information systems within this?

A growing number of studies have called for a more holistic, systemic approach to knowledge. It is not simply a tool or resource so much as a social construct. It is a reciprocal, interdependent process of learning arising from knowledge transfer and information flow and communication.

> Hence the sociotechnical perspective explored in this text, which amalgamates the dualism of people and technology and allows the organisation to adapt to the environment.

The recent book *'The New SocioTech: Graffiti on the Long Wall'* (Coakes, Willis and Lloyd-Jones, 2000) provided an up-to-date overview of modern approaches to the sociotechnical perspective, and this book expands that overview into the modern knowledge management domain. Further, the application of social theory to the domain of knowledge management has not been addressed in any major text to date, but is the subject of a number of journal articles. This text brings together current thinking in this area.

This book, which is grounded in practical case studies and includes a practitioner as well as an academic approach, should appeal to knowledge management practitioners and academics, general managers, management information systems managers, human resources managers and researchers in the field of information systems. The international approach will provide an overview of how knowledge management is addressed across different cultures.

The approach taken of "know-why, know-what, know-who and know-how" takes as its foundation key questions commonly addressed in studies underpinned by a social perspective. The "how" questions privileging a technical view, and the "what" questions concerned with issues of debate in a social environment, may be seen as the foundation of sociotechnical approaches. The "who" and "why" questions seek to determine issues of power, which might be seen as distorting sociotechnical issues. (See Garud, 1997, for a further discussion on this matter.)

The chapter by Coakes clearly sets the sociotechnical framework for the rest of the book. It is by comparison with this work that we can see the sociotechnical aspects more clearly as they are brought out and developed in other chapters.

In the first section, "Know-Why", Binney, Goldkuhl and Braf, Scholz, and Yoo and Ifvarsson each offer their individual perspectives on the sociotechnical approach to knowledge management. Binney takes a strong line on the need and importance of the human factor based on his practical experience. Goldkuhl and Braf offer a focus of organisational ability and introduce a range of knowledge management aspects, individual knowledge, institutionalised shared knowledge, artefacts' functionality, and linguistic and pictorial descriptions of ability, discussing the need for congruence. Scholtz' work looks at a "knowledge business" and examines whether the same knowledge management principles apply here, investigating whether this work can provide guidelines for other organisations. Yoo and Ifvarsson investigate the perennial problem of why large IT investment in information systems fails to produce the expected returns. The sociotechnical nature of organisations forms the core of this analysis, leading to a people-based analysis of how to be effective.

In the second section, "Know-What", Phillips and Patrick, and Pemberton and Stonehouse bring the people aspect under closer consideration. Phillips and Patrick are concerned with a personality type analysis and the effects this has in terms of working patterns, and investigate the possibility of generic knowledge management solutions based on this analysis. Pemberton and Stonehouse address the importance of individual knowledge in organisational development through the "knowledge-centric organisation". The sociotechnical perspective highlights the importance of the interplay between the social aspects of an organisation and the technological infrastructure, forming a means by which new knowledge assets can be created, shared and communicated.

In the third section, "Know-Who", Huang and Pan, Yi, and Ericsson and Avdic bring a case-study focus to the book. All the work is based on current applications of knowledge management, and hence provides the practical dimension which is such a key dimension of this text. Huang and Pan present work based on Boots The Chemists, a knowledge-intensive organisation in the British retailing industry. They emphasise the benefits of a social construction approach. Yi looks at Motorola and a community of practice, an area of great importance for a sociotechnical perspective being concerned with human networks. Ericsson and Avdic take a manufacturing angle, and address IT system design for decision support, looking at how to minimise organisational disturbance to maximise effectiveness.

In the final section, "Know-How", Cuthbertson and Farrington, Kazi, Puttonen, Sulkusalmi, Välikangas and Hannus, Al-Karaghouli, Fitzgerald and Alshawi, and Coakes, Sugden, Russell, Camilleri and Bradburn again take a case-based approach to the issues of technology; organisations and people. The focus here is the capture, sharing and organisation of knowledge in a variety of settings. Cuthbertson and Farrington use an explicitly sociotechnical framework to consider the knowledge management process from initiation to implementation. Kazi, Putonen, Valikangas and Hannus address issues of knowledge creation and management at Fortum Engineering to illustrate the sociotechnical perspective. Al-Karaghouli, Fitzgerald and Alshawi move down the line to the requirements stage of knowledge systems. They stress the need for communication on a human-to-human basis as the only tenable starting point for success, human-to-machine communication being unable to produce an effective system which is then often regarded as a failure. Finally, Coakes et al. take a more in-depth look at tacit knowledge in knowledge-intensive firms by examining two management consultancies in the UK and the USA. They provide evidence of a clear sociotechnical implementation, with the importance of technology for tacit knowledge sharing being found to be of lesser importance than the desire to so share.

All that remains for us, as editors, is the hope that you, the readers, will enjoy and find interesting this new perspective on knowledge management.

Chapter 2
Knowledge Management: A Sociotechnical Perspective

Elayne Coakes

Knowledge comes but wisdom lingers (Tennyson 1842)

2.1 Introduction

This chapter takes a sociotechnical perspective on the organisational issue of knowledge management.

Sociotechnical perspectives can be characterised as holistic, and whilst not being panoptic in character, take a more encompassing view of the organisation, its stakeholders in knowledge and the environment in which it operates, than many other organisational views which are limited by their origins and paradigms.

The word sociotechnical, in its origins, is a combination of two paradigms: the social and the technical. It was thus intended to describe a broader view of the role of technology in an organisation than either paradigm could offer on its own. Technology, it was argued, should be seen, discussed and developed not just as a technical artefact but in the light of the social environment in which it operated.

Thus, it is acknowledged by many writers that strategies today should optimise the contribution of both people and information through technology support.

> The "real" information system is the system built on organisational culture and interpersonal communication (Liebenau and Backhouse, 1990); this "real" information system contains the rich and dynamic tacit knowledge which, when harnessed effectively, can give organisations sector and market advantage.

This chapter discusses the social and technical issues relating to harnessing this knowledge. An overview of the origins of the sociotechnical paradigm is first given, drawing out the common principles that enlighten this paradigm. This is followed by a discussion of knowledge and the management of knowledge, showing this author's argument of where and how these principles are applicable. The chapter concludes with a brief discussion of the author's research in progress and where future research may lead.

This chapter is based on material previously published in OR42 Keynote Papers, edited by S. Clarke. © Operational Research Society 2000. Reprinted with permission.

2.2 The Sociotechnical Paradigm

The term "sociotechnical" is commonly applied to the study of systems, particularly within organisations. The sociotechnical paradigm is now over fifty years old in its application to organisational design, although it is possible to trace the origins of the paradigm back to earlier writers on philosophy such as Edmund Burke and writers on the Industrial Revolution (see Mumford, 1996, for further details on these), and also theorists such as Mary Parker Follett (1920, 1924).

In its best-known incarnation, the paradigm can be located in the work of Fred Emery and Eric Trist at the Tavistock Institute, London, and in particular, in the now seminal Longwall Mining Study of Trist and Bamford (1951), where the researchers identified the need for a sociotechnical approach in which an appropriate social system could be developed in keeping with the new technical system. One definition of the term sociotechnical therefore is:

> the study of the relationships and interrelationships between the social and technical parts of any system.

The sociotechnical perspective was frequently found during the 1950s and later in many Scandinavian industrial democracy studies (Elcon, 1979; Larsen, 1979; Bjerknes and Brattenberg 1995), as well as other European and British studies where the issues of the social systems' relationships to the technical systems within a manufacturing environment were of concern (Cooper and Mumford, 1979; Mumford 1997). A number of local variants of sociotechnical systems (STS) have been produced in Europe, North America and Australia over the fifty years since the work of the Tavistock Institute became well known, but with all, the idea of changing the division of labour within firms to achieve a participatory democracy is a main focus (van Eijnatten, 1993).

In the discussions of the applicability of the sociotechnical principles, it is generally considered that these principles, and the methods of application associated with them, help organisations to explore conflicts and complexity in the human, organisational and technical aspects of change. They relate to how jointly to optimise people and technology within a clear ethical principle:

Sociotechnical principles, therefore, have been discussed and applied to organisational change for the following purposes:

> that the individual's participation in decision making and control over their immediate work environment is enabled and increased.

- the joint optimisation of technology and people to introduce improvement within the organisation;
- the improvement of the quality of products and services;
- the improvement of communications and the relationships amongst organisational stakeholders;
- the improvement of the organisational sensitivity and responsiveness to change in complex environments;

- the enhancement of aspects of individual work such as performance levels, involvement, skill levels, job satisfaction and reward structures;
- the creation of a culture and structure which encourages continuous improvements in effectiveness.

There are several generic principles applied across all STS variants and initiatives. Cherns (1976) expressed the underlying assumptions of sociotechnical design for organisational change to have nine key principles. In his later work (Cherns, 1987) where he revisited his earlier article and commented on the increasing divergence between the Scandinavian and North American approaches and applications, he also revisited his original principles and added a tenth. Table 2.1 shows the original nine principles and their revised order and content from the later work.

Thus, the goal of sociotechnical design is to produce a system capable of self-modification, of adapting to change, and of making the most of the creative capacities of the individual for the benefit of the organisation.

It also evident from the comments shown in Table 2.1 that much of Cherns' work on the sociotechnical principles has a direct impact on our discussion about knowledge management.

2.3 Knowledge and the Management of Knowledge

2.3.1 A Sociotechnical View of Knowledge

> Knowledge is the capacity of an organisation and its staff to act effectively, as shown in Cherns' principles: a sociotechnical perspective.

It has been said (Roth, 1999) that most of our knowledge management efforts have been focused on the codifying, archiving and retrieving of information. Thinking of knowledge as something that can be stored and retrieved confuses it with information.

Nurminen (1987) classifies the sociotechnical perspective for information systems into seven aspects: knowledge, users, actors in information tasks, communication tasks, information technology (IT) systems in organisation, IT systems and organisation, and systems development.

In this classification, the IT system interfaces between the social and technical systems for the users (by user-friendly means of communication and action in information tasks), and knowledge is considered to be objective but instrumental. The social system in sociotechnical terms is here usually considered to be the attributes of people (attitudes, skills, values, etc.), the relationship amongst them, the reward systems and the authority structures. The technical systems in these terms include the processes, tasks and technology needed to perform the organisation's operations.

Table 2.1 Cherns' principles from 1976 and 1987 with comments

1976 principles and order	Brief explanation	1987 principles and order	Further comments
1. Compatibility	"the process of design must be compatible with its objectives" (p. 785)	1. Compatibility	"Design is an arena for conflict" (p. 154). Design has to satisfy an array of objectives which may conflict and therefore decisions must be reached by consensus and not by power plays
2. Minimal critical specification	"no more should be specified than is absolutely essential ... requires that we identify what is essential" (p. 786). What is done not how it is done is important	2. Minimal critical specification	"premature closure of options is a pervasive fault in design; it arises, not only because of the desire to reduce uncertainty, but also because it helps the designer to get his own way" (p. 155). Success is measured less by design quality than by the quantity of own ideas and preferences that are incorporated. Assumptions should be challenged
3. The sociotechnical criterion	"variances, if they cannot be eliminated, must be controlled as near to their point of origin as possible" (p. 787). Variances here mean unprogrammed events, a key variance being one that critically affects outcome. People should be allowed to inspect and challenge their own quality of work and make their own judgements and decisions as to how to improve: to learn continuously	3. Variance control	"sociotechnical analysis does not end with the variance control table. The social system is more than an effective system for the control of technical and raw materials variances" (p. 156)
4. The multifunctional principle: organism vs mechanism	"there are several routes to the same goal – the principle sometimes described as equifinality" (p. 788). The same function can be performed in different ways by using different combinations of elements	7. The multifunction principle	"organisations need to adapt to their environments; elements of organisations need to adapt to their environments of which the most important are usually other organisational elements" (p. 158)

(Cont'd)

Table 2.1 (*Continued*)

1976 principles and order	Brief explanation	1987 principles and order	Further comments
5. Boundary location	"the more the control of activities within the department becomes the responsibility of the members, the more the role of the supervisor/foreman/manager is concentrated on the boundary activities – ensuring that the team has adequate resources to carry out its activities, co-ordinating activities with those of other departments and foreseeing the changes likely to impinge upon them" (p. 789). Boundaries should not interfere with the sharing of knowledge and experience	4. Boundary location	"its essential feature is that boundaries should *not* be drawn so as to impede the sharing of knowledge and learning" (p. 156)
6. Information flow	"information systems should be designed to provide information *in the first place* to the point where action on the basis of it will be needed" (p. 789). These systems should provide sufficient feedback and anticipate the variances that will/might affect their work	5. Information flow	"the principle of boundary location counsels against, if it cannot absolutely prohibit, the interruption of information or the insertion of loops by misplaced organisational boundaries" (pp. 157). Cherns comments here on the information associated with power games that are rife in organisations and the temptation to intervene, harass and usurp control that is offered by the provision of indiscriminate and unnecessary information to management
7. Support congruence	"the systems of social support should be designed so as to reinforce the behaviours which the organisation structure is designed to elicit" (p. 790). These systems of social support would include procedures for selection, training, conflict resolution, work measurement, performance assessment, timekeeping, leave allocation, promotion and separation	8. Support congruence	"support of production teams implies significant and far-reaching changes in reward and information systems, in financial control, and in marketing, sales, purchasing, and planning" (p. 158). Pay people for what they know, not what they do. "their value is what is in their heads" (p. 159). *(Cont'd)*

Table 2.1 (*Continued*)

1976 principles and order	Brief explanation	1987 principles and order	Further comments
8. Design and human values	"an objective of organisational design should be to provide a high quality of work" (p. 790). To provide, for those who want them, responsibility, variety, involvement and growth in their work	6. Power and authority	"the power and authority that accompanies knowledge and expertise" (p. 157). Also, people require the power and authority to command the necessary resources for their work and should take the concomitant responsibility for them
9. Incompletion	"As soon as design is implemented, its consequences indicate the need for redesign" (p. 791). A constant process of evaluation and review is required	10. Incompletion	Cherns also calls this the Forth Bridge principle; "back to the drawing board" (p. 159). He emphasises that all periods of stability are in effect only temporary periods of transition between one state and another. Redesign should be a continuous process and is the function of the self-regulating teams through review, evaluation and negotiation
		9. Transitional organisation	"managing the stress of start-up and shut-down can be prepared for" (p. 159). The transitional organisation is both different and more complex than either the old organisation was, or the new organisation will be, in either situation. The manner of the treatment of staff in selection either for incorporation into the new organisation or in separation from the old demonstrates very clearly the adherence to the sociotechnical principles

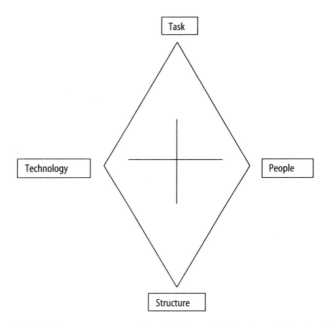

Figure 2.1 The four-component sociotechnical model (Laudon and Laudon, 2000).

A four-component model of the sociotechnical perspective has been developed which relates the technology to task, people and organisational structure (Fig. 2.1).

The author would argue that when considering knowledge management for an organisation a fifth component must also be considered: the environment within which an organisation operates. The environment affects how an organisation can be structured and of what value the technology can be to that organisation. The tasks and technology today are inextricably linked, through processes supported by such technology as intranets, extranets, electronic data interchange (EDI), customer relationship management and supply chain management to the external world. The environment is encompassing and the diamond thus is enclosed within the environment, as shown in Fig. 2.2.

Managing knowledge, therefore, with a sociotechnical perspective, has a wide-ranging necessity to manage the organisation through continuous change and a process of continuous learning supported, where appropriate, by technology. The next section discusses the management of knowledge in more depth and shows the sociotechnical perspective in more detail.

2.3.2 Managing Knowledge

Knowledge management has often been treated as an issue for IT and information systems specialists alone, and the efforts of many of these have focused on data and communication systems. This is witnessed by the name changes of many existing

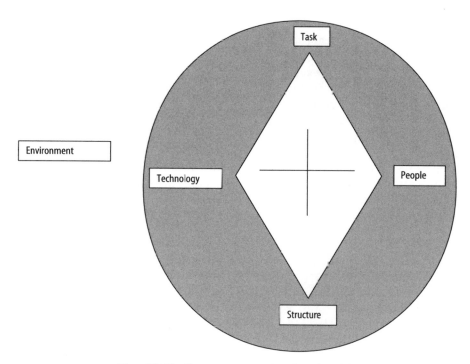

Figure 2.2 The five-component sociotechnical model.

software applications or information communication systems to include the word "knowledge". This can be seen as part of the bandwagon effect whereby the word knowledge, when linked to any system, apparently increases the value of the system in the minds of those viewing it, and thus increasing the likelihood of sales (and often prices).

When considering organisational knowledge and the management of this knowledge, we need to ensure that this is not seen simply as the acquisition of more data and information (Coakes and Sugden, 2000). Effective knowledge management is more about managing the human resource than about managing the technology.

"People will be the biggest factor in determining the success of failure of knowledge management by the quality of their decisions" (Taylor, 1998).

In Garvin's (1993) terms, the "transformation of knowledge" is the most essential activity of a learning organisation, and only an organisation that learns is one that truly manages its knowledge.

Pan and Scarbrough (1999, p. 362) discuss the processual and emergent qualities of the interplay between the technology and the organisation. They emphasise that, "the social aspect of socio-technical needs to be able to embrace the socially constructed aspects of knowledge within organisations." Lisl Klein (1999) also emphasises the interdependencies of both technical and social factors, with writers such as Nonaka and Takeuchi (1995) emphasising the social aspects of knowledge management such as teamwork and organisational culture as being critical for such management. "Motivation is ruled by the soft areas whereas technology rules the ability" (1998), or one could say that technology provides the capability. Allee (1997) also tells us that in a quantum worldview, with new thinking, motivation comes from intrinsic creativity where knowledge is collective and life thrives on cooperation, with workers being multifaceted, always learning, and being managed through insight and participation; in other words, through sociotechnical principles.

In Table 2.2 Cherns' 1987 principles are listed in his order of importance and explained in terms of knowledge management. This perspective on knowledge management differs from the perspective given by Pan and Scarbrough (1999) and

Table 2.2 Cherns' principles explained in terms of knowledge management

Principle	Knowledge management explanation
Compatibility	Design for knowledge management has to account for the social construction of knowledge within an organisation. Conflicts may occur as organisational cultures may not be compatible with the sharing of knowledge (Coakes and Sugden, 2000) The objectives of the workers may not be aligned with the objectives of the organisation. Knowledge management does not, however, demand consensus, although power plays are anti-organisational knowledge management, but these objectives may be individually appropriate depending on the organisational culture
Minimal critical specification	Knowledge is fluid and changing The technology used and the design of such systems for assistance should also be fluid and capable of change. Any rigidity will stifle the necessary creativity. Rules of what should be done, and how, should be minimal Systems should be permissive as opposed to mandatory
Variance control	Knowledge management requires that the social system is the controlling factor in deciding what work should be done, how and by whom according to their requisite knowledge Decisions to a high level of independence and self-management of tasks, etc., should be devolved to the knowledge workers
Boundary location	One can only repeat here what Cherns said in 1987, that boundaries should not impede the sharing of knowledge The organisation structure should be such that knowledge can flow freely and easily as required, to where required
Information flow	For knowledge management to work there must needs be no organisational barriers to sharing of information and knowledge. This would include the breakdown of power plays and resistance to knowledge sharing It would also imply a minimum level of checks and balances by management and especially of "checking-up"
Power and authority	Again, this repeats Cherns' views that people require the necessary power and authority, aligned with the required responsibility, to decide what resources they need to undertake their work

Table 2.2 (*Continued*)

Principle	Knowledge management explanation
The multifunction principle	A knowledge-based organisation needs to be fluid and adaptable to change, especially in relation to the external and internal environment. It would seem that a flat structure with people working in teams across projects and processes might be more appropriate The management of knowledge means looking at an organisation from a cognitive perspective, with the organisation seen as a knowing, sentient organism, and using its resources, both human and technological, to make sense of its environment
Support congruence	The element of reward systems is discussed by Cherns, suggesting that we pay people for their scarce knowledge, not what they do. This obviously will have repercussions when organisations manage this knowledge. Who decides who knows most? How can one judge? Is one type of knowledge more useful to the organisation than another? How should the reward system be devised to be fair and equitable?
Transitional organisation	Taking into account the above comments about the fluidity of the organisation that manages its knowledge in relation to the environment, it follows that the organisation is constantly in a state of transition. Management of staff in such a state of constant flux, and management of their knowledge, are clearly challenging tasks
Incompletion	As discussed in the transitional organisation above, redesign is continually happening as knowledge is constantly changing and the resources that people require to perform their work activities are also in a state of flux. It is important to recognise this and, if at all possible, to embrace this state of flux as being the norm rather than the exception

is intended to align the seminal principles with current organisational requirements.

This sociotechnical perspective shows clearly that in order for organisations to manage and share their knowledge effectively they must first consider, and then organise for, the following:

- aligning the organisational culture for easy sharing of knowledge and information;
- aligning the organisational structure and form to minimise checks and barriers to the sharing of knowledge and information;
- aligning the organisational management to permit a maximum devolution of responsibility and decision making. Managers should become facilitators and holders of wisdom (Coakes and Sugden, 2000);
- aligning the organisational structure and form to permit fluidity of this structure and form as change impacts both the organisational knowledge and the required organisational output;
- aligning the organisational reward system to encourage the development of learning and knowledge;
- finally, aligning the organisational technology infrastructure to permit all of the above.

2.4 Future Research

The discussion above shows quite clearly that it is not only possible but also desirable to take a sociotechnical view of knowledge in the organisation. It also shows how we can manage this knowledge. Knowledge should be strategically valued and the knowledge strategy needs to be future orientated, with strategies optimising the contribution of both people and technology. The development of innovative and creative knowledge requires the culture to support knowledge creation, sharing and learning. The organisation needs a leadership style that is conducive to permittance and acceptance, allowing self-organisation around competencies or expertise.

Future research must take the theoretical into the field of the practical. We need to discover whether what we postulate can translate into actuality. The author is engaged in a number of research projects looking at how organisations are currently using their technology for knowledge management and how organisational cultures impact the sharing of knowledge. In addition, several proposals are being developed where organisational change is taking place in order to undertake knowledge management, and the researchers can participate and/or observe the progress of the projects through action research or ethnographic studies.

2.5 Conclusions

This chapter set out to discuss a sociotechnical perspective on knowledge management. It first discussed the origins of the principles that drive the paradigm and analysed these principles as expressed by Cherns in his seminal chapters of 1976 and 1987. It then applied these principles to the concept of knowledge management, taking into consideration the idea of a five-component sociotechnical model. In particular, the chapter highlights six steps of alignment that an organisation needs to undertake for knowledge management. A sociotechnical perspective is holistic and encompassing and these steps of alignment reflect this viewpoint, showing how the paradigm can effectively assist our understanding of how knowledge can be managed.

> Knowledge alone, however, is insufficient, wisdom is the ultimate goal. For with wisdom comes understanding, and understanding is the necessary prerequisite to creative thought and action.

Part 1
Know-Why

Chapter 3
The Knowledge Management Spectrum: The Human Factor
Derek Binney

3.1 Introduction

Current management theory is urging managers to lead their organisations to become "learning organizations" (Senge, 1990) and proactively to manage knowledge as a strategic element of their organisations' asset base. Some are suggesting that being a successful knowledge-based organisation is both a precondition and a necessary condition to competing and surviving in this century's knowledge-based economy (Drucker, 1988; Edvinsson and Malone, 1997; Sveiby, 1997). Increasingly, these exhortations are highlighting the necessity for the appropriate organisational culture being in place to be successful in the knowledge management arena. This view is well expressed by Tissen, Andressen and Deprez (1998) when they state

"… knowledge is not an asset which can be easily managed like any other asset. Because thinking like that ignores one major fact: and that is the human factor. Knowledge and people go hand in hand. The result is that knowledge-based companies must be human-based companies."

Statements such as these lead to the conclusion that cultural change initiatives need to be included in knowledge management planning for most organisations, as the prescribed knowledge management culture is observed not to be the norm in organisations today.

Theory aside, there is no doubt that knowledge management is occupying significant executive mind-share. In addition to working on Computer Sciences Corporation's (CSC) knowledge management initiatives over the past eight years, the author has had the opportunity to explore knowledge management at operational, tactical and strategic levels with hundreds of customers, from many industries, as they visit CSC's Knowledge Solutions Laboratory (KSL) in Falls Church, USA, to benchmark knowledge management within CSC and to explore knowledge management further. Given a general acceptance amongst these executives for the need for some level of knowledge management investment, the main questions being asked in these sessions seem to fall broadly into two categories: the what and the how.

The knowledge management "what" questions are those such as:

- What is knowledge management?
- What can I and do I want to achieve tactically and strategically through knowledge management?

- What is the appropriate mix of knowledge management applications and technologies for my organisation?
- Where do I start?
- What is or should be my knowledge management strategy?

The knowledge management literature offers a range of often conflicting views and answers to these "what" questions. The knowledge management spectrum (Binney, 2001) was developed to assist in answering these "what" questions. The knowledge management spectrum is a one-page quick reference guide and checklist which provides a synthesised view of the totality and complexity of the various knowledge management theories, applications, tools and techniques presented in knowledge management literature.

The knowledge management "how" questions are those such as:

- How do I justify it?
- How do I achieve the cultural changes which seem to be required to realise my knowledge management investments?
- How do I find the appropriate balance and scale of organisational change versus technology investment?
- How does this vary with different knowledge management applications?

This chapter aims to address the organisational change aspects of this second group of "how" questions by positioning a discussion on organisational change in relation to the knowledge management spectrum. It provides a review of the organisational culture described in the literature as being required for successful knowledge management and provides a summary of the various organisational change options available with their relevance mapped to different knowledge management applications.

This review highlighted two issues. First, the human factor needs to be considered in all types of knowledge management applications: only building the technological mousetrap will not work. However, the types and level of individual involvement in the development and the deployment of the knowledge management applications vary with the type of knowledge management application being considered. There is no general truism or one size fits all organisational change solution for knowledge management. Secondly, where broad organisational change initiatives are described these have a "system"-level focus on organisational change which is at odds with the author's personal experience. This experience shows that system-level changes need to be balanced with a focus on what makes individuals use knowledge management applications and adopt knowledge management behaviours. This experience led the author to the view that change requires individuals to adopt necessary behaviours and that the focus of organisational change initiatives needs to balance between the system and the individual. How do organisations respect the role of the individual in knowledge management applications and any associated organisational change? Recommendations are offered on the importance of personalisation and adaptation in certain classes of knowledge management application. The human factor is considered as ultimately being a focus on individuals and their motivations for adoption or use of the knowledge management applications we are trying to implement. These personal views are supported by further references to current organisational change and knowledge management literature.

These views and recommendations are developed and discussed as follows. Section 3.2 provides a summary of the knowledge management spectrum, describing its elements and how the spectrum was developed. Section 3.3 builds the case for organisational change in the knowledge management context and maps a number of organisational change options as a variable to the knowledge management spectrum. Section 3.4 extends this discussion to recognise the role of the individual in organisational change. Section 3.5 contains a number of observations and recommendations on the need for and how to recognise the human factor in designing knowledge management systems, leading to some concluding remarks.

3.2 A Review of the Knowledge Management Spectrum

This section reviews the knowledge management spectrum as a framework for the categorisation of all knowledge management applications and enabling technologies being discussed in the knowledge management literature. Based on a synthesis of the literature, the spectrum provides a summary of knowledge management applications and enabling technologies not previously provided. The major elements and dimensions of the knowledge management spectrum are first reviewed and its applications discussed before moving on to the main discussion in the current chapter on organisational change: the human factor.

3.2.1 Structure of the Knowledge Management Spectrum

Binney (2001) established that the knowledge management applications discussed in the literature can be categorised. These categories, termed "elements", are defined as: (1) transactional, (2) analytical, (3) asset management, (4) process based, (5) developmental, and (6) innovation and creation knowledge management. The knowledge management application and enabling technology layers of the knowledge management spectrum contain checklists of knowledge management applications and technologies mapped to these elements. The knowledge management spectrum is shown in Figure 3.1.

The elements of the knowledge management spectrum are defined as follows.

Transactional

In transactional knowledge management, the use of knowledge is embedded in the application or technology. Knowledge is presented to the user of a system in the course of completing a transaction or a unit or work, e.g. entering an order or handling a customer query or problem. Examples of transactional knowledge

	Transactional	Analytical	Asset management	Process	Developmental	Innovation and creation
Knowledge management applications	Case-based reasoning (CBR) Help-desk applications Customer service applications Order entry applications Service agent support applications	Data warehousing Data mining Business intelligence Management information systems Decision support systems Customer relationship management (CRM) *Competitive intelligence*	Intellectual property Document management Knowledge valuation Knowledge repositories *Content management*	Total quality management (TQM) Benchmarking Best practices Quality management Business process (Re)engineering Process improvement Process automation Lessons learned Methodology *SEI/CMM, ISO9XXX, Six Sigma*	Skills development Staff competencies Learning Teaching Training	Communities Collaboration Discussion forums Networking Virtual teams Research and development *Multidisciplined teams*
Enabling technologies	Expert systems Cognitive technologies Semantic networks Rule-based expert systems Probability networks Rule induction, decision trees *Geospatial information systems*	Intelligent agents Web crawlers Relational and object DBMS Neural computing Push technologies Data analysis and reporting tools	Document management tools Search engines Knowledge maps Library systems	Workflow management Process modelling tools	Computer-based training Online training	Groupware e-Mail Chat rooms Video conferencing Search engines Voice mail Bulletin boards Push technologies Simulation technologies
Portals, Internet, Intranets, Extranets						

Figure 3.1 The knowledge management spectrum.

management include help desk, customer service, order entry and field support applications.

Analytical

Analytical knowledge management provides interpretations of, or creates new knowledge from, vast amounts or disparate sources of material. In analytical knowledge management applications, large amounts of data or information are used to derive trends and patterns, making apparent that which is hidden by the vastness of the source material and turning data into information which, if acted upon, can become knowledge.

Asset Management

Asset management knowledge management focuses on processes associated with the management of knowledge assets. This involves one of two things: the management of explicit knowledge assets which have been codified in some way (Guthrie and Petty, 1999), and the management of intellectual property and the processes surrounding the identification, exploitation and protection of intellectual property (Teece, 1998).

Once captured, the assets are made available to people to use as they see fit. This element of the spectrum is analogous to a library, with the knowledge assets being catalogued in various ways and made available for unstructured access and use.

Process-based

The process-based knowledge management element covers the codification and improvement of process, also referred to as work practices, procedures or methodology. Process-based knowledge management is often an outgrowth of other disciplines such as total quality management (TQM) and process re-engineering. Process knowledge assets are often improved through internal lessons, learning sessions, formal engineering of process by internal best practice selection, and codification and external benchmarking (Feltus, 1994; Powers, 1995; Hill, 1999; O'Dell and Grayson, 1999).

Developmental

Developmental knowledge management applications focus on increasing the competencies or capabilities of an organisation's knowledge workers. This is also referred to as investing in human capital (Edvinsson and Malone, 1997). The applications cover the transfer of explicit knowledge via training interventions, or the planned development of tacit knowledge through developmental interventions, such as experiential assignments or membership in a community of interest.

Innovation and Creation

Innovation and creation-based knowledge management applications focus on providing an environment in which knowledge workers, often from differing disciplines, can come together in teams to collaborate in the creation of new knowledge. There is still a role for individual innovation; however, innovations are increasingly coming from the marriage of disciplines and teamwork. More and more, turning an individual's innovation or insight into reality requires the power of n.

The main uses of the knowledge management spectrum build on its unique categorisation and inventory of knowledge management applications and enabling technologies. The knowledge management spectrum has proved useful as a more complete framework for better understanding the knowledge management literature, and as a knowledge management assessment and strategic planning tool.

3.2.2 Observations on the Knowledge Management Spectrum

Binney (2001) made six major observations associated with the applications being described in the literature and the significance of their variance across the knowledge management spectrum.

1. There is a grouping of the literature within the spectrum consistent with the author's background.
2. The type of knowledge or information being discussed moves from explicit to tacit.
3. The degree of individual choice, or optionality, increases moving from left to right.
4. The modality of choice increases, moving from left to right.
5. The underlying adoption model changes from left to right.
6. The intellectual capital models proposed by the knowledge management valuationists map to the Spectrum.

Figure 3.2 is a graphic representation of these observations.

Obs	Transactional	Analytical	Asset management	Process	Developmental	Innovation and creation
1	Technologist			Organisational theorist		
2	Explicit			Tacit		
3	Low optionality			High optionality		
4	Single modality			Multiple modality		
5	Technical mousetrap			Cultural change		
6	Structural capital			Human capital		
6	Internal structure			Employee competence		Internal structure

Figure 3.2 Observations mapped to the knowledge management spectrum.

3.3 Organisational Change as a Variable in the Knowledge Management Spectrum

There is consistent agreement in the literature with the view of Senge *et al.* (1999) that any knowledge management-related investments based on the "build the better mousetrap (technological solution) and "they will come" approach are unlikely to be successful or will fall short of achieving the expected investment outcome or potential. If, as it appears, organisational change is indeed required to realise increased returns on knowledge management investments, then to what level, and what type of organisational change or interventions are required?

This section focuses on the "human factor" and "organisational change" interventions associated with each element of the knowledge management spectrum. The first part builds on the observations highlighted in Figure 3.2 by reviewing the implications in organisational change terms. The second part summarises the organisational change interventions discussed in the literature.

3.3.1 Optionality and Modality: Varying Across the Spectrum

The level of optionality and modality of choice can be seen to vary across the knowledge management spectrum as follows.

In transactional knowledge management, the use of knowledge is embedded within the system. There may be a choice as to what the person does with the knowledge presented but its access and presentation is non-optional. This non-optionality is often reinforced by there being only one way of doing a task in transactional knowledge management systems (i.e. the system has singular modality).

In analytical knowledge management, the technology provided by the environment often dictates the options available. For example, in establishing data warehouses or implementing business intelligence systems, decisions on technologies and tools are often made by the organisation, and once the systems have been built and provided for use there is no option at the individual level to use something else or do it in a different way.

In asset management knowledge management, the capturing of assets is often mandated by the management system in terms of definitions, standards or technologies to be used. However, participation rates can vary significantly due in part to the level of optionality associated with the participation in centrally mandated initiatives. The degree of optionality in this element can be influenced by the implementation of workflow and document management systems, which force contribution of assets to the system. The retrieval and use of the assets can, however, be highly optional. This use is considered to be part of the innovation and creation knowledge management element. As with analytical knowledge management, central technology decisions are limiting users' choices and reducing the degree of modality of usage in this element.

In process-based knowledge management, use is often mandated by the system (both management and technology) in terms of definitions, standards or technologies to be used. Participation rates can vary significantly due in part to the level of actual optionality associated with the participation in mandated initiatives (i.e. participation in TQM programs or the use of sanctioned processes can vary significantly at both an organisational and individual level).

There is often a high degree of optionality in the developmental knowledge management element. Organisations often provide a "learning environment" and rely on self-directed learning on behalf of the employees to participate. In the author's experience, the acceptance and participation by individuals varies even in systems where there is encouragement and reward for participation in and the adoption of developmental programs.

Finally, as with developmental knowledge management, there is a high degree of optionality and modality in systems aimed at fostering innovation and creation. For example, an employee may elect to join and actively participate in communities of practice or to seek out and build on the knowledge in an organisation.

> When it comes to knowledge creation, the modality increases as people can choose to use the enabling technologies (even if there is a limited set) in non-prescriptive ways (i.e. people tend to operate in this space in personalised and unpredictable ways).

3.3.2 Organisational Change Emphasis in the Knowledge Management Spectrum

This section looks at the main organisational themes and interventions from the literature associated with the different elements of the knowledge management spectrum.

In the transactional and analytical elements of the knowledge management spectrum the emphasis is on the technology supplemented by training in the use of the application rather than creating an environment that encourages and reinforces usage or participation. Historically, a significant percentage of systems developed by technologists are systems that people have to use once or if they make it into production (e.g. a new online order entry system becomes the only way people can enter orders; there is no choice but to use the system). Techniques are often used to engage users in the design and acceptance of the system, but the organisational change activities have often been limited to training and user manuals. Modern development methods are increasingly incorporating organisational change aspects into system design and deployment (CSC, 1999).

In the asset through to innovation/creation elements of the knowledge management spectrum, the literature focuses on the cultural or organisational change at an organisational or system level. Nonaka and Takeuchi (1995) and Leonard (1999) represent the thinking that companies need to create an environment for successful knowledge management, whatever that may mean for the organisation. Davenport and Prusak (1998) express a view that whilst technology is an enabler, the changes required for successful knowledge management have more to do with the cultural environment that management needs to create to enable knowledge management processes to flourish.

The organisational change initiatives they propose include six main elements:

- reward and recognition programmes;

- creating a "trusting" environment;
- showing alignment with business strategy and goals;
- providing adequate training;
- providing universal access;
- providing management reinforcement and encouragement, in application usage or adoption of the implied behaviour.

The examples and recommendations offered tend to describe an end state with little in the way of prescriptive guidance on the relative mix or timing of these interventions. The success of each of these initiatives is highly dependent on the motivation and willingness of the individual or groups of individuals to participate.

Is this system level approach to organisational change akin to building a better organisational mousetrap and hoping the world will come?

3.4 The Human Factor: The Role of Individuals in Changing Organisations

This section looks at the role of the individual in organisational change and posits the need for increased focus on the human factor at the individual level through techniques such as adaptation and personalisation, especially where there are high degrees of optionality and modality in knowledge management applications. It starts with a selection of views offered in the knowledge management and organisational change literature which highlight the significant role of individuals in change and ends with the individualisation of the "human factor" being added to the knowledge management spectrum.

The author's experience in implementing knowledge management systems with high levels of optionality suggest that creating the correct system or environment for acceptance and usage is not in and of itself sufficient – the human factor requires significant focus on building and supporting individuals' needs for personalisation and being able to adapt aspects of the environment to make it their own. There is little evidence that mandating participation is a sustainable intervention or adoption model.

Organisational change literature recognises the role of the individual in organisational change to varying degrees. This recognition varies from the individual being an important part of a system, as proposed by systems dynamics theory, through to being the system, as proposed by ecological organisation theory. The company is a living being. The decisions for action made by this living being result from a learning process. De Geus (1997) summarises the ecological view of organisations.

Carr (1996) stresses the pivotal role of the individual in organisational change when he says that all change is individual. If countries change it is because thousands or millions of individuals in them changed. If organisations appear to change it is because hundreds or thousands of individuals in them changed.

Carr further proposes that personal advantage is required when he suggests that individuals will perform within an organisation and accept changes or innovations when:

- they have relatively clear and specific goals;
- which are important to the individual;
- which are within their power to achieve;
- for which they have or can develop the required competence to achieve them;
- they can get information relevant to the goals and their progress towards it, and
- they can assimilate feedback.

This requires a degree of personalisation not emphasised in organisational change interventions discussed in the knowledge management literature.

Carr introduces the concept of personal relative advantage. He states that individuals change by making choices. He also states that all organisational change is the sum of the changes made by individuals in the organisation, and each individual will change (or not) based on how the change affects them.

Another view strongly proposed by some of the organisational change community is that people will adopt that which they had a part in defining or can adapt to their situation.

Jacobs (1994) stresses the importance of individuals in making change occur and the resultant change being a sustainable change. Jacobs proposes that real-time strategic change can only be achieved with the mass mobilisation of individuals in the company to understand, define and be part of developing the strategic change design required. His premise is that if individuals had a stake in defining the change or innovation, they would automatically buy in to the proposed change and adopt any associated innovations or behaviours. Jacobs claims that his approach addresses three basic human yearnings: (1) to have their voices heard, (2) to be part be part of something larger, i.e. belonging, and (3) to be part of something successful.

Not all users are able participate in the design of the new system. This is for both practical (scale) and timing reasons; recognising that new staff will join once the original innovation has been designed and implemented. Allowing users to adapt the system to their individual requirements can partly satisfy the benefit associated

Transactional	Analytical	Asset management	Process	Developmental	Innovation and creation
Training and imbedded help assist **ease of use** and therefore usage of the system.					
User involvement in design and development leads to earlier **acceptance** of the system.					
System level organisation change interventions provide **environment for acceptance and** usage.					
Adaptation and personalisation increase **adoption of behaviours and usage** of the system.					

Figure 3.3 Individualisation added to the organisational change mapping.

Transactional	Analytical	Asset management	Process	Developmental	Innovation and creation
	Training and imbedded help assist **ease of use** and therefore usage of the system.				
	User involvement in design and development leads to earlier **acceptance** of the system.				
	System level organisation change interventions provide **environment for acceptance and usage**.				

Figure 3.4 Organisational change initiatives mapped to the knowledge management spectrum.

with being involved in the initial design and taking ownership of the system. Ehlrich (1999) observed a similar phenomenon when studying the use of collaborative technologies by workgroups: acceptance and usage of the systems was higher when people could adapt and personalise the systems provided for their use.

Figure 3.3 highlights the elements of the knowledge management spectrum where, in the author's experience, personalisation[1] and adaptation play a significant part in an individual's decision to use or to participate in the knowledge management innovation. Its inclusion completes the organisational changes mapped in Section 3.2.

3.5 Observations and Recommendations

This section provides a summary of four major observations leading to recommendations on the need to focus the human factor at the individual level when implementing knowledge management applications.

First, if we accept that building the technological mousetrap is not sufficient, then knowledge management initiatives need to incorporate organisational change elements in their design, costing and deployment. This expectation needs to be clearly established from the outset.

The type and degree of organisational change required vary depending on the knowledge management application and where it lies in the knowledge management spectrum. Figure 3.4 provides a summary of this variability, which may assist in better understanding the appropriate mix or emphasis of the intervention described.

Understanding the varying optionality and modality associated with the elements of the knowledge management spectrum allows strategists looking at making knowledge management investments to understand better the total investment required to realise the benefits of any given investment mix.

Secondly, whilst system level interventions are valuable, they are not in and of themselves sufficient. Nonaka[2] (Nonaka and Konno, 1999), representing the eastern school of thought, uses images such as "Knowledge is manageable only in so far as leaders embrace and foster the dynamism of knowledge creation. The role of top management is as the providers of 'ba' for knowledge creation. Their task is to manage knowledge emergence."

As Senge (Senge *et al.*, 1999) proposes, "no one person can train or command other people to alter their attitudes, beliefs, skills, capabilities, perceptions, or level of commitment."

Thirdly, remember the human factor: the literature combined with personal experience indicates that there is likely to be a higher level of adoption when the users have had a part in the design of the system, or are able both to personalise and to adapt the system. Personalisation, which recognises relative personal advantage, further increases individual adoption rates.

Finally, organisational change interventions prescribed for applications in one part of the knowledge management spectrum may need to be complemented with intervention types prescribed for other elements in dependent related elements.

At first sight, the level of organisational change required for transactional systems is training or imbedding help in the system as the level of optionality is low. However, this is only half of the system. The other half has to do with capturing and codifying the knowledge in the first place and ensuring that practitioners use the knowledge provided to them. The processes and the associated organisational change interventions needed to support this part of the system are the same as those needed for the asset management or process-based elements of the knowledge management spectrum.

The preceding discussion is founded on experience that building a better mousetrap does not work for the types of knowledge management application being pursued by businesses wishing to become knowledge based and compete in the emerging knowledge economy. These knowledge management applications have high levels of optionality and modality, which means that individuals and their personal choice need to be considered when making strategic knowledge management planning decisions and implementing knowledge management applications.

As previously discussed, the knowledge management spectrum has a number of immediate applications as a framework for better understanding the knowledge management literature and as a diagnostic and strategic planning tool.

Understanding the varying optionality and modality associated with the elements of the knowledge management spectrum will allow strategists looking at making knowledge management investments to understand better the balance between technology and organisational change required to realise the benefits of any given investment choice.

Additions to or comments about the knowledge management spectrum are welcome. Through such comments and feedback, the knowledge management spectrum will evolve and continue to be of value in assisting our understanding of knowledge management as it develops.

Acknowledgements

I would like to thank Prof. James Guthrie, MGSM, for his thoughts, insights and valuable editorial work. I have been greatly assisted by comments from Dr Eric

Tsui and Mr Geoff Brehaut of CSC. The responsibility for the contents of this paper nonetheless remains entirely that of the author.

Notes

1   This personalisation extends to the technical solutions and portals being deployed: note the 'my.com' phenomenon.
2   Page 53; on p. 40 Nonaka describes "*ba*" as "shared space for emerging relationships ... that at a transcendental perspective integrates all information needed ... as a recognition of the self in all ... that serves as the foundation for knowledge creation."

Chapter 4
Organisational Ability: Constituents and Congruencies

Göran Goldkuhl and Ewa Braf

4.1 Introduction

During recent years there has been an upsurge of interest in knowledge management and organisational learning. But why focus on a subject that, at some level, has been around since the pre-Socratic philosophers? The answer to the question is manifold. One explanation is that knowledge and improvement of knowledge is considered to be crucial for the performance and development of organisations. It is also argued that in our contemporary society knowledge is an important asset in order to reach sustainable competitive advantage (see for example Drucker, 1993; Nonaka and Takeuchi, 1995; Quintas, Lefrere and Jones, 1997; Davenport and Prusak, 1998). One question of concern is what are the implications of seeing knowledge as an organisational asset? When comparing intangible assets, such as knowledge, with tangible assets, such as machines or land, they can hardly be treated as having the same properties. Another question is: how should we relate knowledge to the organisation's total ability to perform actions and deliver value to its customers? Is knowledge the only constituent of organisational ability or are there other inherent parts? The purpose of this chapter is to investigate these questions and thereby develop the notion of organisational ability. In order to do this the chapter begins by looking at some theories around the area of interest.

Owing to the vast amount of available literature it is neither possible nor the intention to explore all existing theories. Instead, some relevant and current notions have been selected that have been used as guidelines for the investigation. These notions include knowledge management, intellectual capital and organisational knowledge. The chapter is structured in the following way. Section 4.2 comprises a theoretical discussion about knowledge in organisations. Section 4.3 draws some intermediate conclusions from the analysis of the selected theories and formulates some objectives for the conceptualisation of organisational ability. Section 4.4, the main part of the chapter, consists of a description of the notion of organisational ability, its four constituents and the relations between them. Section 4.5 summarises the contribution and draws some final conclusions.

> The chapter is based on a pragmatic and sociotechnical perspective. It is pragmatic in the sense that it emphasises organisational action and abilities for such action. It is sociotechnical in the sense that it emphasises the close linkages among human knowledge, intersubjective institutions, language use and technical artefacts.

4.2 Knowledge in Organisations

The existence, use and importance of knowledge itself are not new. Knowledge makes people able to act and perform different organisational tasks. In this way we can say that knowledge is what makes organisations function. What is new, according to Davenport and Prusak (1998, p. 12), is the recognition of "knowledge as a corporate asset". Viewing knowledge as an asset implies efforts to utilise, improve and deploy knowledge in the organisation. Davenport and Prusak mean, "knowledge may be a company's greatest competitive advantage" (Davenport and Prusak, 1998, p. 13). Drucker (1993) fortifies this by saying that knowledge is the only meaningful economic resource.

To take this asset view a step further Edvinsson and Malone (1997) describe how organisations should measure their intellectual capital.

There are two main components of intellectual capital:

- human capital (consisting of individual capabilities, skills, experiences); and
- structural capital (embodiment, empowerment and supportive infrastructure of human capital).

Edvinsson and Malone (1997) emphasise the importance of measuring the intellectual capital and present a measurement model. This model can, however, be questioned. An investment in employees' education will not always lead to increases in intellectual capital as presupposed. Acquired knowledge might not be practicable in the specific work situation or an employee might not be able to understand how to apply it to his or her particular tasks. It is problematic to treat knowledge in the same way as treating tangible assets. It seems as though knowledge is sometimes viewed as a material resource that is easy to externalise. Nevertheless, it is important to evaluate knowledge in some way. One suggestion is to focus on evaluation of the usefulness of knowledge, instead of trying to measure knowledge per se.

> The role of information technology (IT) is said to enable and facilitate the management of knowledge, but technology itself "disappears as a sustainable source of competitive advantage" (Davenport and Prusak, 1998, p. 16).

If knowledge is considered to be the main asset of organisations, what about other capabilities? Or are there no other capabilities or functions that ought to be noticed? Much of the literature around knowledge management and organisational learning emphasises that technology only has a secondary role in the management of knowledge. Davenport and Prusak (1998) expand this by criticising the belief that technology could replace the skills and judgement of an experienced human worker.

The emphasis of the role of knowledge within organisations sometimes seems to be exaggerated to a degree that knowledge is what constitutes the ability of the organisation. This claim for totalisation of knowledge neglects other forms of ability that actually exist in organisations. In contrast to some other authors, Edvinsson and Malone's conception of intellectual capital takes a different stance.

They include the capacity of IT systems
by saying that paying explicit regard to
the fact that employees are not all of
the intellectual capital is an important
contribution. In terms of the structural
capital they include, for example, IT
artefacts as part of the intellectual
capital. In this context one can also
turn to the term "core competency" put

> "organisational capital is the company's invest-ment in systems, tools, and operating philoso-phy ... It is the systemised, packaged, and codified competence of the organisation as well as the systems for leveraging that capability" (Edvinsson and Malone, 1997, p. 35).

forward by Prahalad and Hamel (1990). They define core competence as a unique
bundle of skills and technologies that enables organisations to provide particular
benefits to customers. To this is added the "core performance capability" that
enables organisations to deliver high-quality products to the customers (Allee,
1997, p. 21). Allee defines the notion of core performance capability as generic to
the success of many organisations. The capabilities could be exceptionally efficient
core business processes or enabling technologies that capture detailed information
about the customer.

One limitation of Edvinsson and Malone's view seems to be that they handle the
structural capital (including IT artefacts) more as a leveraging factor than as
something that has a capacity of its own. A similar restriction is found in Prahalad
and Hamel (1990) and Allee (1997). Full consideration is not taken of the different
performance functions that artefacts (e.g. information systems) offer organisa-tions. Technology includes artefacts that support information processing, manu-facturing and transportation. Many modern organisations are dependent on these
different artefacts in order to perform and create value for their customers.
Artefacts therefore need to be taken into explicit consideration when talking about
what organisations can do, i.e. the organisational ability.

In order to manage and create knowledge Nonaka and Takeuchi (1995) put
forward a model for knowledge conversion. The four modes of knowledge conver-sion are socialisation, externalisation, combination and internalisation.[1] Among
those modes, externalisation is seen as the key to knowledge creation.
Externalisation is said to create new, explicit concepts from tacit knowledge. The
mode of externalisation can be compared with terms such as codification of
knowledge (Allee, 1997; Davenport and Prusak, 1998) and encoding of knowledge
(Blackler, 1995). Nonaka and Takeuchi's model is built on Polanyi's (1983) distinc-tion that there are two kinds of human knowledge, explicit and tacit knowledge.
Nonaka and Takeuchi mean that explicit knowledge can be articulated in formal
language and transmitted across individuals formally and easily. Tacit knowledge,
by contrast, is personal, context specific, and therefore hard to formalise and com-municate. Still, tacit knowledge is argued to be the most important kind of knowl-edge and one aim of Nonaka and Takeuchi's (1995) knowledge-creation model is
to transfer tacit to explicit knowledge through the externalisation process.

The notions of externalisation and explicit knowledge are problematic. Authors
such as Nonaka and Takeuchi (1995) and Davenport and Prusak (1998) do not
always seem to conceive that there are translation processes involving language. In
communicative externalisation there is a translation of knowledge into language

and in internalisation there is a translation back from language to knowledge again.

It should be emphasised that when talking about externalised (explicit) knowledge this is not knowledge per se. It is just linguistic descriptions of knowledge, i.e. texts, which need to be interpreted by the receiver in order to become knowledge again. For different reasons the receiver may not be able to understand the intended knowledge meaning of the texts. For example, the receiver may not have the necessary background knowledge or may interpret the meaning in a different way than was the intention of the knowledge exponent. This problem is unfortunately something that is not emphasised sufficiently in the literature. The importance should be stressed of further investigation into the conversion between knowledge and externalised knowledge. Other parts of the organisational ability need to be considered, not only the knowledge part. To do this the authors believe in drawing upon a perspective rooted in the philosophy of knowledge, language and action.

4.3 Intermediate Conclusions and Theoretical Objectives

The above discussion on knowledge in organisations is now summarised in some intermediate conclusions. These conclusions form a basis for elaboration on the notion of organisational ability (Section 4.4).

1. Knowledge should not be totalised as *the* organisational asset. It is important to acknowledge other assets as important for organisational action.
2. When treating knowledge it is important to avoid mechanistic views. It is important to maintain (and thus not blur) distinctions between knowledge as parts of the human mind and its linguistic representations.
3. A proper account of technology for organisational action should be given. This means a balance between two extremes of technology comprehension (items 7 and 8 below).
4. Language should be recognised as having an important role for communicating and bearing organisational ability.

These conclusions will function as objectives for a further theoretical analysis of the notion of organisational ability. Besides these four more objectives are now added for the theoretical analysis:

5. Organisations should be considered as actors without falling into the trap of reification. Organisations act through their human co-workers.
6. The importance of intersubjectivity (shared knowledge) in organisations for coordinated actions must be recognised.
7. Reified and deterministic views of technology should be avoided, i.e. giving it properties on acting and developing totally on its own. All artefacts have a human origin and they always rely on human purposes.

8. The reduction of all technology to mere instruments (enablers) of human action should be avoided. Some artefacts have properties that make them function partially as independent devices and they do not need constant human supervision.

4.4 Organisational Ability for Organisational Action

4.4.1 Organisational Ability as Actable Assets

The notion of organisational ability, which is introduced here, is to be understood as an ability for organisational action. The constituents of organisational ability can thus be seen as assets of the organisation. Not all organisational assets are parts of organisational ability. The assets must be actable,[2] i.e. they must be almost directly transformable into action.

> Human knowledge is an important asset for organisational action. It is an actable asset since it can directly be transformed into action. All human actions are based on the knowledge of the actor.

Some organisational assets cannot be regarded as actable assets, e.g. financial assets must be transformed into other assets in order to be used. Assets such as buildings are not direct actable assets. Buildings are part of the infrastructure of the organisation facilitating different actions. A building is an artefact produced by humans to be used for certain purposes. The non-actable character of buildings can be compared with other artefacts which have actable properties. Production equipment is more than a facilitating infrastructure. Machines for manufacturing make things happen. They are parts in the production of goods and they have a (rather specialised) ability for such organisational action.

Human knowledge is an important organisational ability and asset. It can be seen as the fundamental and original organisational ability. Without human knowledge there will be no organisational action and there will no other abilities. It is, however, too restricted to say that human knowledge is the only organisational ability. There are other important abilities, which are described in this chapter. Organisational ability is considered to consist of, and thus depend on, the following parts:

- individual knowledge;
- intersubjective institutionalised knowledge;
- artefact functionality;
- linguistic and pictorial descriptions of abilities.

Organisational ability is what makes the organisation able to create value by action for its clients or customers.

4.4.2 Knowledge and Artefacts

A competent act is an act based on adequate knowledge. The knowledge is used for performing the action. Human knowledge is expressed in action. This is the case both for motory–material action (e.g. driving a nail) and for social–communicative action (e.g. ordering nails).

For many actions humans use artefacts. We use a hammer to drive a nail into a wall. The hammer, as an artefact, extends the ability of a person. A human can perform acts with the aid of artefacts. Some acts can be improved by using tools and certain tools enable other acts. Some acts cannot be performed without the use of appropriate tools: the artefacts are necessary for action. To perform tool-based actions people need to have knowledge about the tools and how to use them. They must be competent tool users. The tool must have adequate properties for the kind of intended action. The properties of a tool (artefact) are not called competence; these properties that make the action possible are called the functionality of the tool.

There are many artefacts for material actions and they play an important role in manufacturing and other enterprises. There are also important tools for communicative and informational action. Computers and other instruments of IT are important artefacts for such action. The computer has properties (functions) for data manipulation, storage, transfer and presentation. It extends the ability of people through such properties. There are similarities between the computer and a material tool such as a hammer, but also important differences. A hammer and a computer can enable certain actions performed by humans. Of course, they enable different types of action. But there is also another fundamental difference between these kinds of instrument. A computer has properties of independent performance which a hammer is lacking. Following the program code, a computer can execute operations without human presence or surveillance. A computer can perform tasks (partially) independently. A hammer does nothing by itself.

In some situations we use the computer as a tool; we perform actions with the interactive support of the computer. In other situations the computer is used as an independent device, performing tasks automatically and thus independently. Weizenbaum (1976) distinguishes between prosthetic tools and automatic machines. A prosthetic tool extends the ability of humans, as described above. The automatic machine has an autonomous ability to function on its own. This autonomy is restricted and conditional. The conditions for action are expressed in the program code, written by humans, and governing the performance of the computer.

When designing a computer-based information system, humans create an action repertoire of the system to be used interactively or automatically (Goldkuhl and Ågerfalk, 2000). The computer systems (as designed artefacts) have been given an action ability. They can perform, on their own or together with users, organisational actions of informational or communicative character. Their performance of organisational action is conditioned by the programming made for them. Computer-based systems have a functionality which can be directly transformed into organisational action. This means that such systems are considered as organisational actable assets.

IT is thus seen as an important part of organisational ability. Other types of technology also have important roles in organisational performance. The presentation above focused on IT. Much of what has been said about computers, including their character and ability for tool-supported action and automatic action in organisations, is, in principle, also valid for other technologies.

Knowledge makes people able to act and perform important tasks in the organisation. What is performed within an organisation is, however, not only restricted to knowledge-based action of people. Technology has great importance in most companies today (Latour, 1992). The performance of organisations is usually dependent on different kinds of equipment, i.e. information, manufacturing and transportation technology. The use of equipment (different artefacts) makes the organisation able to create value to its clients or customers. Organisational action can be performed by people or by artefacts created and arranged by people.

Knowledge is primary and artefact functionality is secondary. Human knowledge is expressed and externally manifested when people create artefacts. Human knowledge is built into the artefacts. The performance of the artefacts will be in accordance with the knowledge and intentions made explicit during their design and transformed into them. Their performance will also be dependent on the material conditions of their construction.

4.4.3 Organisations as Actors: Humans as Organisational Actors

The claim has been made that organisations act; that organisations should be seen as actors. Is this not a reified[3] position? a view that organisations have been given an ontological status of their own outside the realm of human originators? It is being claimed that organisations are actors, but they are not actors on their own. They always have a human origin and purpose.

> Organisations are created by humans and for purposes of those humans. And the organisations act always through their human co-workers or through artefacts arranged by humans. They cannot act themselves but only through humans (Ahrne, 1994; Goldkuhl and Nilsson, 2000).

The co-workers act on behalf of the organisation (ibid; Argyris and Schön, 1996); they act in the name of the organisation. An act performed by a human co-worker is always dual. It is both an action performed by a person end an action performed by the organisation. People act in organisational roles; their action is representative. They represent the organisation when acting.

It is important to conceive of the organisation as an actor because otherwise it would not be appropriate to talk about organisational ability for action. Such an organisational ability goes beyond the abilities of individual humans. Organisational ability can be manifested in artefacts outside humans (Section 4.4.2). Organisational ability can also be manifested in organisational institutions (Section 4.4.4) and expressed in linguistic and pictorial descriptions (Section 4.4.5).

4.4.4 Individual versus Institutionalised Knowledge

Viewing the organisation as an actor means that its human members perform different acts in the name of the organisation. These different acts (by different humans) must be coordinated to a certain degree. If different acts are not coordinated enough there will be problems in creating products of high quality for customers. What is said and done, on different occasions, to one customer must be in alignment, otherwise the customer will be confused and perhaps suspicious concerning the trustworthiness of the organisation.

To perform coordinated actions, there is a need for intersubjective knowledge within the co-workers of the organisation. The knowledge of products, production processes, marketing principles and many other aspects of the organisation must be shared among different members of the organisation. An efficient organisation requires typical ways (routines) of performing recurrent actions. These action patterns and the knowledge about them are being institutionalised into a common stock of knowledge within the organisation (Berger and Luckmann, 1967; Scott, 1995). This means that knowledge about organisational actions and action conditions is, to a large degree, shared among its members. Conceptions, objectives, norms and rules are shared among humans. Fundamental for this knowledge sharing is the existence of a common organisational language. The categories and terminology of such a language are used to perform and describe many organisational tasks.

It is not claimed that there is a total match of the organisational knowledge among all its members. In organisations there will be different "knowledge provinces" due to different task areas. Even between members of a work team degrees of intersubjectivity may result from differences in personal history and organisational commitment.

Institutionalised knowledge has an origin within individual subjects. Individual ideas and experiences, with a value for the organisation beyond their individual originator, can be shared with other members, and thus become intersubjective and institutionalised. Such knowledge is not always deployed through an explicit and linguistic communication process. Tacit knowledge of a worker can be shared among fellow workers only by working together. Not all knowledge is codified into linguistic categories; much knowledge (both individual and intersubjective) is kept in "practical consciousness" (Giddens, 1984).

Every human actor within an organisation must be knowledgeable in order to perform actions. He or she must rely on his or her subjective knowledge. In order for actions to be coordinated, different actors must be knowledgeable in a joint way. They must share knowledge, i.e. such knowledge is intersubjective between the different actors. By individual knowledge is meant knowledge residing within a human subject. By intersubjective knowledge is meant such knowledge of individuals which is shared among them.

4.4.5 Descriptions of Organisational Ability

Knowledge is considered to be located within people, whereas on the outside are externalisations and manifestation of knowledge. Artefact functionality is a manifestation of knowledge which is discussed above (Section 4.4.2). Human knowledge is constantly being expressed in utterances and messages. When we talk and write, we express parts of our knowing, and through the use of language this knowing can become shared with those listening to us.

Knowledge as an ability for organisational action can thus be expressed in order to be shared among other members of the organisation, as described in Section 4.4.4. Such descriptions can be kept and saved over time. For descriptions to have permanence, i.e. going beyond oral and casual communication, there is a need to use written descriptions or descriptions recorded in other ways. Language is an efficient way of transferring knowledge of possible ways to act. Verbal descriptions may be enhanced by using pictures expressing how to act.

Such linguistic and pictorial descriptions become an external collective memory of the organisation concerning its ability. Organisational members can learn how to act in different situations. They can also recall knowledge that has been forgotten, through reading instructions how to act. Such descriptions have thus a prescriptive and reminding function for organisational ability and the expected action.

Organisational ability can be described in manuals, handbooks, job descriptions and many other organisational documents. Such descriptions do not have the same directedness to action as knowledge and artefact functionality. The descriptions must be perceived, interpreted and understood to result in action. Further, they may be considered as part of the organisational ability and thus as an actable asset. The purpose of descriptions is that they should be used as an aid for organisational action according to institutionalised and prescribed ways of action.

4.4.6 Relations and Congruencies

Four kinds of organisational ability have been described which are transformed into everyday organisational action. They are not unrelated to each other. Primary to all other abilities is a person's individual knowledge. Without knowing subjects there will be no intersubjective knowledge,[4] no artefacts and no descriptions. But an organisation cannot exist without having individual knowledge shared into a common stock of institutionalised knowledge. People can create artefacts based on their own subjective knowledge, but usually such artefacts rely on intersubjective knowledge within and outside the organisation. Engineering equipment is built based on technical knowledge which, to a large degree, may be outside the organisation. An organisation procures production equipment, with packaged knowledge manifestations of technical–material character. An organisation usually procures such equipment because it lacks the knowledge (or other ability) to create it within the organisation.

Sometimes computer-based information systems are created within the organisation. That is the case if the organisation has enough systems development ability. The knowledge built into such an IT artefact is of other character than a manufacturing artefact. What is built into an IT-based system is parts of the institutionalised knowledge of the organisation It is thus possible for the organisation to create such artefacts if they have enough knowledge of how to formalise and renew such institutionalised knowledge and transform it into computer code.

The institutionalised knowledge must continuously be exercised in action, otherwise certain parts of this institutionalised knowledge might be (at least partially) forgotten and thus distorted in action. Linguistic descriptions often constitute a necessary external memory for the institutionalised knowledge. People can be reminded of what kind of actions to perform, and the norms and principles for their execution.

Relations between the four constituents are described in Figure 4.1. This model also describes the relations to organisational action. The kind of action performed has been characterised based on a certain type of ability. In many situations the actions performed are based on several parts of organisational ability. For example, assume a situation where a market assistant is handling a customer order and creates an order confirmation with the support of an interactive computer-based system. To perform this action with success, it must be exercised in a competent

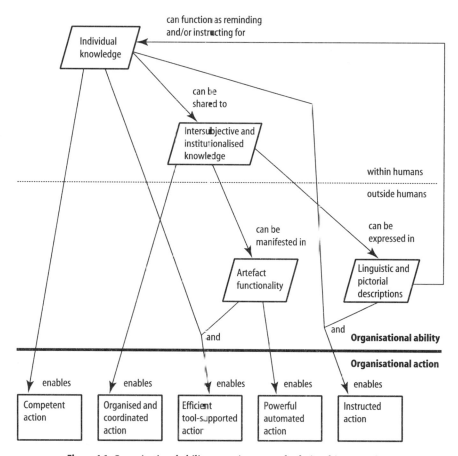

Figure 4.1 Organisational ability: constituents and relationships to action.

way, based on the knowledge of the market assistant. This knowledge must be in alignment with the institutionalised order procedures of the company, i.e. the order confirmation must be coordinated with other actions and thus be based on this kind of institutionalised knowledge, of which the market assistant must be a bearer. To ensure that he performs this action correctly, the market assistant checks a manual containing descriptions of the institutionalised order procedures of the company. He makes the order confirmation with the interactive support of a computer-based order system, i.e. the performance of the order confirmation is a tool-based action and must rely on both human knowledge and appropriate artefact functionality. As seen from this simple example, to perform one single organisational act there is a combined application of several parts of organisational ability. One can speak of multicapable actions. Through this example it is also obvious that there must be congruence between different organisational abilities.

To perform an organisational action, the knowledge of this person must be in alignment with institutionalised knowledge in the organisation. The intersubjective organisational knowledge also needs to be aligned with functionalities of different artefacts within the organisation. People must know what different artefacts are capable of doing and they must also possess enough knowledge to manage them. The descriptions of human and technical ability must be correct, otherwise people may perform inappropriate actions when trying to follow the instructions.

The importance of congruence between different organisational abilities has been stressed; however, most organisations do not have a total congruence of abilities. Organisations evolve over time and their abilities are gradually changing. Through learning and innovation human knowledge is changing, but other parts of organisational ability may not change at the same pace. There may be different incongruencies between the organisational abilities. There may be a mismatch between parts of the institutionalised knowledge and the descriptions of how to act, which may be due to obsolete descriptions that have not been updated. The mismatch may be the other way around: intersubjective knowledge that has not been adapted to new descriptions. There may be a delay in learning new procedures or resistance to change when management is trying to implement new ways of working.

Ability incongruencies may cause serious problems for the organisation. Organisational performance may be happened in different ways. It is, however, important to see that an identified incongruence is an incentive for organisational change and learning.

> Organisational change is a never-ending chase between different organisational abilities to keep in touch with each other.

An organisation is gradually changing through changes in its different abilities, which must be in accordance with each other. In change processes one ability can be "moved forward" and as a result others need to be changed. A jump (i.e. a positive shift) in one organisational ability may trigger other abilities to change, then another ability can jump in front of others and thus trigger further changes. A fundamental hypothesis about organisational change is that it is due to two main forces within organisations, the impetus for organisational change to be an effective actor in society (and thus change its organisational abilities) and the impetus to establish congruence between different organisational abilities.

4.5 Organisational Abilities: Towards a Sociotechnical Balance

To perform an organisational act is to exercise ability. In this chapter the notion of organisational ability has been defined. This ability consists of four principal constituents, which exist on different ontological levels (Goldkuhl, 1999):

- subjective level: individual knowledge
- intersubjective level: institutionalised knowledge
- technical level: artefact functionality
- semiotic level: linguistic and pictorial descriptions.

It is important that there is enough harmony and congruence between the different abilities. Too much mismatch and conflict can have severe negative consequences for organisational performance. The view of organisational ability presented in this chapter emphasises a combined approach, comprising developing human knowledge, intersubjective institutions, technical artefacts and linguistic descriptions as an endeavour for a sociotechnical balance.

One key argument in this chapter is that knowledge management cannot be seen in isolation. A contextual approach is required which recognises the relations between knowledge and other parts of the organisational ability. A sociotechnical and pragmatic approach has been adopted here. A sociotechnical view incorporates both ontological and ethical considerations. The main emphasis here has been on ontological issues. This text has tried to describe the meanings of and relations among the human level (individual knowledge), the social level (intersubjective knowledge and linguistic expressions) and the technical level (artefact functionalities). This kind of ontological clarification is of great importance in developing organisations through knowledge management and other related activities.

The ethical aspects of the sociotechnical approach have not been explicitly touched upon in this chapter. The key ethical principle of the sociotechnical approach[5] is "that the individual's participation in decision-making and control over their immediate work environment is enabled and increased" (Coakes, 2000). The authors fully adhere to this being an important principle of participation.

> Knowledge management in terms of knowledge development is not possible to perform without the participation of those knowing. Knowledge management without user participation seems to be self-contradictory.

This chapter concludes with some general advice following the lines of thought presented herein:

- An isolated development of knowledge should be avoided.
- Development of knowledge should be performed in combination with external supports of technical and semiotic character.
- Development or procurement of technical artefacts should always be supplemented by development of knowledge on how to use the artefacts.
- One should try to establish a balanced development of different organisational abilities.
- Any imbalance in different organisational abilities should be used as a trigger for organisational change.

Notes

1 Socialisation means transferring tacit knowledge between actors, externalisation means making tacit knowledge explicit, combination means combining different kinds of explicit knowledge and obtaining new explicit knowledge, and internalisation means embodying explicit knowledge to tacit knowledge (Nonaka and Takeuchi, 1995).
2 The notion of actability (in relation to information systems) is treated in Goldkuhl and Ågerfalk (2000). Here the use of actability is broadened to other organisational abilities and assets.
3 Berger and Luckmann (1967) describe the meaning of reification and the problems and dangers of reifying social phenomena, i.e. disregarding the human origin of socially constructed products.
4 This is not to deny the dialectical relation between subjective and institutionalised knowledge (Berger and Luckmann, 1967). For a new employee coming into the organisation, the institutionalised knowledge within that organisation is prior to his acquaintance (knowing) of that knowledge.
5 Summaries and overviews of sociotechnical change principles can be found in Mumford (1984) and Coakes (2000).

Chapter **5**
Managing Knowledge in a Knowledge Business
Vicki Scholtz

5.1 The Importance of Managing Knowledge

Evans and Wurster (2000, p. 20) argue that while "information ... may be the *end product* of only a minority of businesses, ... it glues together value chains, supply chains, consumer franchises, and organisations across the entire economy. And it accounts for a grossly disproportionate share of competitive advantage and therefore of profits" (emphasis in original). It clearly makes good sense for all businesses to take information, and knowledge, seriously.

While Earl (2000, p. 16) asserts that "every business is an information business", some organisations have traditionally been more explicitly focused on the creation, dissemination and evaluation of knowledge than others, universities being an extreme example of this type. Drucker (1988, p. 2) predicts that organisations of the future (Fig. 5.1) will resemble the university: they will consist of specialists or knowledge workers grouped together in transient task forces, coordinated rather than managed, and united by a common objective (which he likens to the score used by an orchestra). This is consistent with the sociotechnical perspective, which values small, independent work groups engaged in highly varied tasks, managing their own activities and often supported by technology. An examination of knowledge management practices and problems at universities may then offer some usable guidelines for other organisations.

5.2 The Academic Business

While Drucker's impression of the university is flattering, particularly the notion of specialists united in their pursuit of a common vision, the reality within universities reveals a shift in the opposite direction. Worldwide, universities are restructuring in response to the demands of the global economy. Resources, including state subsidisation, are declining, forcing universities to become lean, mean teaching machines, or to seek niche markets in order to survive (Cameron and Tschirhart, 1992; Slaughter and Leslie, 1997; see Clark, 1998). With the noose of financial constraint tightening, they have recently begun adopting a more business-like orientation, accompanied by the review and reorganisation of administrative and management processes and structures (Fig. 5.2).

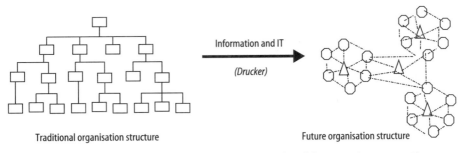

Traditional organisation structure   Future organisation structure

Figure 5.1 Organisational structure development (developed from Drucker, 1988, p. 2).

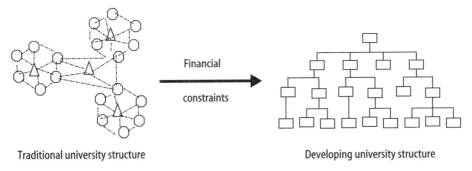

Traditional university structure   Developing university structure

Figure 5.2 University structure development.

In South Africa there have been similar trends, exacerbated by the need to transform the legacy of the apartheid provision of tertiary education. Most major South African cities have several universities within spitting distance of each other, originally designated for use by different "race" or, occasionally, language groups. Skewed resourcing has allowed historically white universities, including the University of Cape Town (UCT) to thrive, while neighbouring historically black universities have struggled.

At UCT, fundamental restructuring of the teaching curriculum into programmes was recently instituted, creating parallel structures and administrative breakdown. Motivated both internally (an audit and integration of management systems process has been undertaken), and externally (to conform to new legislation on matters such as employment equity), the institution is attempting significant restructuring. Early reports which fed into this restructuring process describe the university thus:

"The University is over-administered and rather seriously under managed. It is highly bureaucratic in its decision-making style and its decision-making culture does not encourage enterprise" (Shattock, 2000).

"Committees proliferate and their frequency is increasing while their agendas swell. It appears that the processes by which the University makes its decisions are overwhelmed" (Fielden, 1996).

Moving from a *laissez-faire* to a more formal management style presents unique challenges to those in information management positions, whose jobs are often evolving from managing technology to managing knowledge.

Within universities, information technology (IT) is universally equated with administration, but less so with core business (Scholtz, 1999), i.e. teaching and research. There has thus been a marked absence of effort to create information systems or knowledge repositories concerned with core business. Knowledge, whether tacit or explicit, tends to reside with individuals, where it is jealously guarded. With "rightsizing" and the accompanying loss of expertise, the management of organisational transactive memory (Nosek and Grillo, 1996) becomes critical.

How can this be done? Davenport and Prusak (1998, pp. 146–150) list a number of different types of knowledge management projects to be encountered, including:

- knowledge repositories, containing external knowledge, structured internal knowledge such as documents and reports, informal internal knowledge such as "lessons learned" knowledge bases, and high-level descriptions of the knowledge management process;

- knowledge transfer and access, including maps of knowledge sources and the building of expert networks;

- creating a knowledge environment, including process improvement, increasing recognition of the value of knowledge capital, the creation of new knowledge and the establishment of evaluation and reward systems to change behaviour.

The almost total absence of knowledge management projects within the university arises largely from the process of knowledge creation, which in a university is individual rather than social. Whereas with concrete products, processes are easier to document and thus to understand, automate or redesign, the individual production of knowledge is typically regarded as a black box (Fig. 5.3).

Within academia, "know-how" (and "know-who") is as important as knowledge (or "know-what") but less easy to capture in a system. This resonates with the argument of Nonaka (1998, p. 22) for the importance of recognising "soft" knowledge (tacit knowledge, insights, ideals) as well as more explicit knowledge. This "soft" knowledge is spread, according to Nonaka (1998, p. 37), through built-in redundancy, allowing for dialogue and communication, which are essential for mentoring. This highlights another issue: capturing what Nonaka terms "soft"

Figure 5.3 The knowledge production process.

knowledge is impossible without the full cooperation of the knowledge holders and learners.

Given the extent to which knowledge is bound up with identity in the academic context, the design and implementation of sound and sustainable knowledge management systems and processes demand close attention to and capacity in both technology and people issues. Negotiating the sharing and systematic integration of knowledge requires us to cultivate sensitivity in retaining the dynamic integrity and context of the knowledge, in addition to the usual system requisites of usability, robustness and security. Technology needs to be used to support work groups in the management and execution of their tasks, without threatening their autonomy or variety, to retain their interest in the work.

5.3 Managing Knowledge Workers

Knowledge workers, as is implicit from Drucker's prediction, require a different style of management. In fact, they thrive best by being left alone to direct their own work, with sufficient resources and support available if they require them. Direct attempts at "managing" them tend to breed resentment and demotivation, and are interpreted as undermining their professional judgement. But while the traditional university model of collegiality and autonomy allows knowledge workers to flourish, it can also facilitate the establishment of a forest of "dead wood". A management approach which combines high levels of autonomy and accountability needs to be explored: an approach which values and acknowledges the skill of the knowledge workers while motivating them to produce (Table 5.1).

Quinn, Anderson and Finkelstein (1998, pp. 183–184) describe this "skill" as "professional intellect" and identify four aspects thereof in order of increasing importance: cognitive knowledge (described as know-what), advanced skills (know-how), systems understanding (know-why) and self-motivated creativity (care-why). They argue that the last of these is particularly important to nurture, as it generates and renews the preceding three. The authors assert that this nurturing should be conducted though the provision of software tools to capture

Table 5.1 Characteristics of different management styles (synthesised from sources cited in the text).

	Strength	Potential weakness	Reporting	Makes use of	Encourages
Traditional management style	High accountability	Low self-motivation	Hierarchy	Directives, metrics, appraisal	Directed performance
Traditional university style	High autonomy	Low accountability	Collegial	Recognition, Collegiality	Creativity, pride in work
Knowledge nurturing style	Autonomy, self-directed motivation	High accountability	Network	Incentives, tools	Self-motivated creativity

knowledge, incentive schemes to encourage sharing of information, and appropriate organisational design such as self-organising networks.

Drucker (1988, p. 12) identifies a number of issues pertinent to this new organisational form. There needs to be an appropriate reward and recognition system for specialists. These specialists need to be motivated by a unified vision and managed by an appropriate management structure, which should provide for the supply, preparation and testing of the top management stratum.

5.4 Managing Knowledge Processes

Bukowitz and Williams (1999: pp. 9–12) outline seven phases in the knowledge management process (get, use, learn, contribute, assess, build and sustain, and divest). While the first four take place at a tactical level, the last three happen at the level of strategy. Following their stages, the discussion below examines some of the issues that arise during these activities as manifested within the knowledge processes in the university.

Before one can "get" knowledge, clarity is needed on what it is that people want (or need) to know, and in what form. Davenport (2000, p. 8) uses the term "information ethnography" to describe the paying of attention to the way people actually use information, rather than relying on technical means to deduce this. While software can, for example, record the URLs of websites visited during a session, it tells us little about what was really being sought, what of this was found, what was useful, or why.

Despite the abundance of information available, or perhaps because of this, many people complain that they have to spend too long searching for the information they need, when they need it. The situation reminds one of the "Help" function, standard with any computer application: if you can understand it, you do not need it; and by the time any "help" is given, the time allocated to complete the task has all but elapsed.

Rayport (2000, p. 42) suggests a strategy which does not attempt to do so, but rather leverages what people are currently using or doing, however trivial, to retain their attention. Thus, if academics have mastered e-mail and have come to use it for play as well as work, a knowledge management system based on e-mail is likely to be supported and used.

Can knowledge needs be anticipated so as to make the required knowledge available proactively (using push rather than pull technology) without the interface being too intrusive? Given the very real context of information overload, and the scarcity of attention (see Davenport, 2000, p. 46), how does one separate the wheat from the chaff?

Having identified the content and the form, one needs to identify potential providers: is it available in some repository, or who has the knowledge that is being sought? In what format is the knowledge currently stored? At this point, issues relating to context, ideology, and barriers of discipline and department have to be carefully negotiated during the translation of content, while retaining the integrity of the knowledge. Often those receiving the recycled knowledge are as reluctant to use it as the protective originator is to share it, preferring to generate their own knowledge *de novo* instead of adapting something generated elsewhere in a context that may not feel comfortable to them.

Another serious barrier to reuse can be the very technology designed to facilitate it. Many academics, specialists, professionals and other knowledge workers are not "techies", and may be disinclined to participate in processes that involve grappling with yet more technology. Scholtz (1999) found, in a university setting, that contrary to patterns for administrative staff where seniority correlated positively with high levels of self-reported comfort with and competence in IT, the reverse held true for academic staff. The more senior staff described themselves as "technophobic", while greater numbers of more junior academic staff felt that they were "competent" or even "expert" in this regard.

If the knowledge required is truly not available, it needs to be generated. When dealing with knowledge pioneers rather than knowledge wheelwrights,[1] one needs to build in a mechanism to record the lessons learned, so that organisational learning can take place.

Garvin (1998, p. 51) defines a learning organisation as "an organisation skilled at creating, acquiring, and transferring knowledge, and at modifying its behaviour to reflect new knowledge and insights." Most universities would qualify as "learning organisations" according to the first part of the definition, but not the second. Kleiner and Roth (1998, p. 138) argue that the reason that learning from experience is not exploited is because there are few management tools aimed at this. They present MIT's "Learning History" as a solution. Of course, if the knowledge production process is social rather than individual, the lessons learned are more likely to be explicit, and thus more easily captured through a knowledge management tool.

However, in the academic wilds, sharing the "lessons learned" is generally regarded as a sentence or two in a research report: low priority, with no reward. Defensiveness also becomes an issue, as admitting to mistakes reduces a person's status in the eyes of their peers. Running the risk of having an idea one thought brilliant being reduced to "old hat" by scoffing peers requires brave, committed participants.

On the technical side, there are issues of outcome: while careful planning would be anticipated to provide criteria against which to assess knowledge products, one should not underestimate the role of those catch-phrases for our time, synergy and serendipity. On the political side, the question of who evaluates the knowledge product, and against which criteria, becomes important. If usefulness is important, does "pure" knowledge, for which an application is not yet apparent, become less valuable?

> Evaluating knowledge is a political as well as a technical issue.

One of the drawbacks of a peer-regulated knowledge assessment system is that true creativity may not be recognised; conformity rather than deviance is encouraged, with the result that much research is replicative rather than innovative. Research in the mould of previous research reinforces, and reproduces, the research system as well as its products, and is therefore less threatening and more likely to gain acceptance from the assessing peer group. Furthermore, are peers, located within the discipline but also within the same context of competition for resources, promotion and recognition, the best placed to grade the product good or bad?

The allocation of resources to "build and sustain" presents further political problems. The decision as to which activities, departments or disciplines are considered "strategically important", and will therefore benefit from resource allocation, will advantage some at the expense of others. This generates or entrenches divisions, mistrust and even blatant hostility between departments, and minimises the chances of Drucker's unifying vision.

Resources such as the freedom to pursue knowledge creation on an individual level are also highly valued. Currently, the issue of the grading of academics is generating much discussion. Much of the discussion centres around the classification of some academic staff as active researchers, whose teaching load is then reduced to allow them to continue researching actively. This classification tends to entrench the status quo, as aspirant active researchers are too busy teaching to establish themselves in the research domain, and undermines any efforts made in the direction of equity. It is also contrary to the ethos of the "knowledge creating company", which regards everyone as a knowledge worker (Nonaka, 1988, p. 25).

The allocation of resources leads to questions of ownership of the knowledge produced. The ownership of knowledge is particularly relevant where knowledge is the product, and not merely a by-product. Bukowitz and Williams (1999, p. 321) refer to the "opportunity cost of retaining knowledge" which has to be maintained, but in a system where performance is evaluated on the basis of individual achievement rather than on contribution to a group, the cost of retaining ownership of a knowledge product, even if one has to invest time and money in its maintenance, may be significantly lower than the opportunity cost of sharing that knowledge.

5.5 Summary

It would appear that, despite Drucker's analogy, universities in many ways fall short of the ideals of "knowledge organisations", even though knowledge is their overt product.

This tacit knowledge is best transferred through tacit means, such as mentoring, which requires higher levels of redundancy in the organisation than management would like, as well as the willing cooperation of both the knowledge holder and the learner. Because recognition, appraisal, autonomy and reward depend on individual performance, knowledge workers are unhappy about sharing their knowledge as well as reluctant to recycle and adapt the knowledge produced by others in other contexts.

Most of these shortcomings relate to the individualised culture of the university, with knowledge being produced individually through black-box processes that cannot easily be replicated, mapped, automated or redesigned by others who are not in the know.

5.5.1 Suggestions for Improvement

Universities are blessed with a collegial ethos, whilst being fiercely competitive. This should be built on rather than undermined: it is in everybody's interest for the department, discipline or organisation to be highly rated. However, for this tightrope between competition and collegiality to work to the benefit of more efficient and more creative knowledge production, greater value needs to be placed on teams: teams should be the basis of recognition and reward, albeit without dispensing with individual recognition entirely. Rather, individual recognition can be based on the role played within the teams, with facilitative behaviour as well as productivity being rewarded. Recognition of professional intellect and skill, and respect for specialists, should be entrenched and not threatened by the management structure. The autonomy and independence of teams should be supported by technology, allowing them to manage their own work and to maintain high levels of variety and complexity.

5.5.2 General Recommendations

Some insights and guidelines can be distilled from the academic environment and applied, adapted and integrated within other organisational contexts where knowledge is regarded as an important asset. A philosophical shift is required in certain areas and certain assumptions need to be challenged:

- Value innovation not just successful reproduction. Truly creative knowledge generated may not immediately be evident as such.
- The nature of knowledge production processes needs to be examined. Social rather than individual knowledge generation aids organisational learning and builds organisational transactive memory.
- Recognition should be based on contributions to knowledge and sharing, as well as other more traditional measures of productivity.
- Recognition should also be given to creative application or adaptation of existing knowledge.
- "Failure" or frustration should be regarded as an opportunity for learning: where positive and useful contributions to a "lessons learned" knowledge base can be demonstrated, there should be no negative consequences for not having attained objectives.
- Feedback, reports and lessons learned need to be captured systematically without over-bureaucratising the system.
- New processes and system should build on, rather than seek to replace, existing organisational culture. If the change is seen to be too drastic, people will feel threatened rather than motivated.
- Systems to support new ways of working (such as Lotus Notes, intranets or extranets) should be populated by contributions and requests rather than "information for information's sake", which may never be used.

- Systems should be intuitive with the interface not "in your face", as few people are willing to grapple with new technology when there is a task to be accomplished, and the technology could detract from the very objective it seeks to facilitate.

Note

1 Endlessly reinventing, or refining, the wheel.

Chapter 6
Knowledge Dynamics in Organisations
Youngjin Yoo and Christian Ifvarsson

6.1 Introduction

Many organisations today are making large investments in their information systems to enhance the creation and sharing of knowledge among individuals in the organisation. Despite such large investments and concerted efforts by managers, many of these attempts to build corporate knowledge management systems (advanced information systems built to support systematically a company's effort to manage knowledge) have not been able to produce the intended return on investment. The symptoms of wasted investment vary from a total abandonment of the system to the accumulation of a large body of irrelevant and outdated static documents that yield little practical value to the intended users.

This chapter aims to enhance our understanding of the dynamic nature of knowledge in organisations.

Organisations consist of four basic elements that operate in an environment: social structures, social actors, goals and technology (Scott, 1998). Together they make up a system, which could be called sociotechnical, and knowledge in organisations is embedded in this system. Almost all aspects of organisations are facilitated by both social and technical subsystems, although with different emphasis on these elements in different systems. However, sociotechnical aspects of knowledge in organisations have not been well articulated in the literature. On the one hand, while the literature of social network and social capital emphasises the "social" aspect of knowledge in organisations, it lacks the technical element. Although the importance of the social aspect of organisation has not diminished, the increasing use of various technologies to support the management of knowledge in organisations has made the technical aspect increasingly important. On the other hand, however, the recent literature on information technology (IT) and knowledge management does not pay enough attention to the social aspect of knowledge in organisations.

> One important factor contributing to this failure is our lack of understanding of knowledge in organisations. In particular, the dynamic and holistic aspects of knowledge in organisations need to be incorporated into the design of the systems intended to support knowledge creation and sharing.

To be strategic and effective, organisations need to pay equal attention to both aspects of knowledge.

The purpose of this study is to present a normative framework on knowledge management in organisations, drawn from sociotechnical perspectives. Specifically, knowledge in organisations is conceptualised as distributed among individuals and technology embedded in sociotechnical systems, and the dynamic duality of knowledge in organisations is discussed. From this framework, a specific set of design principles is developed for the management of knowledge in organisations and sociotechnical systems to support it.

6.2 Knowledge in Organisations

The current literature provides two contrasting pictures of knowledge management. One perspective views knowledge as an object that can be controlled and transferred in the hierarchical structure (e.g. Davenport and Prusak, 1998), and the other considers knowledge as socially constructed (e.g. Lave and Wenger, 1991; Wenger, 1998). Both perspectives provide only partial views of knowledge in organisations; thus, these perspectives need to be considered equally to complement each other. The first perspective fails to explain how new knowledge is constructed, while the second fails to explain coherence and consistency in organisations.

Another limitation of the current literature on knowledge management is that it treats knowledge in organisations as if it were a sum of individual knowledge, without considering institutional aspects. For example, Simon (1991) stated that learning occurs in individuals' minds. A similar perspective is expressed in Huber (1991), whose focus was the process by which individual knowledge is organised and managed in an organisational context. These statements represent the general tendency to treat learning and knowledge as phenomena occurring on an individual level, even in the context of organisations. To fill these gaps, an attempt is made to enrich our understanding of knowledge in organisations by discussing its supra-individual aspect.

6.3 Organisations as Distributed Knowledge Systems

This perspective of knowledge in organisations draws upon perspectives that view organisations as distributed knowledge systems (Weick and Roberts, 1993; Boland and Tenkasi, 1995; Hutchins, 1995) and sociotechnical systems (Scott, 1998). In this perspective, the organisation is conceptualised as a system of technology and purposefully cognising human individuals throughout which knowledge is constructed and distributed in time and space. One of the important aspects of knowledge in organisations, as opposed to individual knowledge, is that it includes not only content possessed by individual agents, but also the connections among these agents (Hutchins, 1995; Morgan, 1986, pp. 77–109). According to Tsoukas (1996), knowledge in organisations manifests itself in the manner in which individuals interrelate their actions. It is also important to note that the patterns of connection among individuals are not always deterministic, but rather emergent and dynamic.

Although individual knowledge is an essential part of knowledge in organisations, it cannot by itself fully explain collective actions in organisations. There are numerous examples where a group or an organisation of highly capable individuals with expertise in their respective knowledge areas was not able to live up to the expectations held by the individual members (Janis, 1972). In the social psychology literature, these failures of collectives have often been attributed to poor "social" processes such as group-think, confirmation pressure, social influence, social loafing and crowding (Levine, Resnick and Higgins, 1993). However, recent findings in social cognition research (Weick and Roberts, 1993; Hutchins, 1995; Liang, Moreland and Argote, 1995; Moreland, Argote and Krishnan, 1996) indicate that failures by groups and organisations can occur independently of such social processes.

> Therefore, sociocognitive processes by which individuals co-ordinate their knowledge and interrelate their actions are as important as social processes in understanding why knowledge in organisations can be more or less than a sum of individual knowledge.

According to this perspective, no one holds the knowledge in an organisation in its entirety, although portions of it are held differentially by all (Tsoukas, 1996). Thus, it is argued that group performance is often related to the way in which individuals interrelate their knowledge with each other to perform the task. For example, Faraj and Sproull (2001) found that the ability of software development team members to co-rdinate expertise among themselves significantly influences team performance. Weick and Roberts (1993, p. 363) argue that individuals construct their actions while envisaging a social system of joint actions, and interrelate that constructed action with the system that is envisaged. These processes are distinct from social processes that were examined by traditional social psychology scholars in that they are "cognitive" processes occurring among individuals distributed within social entities such as teams and organisations. Liang, Moreland and Argote (1995) have shown that the sociocognitive aspect of group interaction (i.e. transactive memory) explains the effectiveness of team training better than the traditional social aspect of group processes such as trust and group cohesion.

Another important aspect of an organisation as a distributed knowledge system is that it is a sociotechnical system (Scott, 1998). As such, knowledge in organisations is made up of both social and technical subsystems (Lam, 1997). In reality, these two subsystems are interwoven in the dynamic and complex social fabric of organisations. No knowledge in organisations can be found in either purely social or technical form; rather, these two subsystems always coexist, without a clear boundary between the two, as illustrated in Figure 6.1.

Taken together, organisations may be conceptualised as distributed knowledge systems with two modes, content and connections, within two different subsystems, the social and the technical. While this conceptualisation may appear static at this point, the framework will be expanded later in an examination of the dynamic aspect of knowledge in organisations. However, first, each of these components of the model will be discussed in detail.

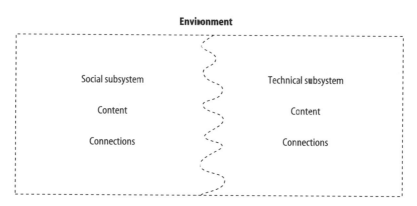

Figure 6.1 The knowledge system with its two subsystems and modes of content and connection.

6.4 Structure of Knowledge in Organisations: Content and Connections

As noted above, when organisations are viewed as distributed knowledge systems, one can differentiate two different modes of knowledge in organisations: content and the connections among the contents. Although it may seem convenient to view this as a network, the network view does not adequately capture this model since, as will be discussed later in the chapter, the distinction between content and connections is dynamic. For the purpose of this discussion, however, the model will be developed with the assumption that content and connections can be clearly distinguished. Once each mode has been discussed fully, the full dynamic picture of knowledge in organisations will be discussed.

In research on social systems, the primary focus has been on the connections between individuals (Blau, 1977; Granovetter, 1985; Scott, 1991; Hansen, 1999). These researchers often discuss these connections in terms of how they are formed and how tight or loose they are. In so doing, they do not explicitly consider the knowledge that is transferred in such interrelations.

Rational and analytical perspectives, by contrast, do not consider the connections but are instead interested in the content of individual knowledge and believe that such individual knowledge is feasible to construct, collect, analyse and restore. The early perspective on human cognition focused on a stimuli–response mechanism, which later resulted in a cybernetic perspective that considered people as information users and transformers in such information systems. In this perspective feedback loops of information were thought of as the source of learning. However, in the literature (Berger and Luckmann, 1967) human knowledge has more and more been considered to be a result of social construction in interactions between a technical and social reality based on intentional consciousness (Searle, 1998). With this in mind, the following paragraphs discuss how knowledge in organisations is constructed and manifested in content and connections, and consider how these modes appear in the technical and the social subsystem.

6.4.1 Content in Social Subsystems

Content in social subsystems refers to mental models, schemata or beliefs that individuals hold and impose on an information environment to give it form and meaning (Polanyi, 1962; Walsh, 1995; Checkland and Holwell, 1998). It includes both explicit paradigmatic knowledge such as scientific theories and formulae, and tacit knowledge such as stories and metaphors (Polanyi, 1962; Boland and Tenkasi, 1995). Kolb (1984) argues that it is possible to identify two types of knowledge: personal and social. Content in social subsystems is consistent with what Kolb refers to as personal knowledge. When personal knowledge is shared by connections (either social or technical), it becomes social knowledge.

6.4.2 Content in Technical Subsystems

Content can also be embedded in technology artifacts such as tools, transaction processing systems, robots and databases. For example, machinery tools that have controlling algorithms or automatic teller machines with routinised authentication and calculation procedures make up a portion of knowledge in an organisation. Although the individual knowledge in technical subsystems is socially constructed out of human cognition (Fulk, 1993; Bijker, 1995), it is experienced as a subjective unit. For example, a database that is accessed by several people appears to the single user to have its own life as it continuously changes. Also, a user of a malfunctioning computer or other technology will be likely to get angry with the computer, not with the constructor of the technology. As such, a single technology represents knowledge that can be accessed and transferred in time and space by connections to it, which can be either social or technical.

6.4.3 Connections Through Social Subsystems

Connections refer to the ways in which content embedded in both social and technical subsystems are interrelated with other contents. Examples of connections via social subsystems include personal and social relationships such as power and authority, accountability practice, trust and informal conversation. These connections tend to be imaginary. This is due to the fact that knowledge is distributed among individuals in the collectives and members neither fully nor equally know the way it is distributed. Social knowledge is independent of a single individual; it is transmitted by and embedded in systems of words, symbols and images. When individuals reach out in discussion, they build connections through social subsystems. Czarniawska (1998) states that spoken stories are the most important holders of knowledge in our society. Often in team sports, players talk about "being on the same page" or "reading others' minds". These phrases, although not well articulated, underscore the distributed nature of knowledge in collectives, that people know what they know and what others know, and the importance of connections. By using this knowledge, people can co-rdinate their connections in a goal-oriented way. In such manoeuvres, knowledge is constructed and distributed within the system. This conceptualisation is consistent with the notion of socially distributed cognition (Hutchins, 1995), collective mind (Weick and Roberts, 1993) and transactive memory (Liang, Moreland and Argote, 1995; Moreland, 1999).

6.4.4 Connections Through Technical Subsystems

Connections through the technical subsystem are defined as relations made via physical artifacts, often embedded in technology. Technical aspects of connections are best exemplified by the physical medium and technology used to create electronic communication and networks. Cables, routers and radio communication transmitters are examples of the tools used in these connections. Written documents and tools can be seen as technical aspects of connections as well. Archive material, books and databases can be used as connections to content produced in the past.

6.5 Duality of Knowledge in Organisations

Knowledge in organisations in its content and connection modes, like social structures in general, simultaneously enables and constrains individuals in the organisation (Giddens, 1984). It underscores the oscillating movement between treating knowledge as given (applying the existing stock of knowledge and thereby further reinforcing it) and treating knowledge as flexible (creating new knowledge and changing existing knowledge). It should be noted here that when people perform routinised and familiar tasks they meet the enabling face of knowledge, whereas when they perform novel and unstructured tasks they face the constraining aspect forcing them to connect, be creative and change.

For example, a formalised methodology employed by a company enables the employees of the company to perform tasks in a consistent manner, while at the same time constraining them from being creative. Also, face-to-face communication is enabling in the sense that it represents the richest form of connection that allows simultaneous co-ordination of knowledge between participating individuals. It further enables in the sense that it allows for the creation of new connections. At the same time, face-to-face communications limit our ability to reach out to other individuals located in different places. Therefore, connections through social subsystems have a strong potential to provide a rich medium for knowledge in organisations. However, they have considerable limitations in supporting knowledge sharing and transferring over distance in organisations. Similarly, connections through technical subsystems such as electronic communication also exhibit both enabling and constraining characteristics in organisations. Electronic communication technology allows people in different locations to communicate and share knowledge. However, it constrains rich sharing and transference of knowledge between different individuals with emerging needs in distant settings.

6.6 Knowledge Dynamics in Organisations

So far in this chapter, organisations have been conceptualised as distributed knowledge systems that have social and technical subsystems with loose and emergent structures between them. It was shown that knowledge in organisations has two modes: content and connections. Both content and connections simultaneously enable and constrain human actions in organisations. Knowledge structures are continuously constructed and reconstructed by the actions performed by the individuals in the organisation. Individuals tend to move within these structures in their daily work, represented by organisational procedures in routines (Nelson and Winter, 1982), rules, norms and informal roles (Scott, 1995). The dialectic contrasts of these structures are represented in knowledge dynamics in organisations. Accordingly, the final step in this theoretical discourse of knowledge in organisations is to discuss the dynamic duality between content and connections in the subsystems. In so doing, the discussion draws on experiential learning theory (Kolb, 1984).

Grasping experience can be achieved through comprehension, a process relying on conceptual interpretation and symbolic representation, or apprehension, a process relying on tangible, felt qualities of immediate experience. These are two dialectically opposed forms of the grasping dimension.

> According to Kolb (1984), learning is "the process whereby knowledge is created through the transformation of experience. Knowledge results from the combination of *grasping* and *transforming* experience" (Kolb, 1984, p. 41, emphasis added).

Similarly, the transforming dimension also includes two dialectically opposed modes of transformation of experiences: one through intention, a process relying on internal reflection, and the other through extension, a process relying on active manipulation of the external world (Kolb, 1984).

While equally important in the learning process, grasping and transforming dimensions cannot be experienced by individuals at the same time. Instead, individuals constantly move between these two modes in their learning processes, and through these movements they come to experience different modes of the same knowledge. Thus, through the grasping dimension, the content mode of knowledge in organisations becomes connections, and through the transforming dimension, the connections mode of knowledge in organisations becomes content. Recall that connections refer to the way in which contents are interrelated in social and technical subsystems. An individual's grasping experience (of either technology artifacts or other individuals) in an organisation, therefore, brings about changes in the pattern of interrelations among contents. That is, either a new connection is made or an existing connection is strengthened (or weakened, depending upon the nature of the grasping). In this process, through the grasping mode, content knowledge is experienced as new connections. In addition, an individual's transforming experience brings about changes in the cognitive makeup of the individual. That is, new connections to other individuals and knowledge embedded in technology artifacts, through the transforming mode of learning, influence the individual's cognitive makeup (Hutchins, 1995). While the content mode of knowledge has a permanent form of existence, connections exist temporarily as they occur. The following example from a field study conducted by one of the authors further illustrates these arguments.

A large global consulting company implemented a "knowledge repository" to facilitate the sharing of knowledge among consultants working in different countries. Various project-related documents such as proposals, interim worksheets, presentations and final deliverables are stored in the system. In most cases, consultants create these documents not through their own invention, but through collaboration with other people. Sometimes such collaboration takes place face to face, but more often than not it takes place via e-mail, telephone, or simple exchange of written documents or software codes. Here, the connections (i.e. collaborations) become content (i.e. documents) through the transforming of the experiences. Once stored, however, these documents are often used by other consultants as a way to find a piece of information or the right person to contact. Here, the content becomes connections through grasping.

For example, one consultant spoke of her experience of making a new connection to new pieces of information embedded in technology:

Another consultant shared his experience of making connections with other people through the same technology:

"It was something I needed to search and find that we had posted out on our internal Web page, so I needed to take the tons of information out on the Web and find it, kind of sift through that to make sure that I'm not overloading people with lots of details. But I did have to go out to a Website and navigate through that for this particular project."

"In some instances it's been helpful because I can then contact the author to maybe get more information about the area that the author, that they did not include into, that they did not post to [the firm's knowledge management system]."

Furthermore, in this interpretation of experiential learning theory, individuals orient themselves toward content and connections in certain ways. According to Kolb, in grasping, some prefer apprehension, while others prefer comprehension. Also, in transforming, some prefer intension, while others prefer extension. Based on this, Kolb observes that there are four dominant learning styles: diverging, assimilating, converging and accommodating. Therefore, individuals with different learning styles will gravitate towards content and connections in different manners. Individuals with converging or assimilating styles will prefer to transform content, while individuals with accommodating or diverging learning styles will be more oriented toward connections. It is possible to organise connections between these styles in two distinct ways, namely, by social and technical subsystems. Individuals with the accommodating style prefer social subsystems such as hands-on experience and acting on feelings, since they rely on personal rather than on technical information to solve problems. Those with the diverging style prefer working in groups and viewing concrete situations from several angles such as "brainstorming", where they listen and talk openly and receive personalised feedback. Those who exhibit the converging style are focused on connections in technical subsystems by practical applications of ideas and theories, but are most interested in technical problem solving such as experimentation, simulation and laboratory assignments. The assimilating style is even more oriented towards connections of abstract concepts and theories, and those with this style prefer reading, lectures, exploration of analytical models and spending large amounts of time in thinking. These aspects of content and connections on the cognitive level drive structures where learning preferences "control" knowledge patterns in organisations. For example, it is typical for managers, when recruiting new managers and employees, to select and, in doing so connect to, individuals with learning styles similar to their own. However, newer research on experiential learning indicates a need for an integrated cycle where individuals "touch all the bases" of content and connection to accomplish balanced and integrated knowledge development (Kolb, Boyatzis and Mainemelis, 1999) in organisations.

Furthermore, it is important to recognise that connections can be established in three different layers of individuals' cognitive makeup, as suggested by Giddens (1984): unconscious, practical and discursive consciousness. The connection at the unconscious cognition layer is often discussed in terms of institutionalisation, where individuals interrelate their actions without reflection, often based on habits. When asked why they do things in a certain way, a common statement is, "this is the way we do these things". A social identification through a cultural immersion would be a good example of connections at this layer. The connection at the practical consciousness layer is based on reflective action where individuals continuously monitor their own and others' actions in mimetic behaviour. Much of the knowledge at this layer remains in its tacit form (Polanyi, 1966). As such, at this level, individuals use socially constructed scripts to act upon and interpret others' actions in making connections. At the discursive consciousness layer, individuals rationalise their actions in the organisation. Knowledge is represented in the most explicit form at this layer. By using their linguistic skills, they talk, write and reflect about the different aspects of connections in organisations.

At the aforementioned consulting firm, all three levels of connections could be found. At the unconscious cognition level, the firm vigorously promotes its culture. The culture is often referred as "[the firm's name]'s way". It is not a particular methodology or tools that the firm uses; rather, it is the strong image that the firm wants to project to its consultants and clients. It is reinforced through the consultants' behaviours and demeanours, as well as their approaches to problems that they need to address. At this level, most of the connections are made through social subsystems. At the practical consciousness level, both technical and social subsystems are used to make the connections. For example, much of the tacit knowledge is shared in the form of one-on-one mentoring relationships. Even though the firm has developed global knowledge management systems, many consultants still turn to their superiors to gain the benefit of their insights and experiences. At the same time, in some cases, consultants try to embed their tacit knowledge into automated tools so that other consultants can leverage the tacit knowledge in practice without necessarily understanding it fully. For example, one consultant developed a program-testing module that incorporated not only the firm's programming standards but also his own years of programming experiences from various different projects. According to his account, the testing module was used by 25 new consultants to help to find errors with the programs they were developing that otherwise would have not been found, saving a lot of time and money for the firm. In this case, the connection was made via the technology subsystem. Finally, at the discursive consciousness level, the firm's knowledge management system is frequently used to help consultants to make connections to documents and other consultants through explicitly articulated documents.

Figure 6.2 illustrates the dynamic and distributed nature of knowledge in organisations by the interplay between technical and social subsystems. The arrows indicate the interplay between the grasping and transforming acts that interconnect content and connections in both social and technical subsystems. As explained above, through grasping and transforming, knowledge is experienced as either content or connections, in either social or technical subsystems. Further, connection and content represent a dynamic duality of knowledge in organisations. As noted in the figure, the content mode of knowledge in social subsystems spans the three layers of human cognition, with each layer having a different degree of tacitness. Finally, it is noted here that the connection mode of knowledge, particularly in social subsystems, exists only temporarily through reification processes by individuals (Wenger, 1998), while the content mode, particularly in technical subsystems, has a more permanent existence.

It is important to notice that these dynamics always exist as long as individuals confront and connect to each other at different layers of cognition in social routines and through technical subsystems. It also shows that a change in technical subsystem is always accomplished in interaction with social subsystems. When humans connect to technical subsystems, they also change their cognitive maps by learning, and knowledge is constructed, manifested and shared. Moreover, distributing knowledge in the technical subsystem enables the quick and easy use of the knowledge by others in the organisation.

The fact that knowledge is dynamic underscores the need for reflexivity and conscious actions from each individual in the organisation. By questioning existing

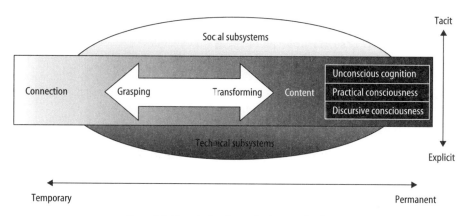

Figure 6.2 Knowledge dynamics in organisations.

structures in grasping and transforming experience and by stepping aside from the structures, individuals create dynamics that enable new knowledge to be constructed. In considering the oscillating movement between content and connection in the two subsystems, it is possible to see such dynamics.

The framework might seem somewhat simple, but when the numbers of subsystems with content interconnected to others are increased, the complexity increases exponentially. And unlike individuals, where the cognitive makeup of knowledge creation by grasping and transforming is tightly coupled in a given context,[1] organisations are loosely coupled, so that different modes of knowledge can coexist, albeit within the organisation's constraining and enabling structures.

6.7 Managerial Observations and Design Implications

The theoretical discussion thus far provides a normative framework of knowledge in organisations that suggests several ways to improve organisations' ability to manage knowledge. This analysis suggests several practical implications for the design of knowledge management systems and knowledge management policy.

6.7.1 Recognise the Subsystems of Knowledge in Organisations

Organisations can build different knowledge systems. Social and technical subsystems are more or less suited for different purposes and tasks. Organisations can thus have a portfolio of different types of subsystems within the organisational boundary. Instead of trying to build the knowledge in organisations based on either one of these two (Hansen, Nohria and Tierney, 1999), this theoretical framework suggests that there can be pockets of subsystems with different emphasis. Managers in organisations need to realise that within an organisation there are multiple knowledge systems, some primarily technical and some primarily social (Boland and Tenkasi, 1995; Wenger, 1998). For example, the aforementioned consulting firm fits the description of a technology-oriented knowledge management strategy according to Hansen, Nohria and Tierney (1999). However, a research and development group of the firm primarily uses connections via social subsystems and seldom uses the firm's global knowledge management systems, yet this group plays one of the most significant roles in the firm's global knowledge management initiative. Just as individuals' learning can be enhanced by touching all the bases of the learning cycle, having these multiple knowledge systems with different emphases in an organisation would enhance organisational learning.

6.7.2 Recognise the Different Modes of Knowledge in Organisations

It has been shown that knowledge in organisations has two modes, content and connections, and that while the content of knowledge is important, connections among the content knowledge are what makes knowledge in organisations distinct from individual knowledge. While the content of knowledge concerns know-what, know-how and know-why, connections concern know-where and care-why. Although the importance of these different aspects of knowledge management in organisations is well understood in the literature, the current prevailing design philosophy of knowledge management systems is preoccupied with the content mode of knowledge. It is the idea of building a "knowledge repository" where individuals can stack up their content knowledge for future reuse by unknown others. While undoubtedly useful, this approach does not recognise the other equally important mode of knowledge in organisations. Ironically, people often use the technology that was built explicitly to support the content mode of knowledge to make connections, as shown in the case study. Here, there is a need for a paradigm shift in the design approach of knowledge management systems, to see systems that explicitly recognise both the content and the connections mode of knowledge. Recently, the firm studied started virtual communities of practice to support informal connections among consultants across the world who share common interests. They are enabled and maintained through communication and collaborative technology. The firm also introduced a new software tool that helps consultants to recognise and maintain webs of connection among consultants, documents, specialties, clients and projects. Building on the firm's global knowledge management system, this tool allows consultants to "visualise" how these elements are connected to each other.

6.7.3 Recognise the Duality of Knowledge

Knowledge in organisations has different faces, and it is important to recognise that it has both enabling and constraining aspects. All too often managers and researchers follow trends (Czarniawska and Joerges, 1996) without reflection in their search for excellence. Instead, managers need to focus on their own businesses and try to find their enabling aspects. In contradistinction to Nelson and Winter's (1982) suggestion of replication being the best strategy, in the long run organisations may benefit more by defining and constructing their own market, which is possible if they consider knowledge as important in the interplay with their environment.

Explicitly recognising the constraining aspect of knowledge in organisations can help companies to avoid the pitfall of simple transfers of "best practices". While the enabling aspect of best practices can help individuals and groups to solve their problems quickly, their constraining aspect can limit people's ability to come up with the "right" solution, which may not exist in the company's existing best practice database.

6.7.4 Recognise the Dynamics of Knowledge in Organisations

Finally, content and connections are not two separate entities. Rather, they are two faces of knowledge in organisations. If organisations take into account the dynamics of knowledge in organisations, it would be possible, in a more explicit way, to use knowledge also appearing outside the formal structures of the organisation. In the past, organisations often focused on job rotation, enrichment or buy-ups to create dynamics and new ideas. In addition, it is important to focus on the capacity for knowledge creation and transfer in such arrangements, considering the different aspects of content and connections. Other examples of knowledge constructing procedures could be to involve customers and suppliers in the product development process or to set up organisational teams where newcomers are involved and therefore in need of connecting and integrating content (Louis, 1980). This drives situations where new individuals confront each other with loose knowledge structures that enable the construction of new combinations of content and connections. Although these arguments and ideas are not new, a shift in focus is needed. By considering the dynamic duality of connections and content in social and technical subsystems, it would be possible to construct organisations that are more vital. In so doing, managers could call their organisations distributed knowledge systems.

6.8 Conclusion

This chapter finishes with an image of organisations as dynamic and colourful emerging patterns, as opposed to an image of a static organisational chart. In this dynamic image of an organisation, each node determines its own colour in an enactment process in which it develops its understanding of emerging local patterns of which it is a part. Through this enactment process, a coherent global, yet dynamic, pattern emerges (as opposed to being drawn). Thus, an organisation is not a collection of thousands of idiosyncratic local actions, but a system of people and technology in interplay with each other. Hopefully, this image will inspire managers and scholars to think and act with a more dynamic and systemic perspective on knowledge in organisations.

Note

1 According to social psychology literature (Billig, 1988), the human cognitive process adapts and changes according to context. That is, different contextual cues can trigger different schemas which would then trigger different actions. Research has shown that individuals comfortably ignore different schemas they apply in different contexts. However, within a given context, people tend to show consistent patterns of cognitive and behavioural attributes.

Part 2
Know-What

Chapter 7
Personality Type and the Development of Knowledge Evolution

Nigel Phillips and Keith Patrick

7.1 Introduction

The effective design of usable information systems has been a particular challenge in recent years. The initial effect of the introduction of computer systems into organisations was to reduce greatly the socialisation opportunities inherent in a working situation. The incorporation of organisations' information systems into communication networks is introducing new forms of distance and distributed socialisation, the dynamics of which are currently still emerging and little understood.

> The sociotechnical systems approach is concerned with identifying and creating the conditions that lead to a "good fit" between people and technology. Central to this approach is the observation that the most efficient technical system is not, typically, the most effective sociotechnical system.

The vast increase in computational power enabled both researchers and managers to develop detailed animated models of social interactions that hold the potential for answering many questions about organisational structure and form and the effects of change. Such developments are still quite crude but there is no technological barrier to their continuing development. The term virtual community is usually applied to groups of people who meet and interact via the internet, but agent-based modelling approaches enable another type of virtual community to be developed, one in which software agents are constructed to behave like people. By a process of incrementally increasing the level of isomorphism between such models and real community behaviour testable, realistic models of organisational behaviour are a real prospect.

This approach is particularly useful when exploring questions concerning the management of organisational knowledge where the aim is to determine the organisational structures and forms that enhance the creation and sharing of knowledge that supports the sustainability of an organisation.

In this chapter an example of exploring the relationship between aspects of cognitive style and effective group performance is used to develop a methodology for the rigorous development of such models. Section 7.2 briefly introduces the theory of cognitive style. Section 7.3 discusses agent-based modelling and presents the underlying model of knowledge evolution that provides the theoretical grounding for the computational model. Section 7.4 presents the main elements of the model for investigating the dynamics of group formation under the influence of cognitive style. The final section offers some critical comments on the approach and indicates possible future developments.

7.2 Cognitive Style

The development of a clear understanding of the process of growth and maturity that leads to the autonomous responsible individual is one of the major scientific successes of the twentieth century (De Board, 1978). Central to this understanding is an appreciation of the interrelationship between the individual and the group. The development of individuality is a process that distinguishes self from others and defines self through alignment with others. It is only within a group that a person can be appreciated as an individual. Only through relationships does autonomy have meaning and only by autonomous self-control in cooperating with others can a person demonstrate his or her responsibleness. Individuality is realised and expressed through a number of different characteristics that can be broadly classified as abilities, competencies, personality and style.

Individuals vary in terms of a number of basic abilities that contribute to their individuality, such as strength, agility, dexterity, intelligence and creativity. People's abilities distinguish them from others and affect how they are valued and appreciated by others and how they value and appreciate themselves. The extent to which self-image is enhanced or deprecated by the perceived value of these abilities influences the aspects of personality that are relied on in a given situation. People naturally seek to place themselves in situations where they can be most valued and avoid circumstances in which they lack confidence (Argyle, 1989).

Psychologists have amassed considerable evidence for the existence of distinct preferences among individuals in how they perceive, represent and reason about the world. These differences are manifest in personality types and cognitive styles. Psychological constructs develop either innately or at a very young age. These constructs determine the preferences that will develop for conducting personal interactions and modes of learning. How people prefer to approach the world, whether they are introvert or extravert; how they prefer to represent the world, verbally or with images; how they reason about the world, whether analytically or holistically; and how they respond to the world through judging or perceiving have all proved useful guides to personality that emerge at an early age and persist throughout life (Riding and Rayner, 1999).

Regardless of an individual's preferences, the process of personal development enables the development of strategies for coping with many different situations. Therefore, within the limits of social mobility people naturally cluster into groups that reinforce their preferences and about activities with which these preferences are suited to dealing. Likewise, strategies are developed for dealing with those unavoidable situations that do not suit these preferences.

> People are naturally attracted to those situations that suit their preferences and to those people who share their modes of expression.

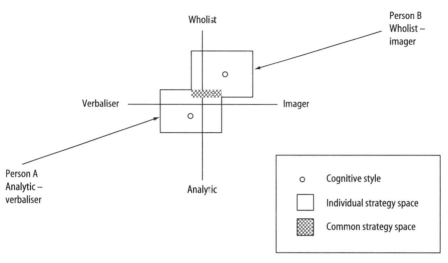

Figure 7.1

Riding and Rayner (1999) identify two dimensions of cognitive style along which any individual can be positioned:

Wholist–Analytic and Verbaliser–Imager

In addition, individuals have learning strategies that extend their learning range in each direction away from their base preference (Fig. 7.1).

These preferences shape and colour the theories that people develop about the world, the types of models and explanations that they prefer, what they pay attention to and consider worth measuring, and the types of solution that they propose to address their problems. The establishment of distinct and immutable personality types at an early age ensures a diversity of opinion in society and increases the chances of finding useful solutions.

7.3 Agent-based Modelling

Traditionally, there are two basic reasons for building a model:

- to increase our understanding and ability to predict and control the behaviour of some real-world phenomenon of interest;
- to design a system the behaviour of which conforms to some preconceived plan, i.e. to create a real-world phenomenon that can be predicted and control.

The advent of cheap computing power enables a third approach:

- to explore the intrinsic organisation of multiple interacting components.

In particular, models can be used to explore the large class of natural phenomena that contain too many components with too many combinations to be treated exhaustively but insufficient numbers to be treated statistically.

Agent-based modelling techniques enable the validation of theories of behaviour in complex systems:

- given a particular environment, what (if any) collection of agents obeying simple rules will lead to a particular type of behaviour, or alternatively,
- given a set of agents obeying simple rules, what environmental factors (if any) will lead to a particular type of global behaviour?

Agent-based models enable researchers to look both ways at once: to explore both individual algorithmically defined behaviours and collective structural constraints. More importantly, any well-defined theory about the behaviour of autonomous individuals in given environments can be mapped into an agent-based model and the predictions of the theory tested. This is particularly useful for validating models where experimentation in the real world would be too difficult or ethically questionable.

It is necessary to highlight the theory underpinning the basic elements of the model to make clear what metaphysical assumptions are made about real human social behaviour and to what extent the model elements are true to, or approximations of, those assumptions. This is important both to ensure that the model and the conclusions drawn from it are consistent and that comparisons of different models do not inadvertently ascribe metaphysical assumptions not entertained by the original modellers. Should logically equivalent models be found that differ in their underlying metaphysical assumptions then interesting questions can be asked about those assumptions: whether they too are logically equivalent or whether the models truly capture them.

7.4 The Evolution of Working Knowledge

In evolutionary terms, success is the production of viable offspring. That is, offspring that are themselves capable of producing viable offspring. Living systems are constrained in their ability to accommodate the perturbations of their environment by their structural organisation. Environmental perturbations trigger changes of state. Changes of state are destructive if the system cannot maintain its integrity, i.e. continue to be organised, in that new state. To maintain its integrity a system must be able to repair and reproduce its parts, including its boundary with the environment. Evolution occurs when systems produce copies of themselves that are similar but not the same; this can be thought of as variations on a theme. These variations may be better able to maintain their integrity than their progenitors in particular environments. The predominance of particular environments will induce a drift in a population of organisms towards those that can best maintain their integrity in those environments.

For an organism to change and evolve its job within its group those jobs must become vacant. For offspring to take over from their parents the parents must die.

Job design by evolutionary selection in animals is widely accepted and often cited as evidence of the naturalness of the division of labour in human society. However, the mechanisms by which jobs in human society are decided are generally held to be the result of learning, which is different from and independent of evolution.

7.4.1 Knowledge Transmission, Learning Transition and Evolution

Humans are characterised by their ability to make and use tools. Technologies greatly enhance the ability to confer privilege in human society. As the number of different types of technology has increased so have the number and variety of specialist roles in human society.

Tool making and tool using both require considerable learning and therefore require their own distinct privileging behaviours to reproduce and evolve from one generation to the next. In human society, this behaviour has led to the emergence of distinct subcultures centred around trades and professions. The creation of master craftsmen through apprenticeships is a good example of a community of practice. Lave and Wenger (1991) have shown that the same features are found in communities of practice across all cultures. This suggests that communities of practice are a natural attractor in human social systems. African tailors, Mexican midwives and Alcoholics Anonymous all pass on their knowledge in the same way. They term this mechanism "legitimate peripheral participation". Inexperienced members get to see what more experienced members do and how they reason about problems by participating in those activities performing peripheral but necessary (and hence legitimate) tasks. The process of development from apprentice to master echoes that of birth to maturity. The success of the masters lies not merely in their ability to apply their tools and survive the perturbation of the environment, but in their ability to pass that knowledge on to a new generation. Knowledge evolves through a process of reproduction from moment to moment and from generation to generation. Knowledge is transmitted from master to apprentice not by direct communication but by experiencing the process that the master creates. Learning is a transition from neophyte to master marked by a deepening understanding of the process.

> Trades and professions form communities of practice that reproduce the working knowledge of tool making and use. Such communities of practice also reproduce the working knowledge of the reproduction process: they possess operational closure.

The knowledge of every new master is a variation on the theme of his or her master's knowledge. New ways of doing things, new tools or new applications of old tools, evolve that are better able to cope with the environment, and old ways die out. The evolution of tools and jobs is complicit. The discovery of new tools and new ways of using tools creates a space of possibilities: new environmental niches to which jobs can adapt.

Closure

A system of transformations has closure if every state generated by those transformations can be used as further input to those transformations. A set of operations together with some set of states to which the operations can be applied has closure if every new state generated by the operations is also a member of the set. For any set of operations there must always be some set of states with which they form a closure: the set of all possible states if no other.

Fields

A field is a set of states that is closed under some set of transformations. That is, any state can be transformed by any combination of transformations from the set and the result will be another member of the set. Adaptation is the process of seeking a set of transformations that will generate a field of viable states: states in which the adapting agent can continue to be and to apply the transformations.

Fields of knowledge consist of a set of ideas and the operations are the methods, tools and techniques that can be applied to those ideas to generate new ideas. New tools may extend the field so that the original becomes a subfield. New ways of applying existing tools may explore new areas of the field.

Work

Humans work to increase their identity. They seek behaviours that will produce closures in their life-space. The better the closure the more identity they gain, the more confidence they have in their expectations (the better they are able to predict outcomes), the lower the cost of regulation (information processing) and consequently the better their ability to control their circumstances and hence the better their ability to survive. People have to work to survive. The usefulness of work is measured by the degree of closure it achieves and the consequent strength of identity gained.

Individuals

It may be assumed that all social interactions take place between individual workers, where a worker is an autonomous agent that seeks to generate fields which lead to closures in its wider environment that enhance its viability.

Groups

At its simplest, a group is a collection of workers where members of a group are more likely to interact with each other than with other members of the population.

Each worker is able to join and leave as they please. From the second and third person perspectives, a group constrains the interactions between the workers in a population. From the first person perspective a group is an identity for a cluster in the interactions of the population.

Membership

People naturally participate in many different groups and each group will have different rules governing membership in particular rules for joining and leaving. These rules are often interdependent membership of one group is dependent on (or excluded by) membership of another. Groups may be of fixed or variable size. In either case, joining and leaving might be a matter of individual choice, group decision, random events of some combination of these three.

Interactions

Depending on the viewpoint adopted, groups either determine the probability of interactions between agents or identify agents with high probabilities of interacting. Structural relationships within groups constrain the possibilities for interaction. A manager in a formal setting may regularly communicate with each other member of the group but will receive the majority of communications from just a few other members. Groups therefore define the opportunities available to their members for interaction.

Taxation

For groups to be more than mutual appreciation societies they must have associated activities that require particular strategies for dealing with them. It is also important to ensure that knowledge transfer is not, inevitable; for instance, by assigning or evolving cooperation strategies similar to Axelrod's (1997) approach to the iterated prisoner's dilemma.

7.5 Agent-based Investigation of the Effects of Cognitive Style on the Development of Groups

The process of developing an agent-based model to explore the dynamics inherent in any theory of systems behaviour is quite straightforward. It starts with a statement of a theory and identifies the features of the system that it defines, the entities that these features distinguish, the associations between these entities, and the effects of their interaction. Then, software objects are designed that are isomorphic with the behavioural descriptions provided by the theory. Next, the conditions of the real-world system that the theory seeks to explain are included and a number of scenarios developed. From these scenarios agent-based models are constructed and their states allowed to evolve for a period of time. Depending on the expected behaviour, this might be until a steady or cyclic state is reached, or for a given number of steps, or until some particular condition is true of some arbitrary measure of the state.

Any phenomenon has an effectively limitless number of features that might be used to describe it. The purpose of scientific investigation is to determine some minimal set of features that provide sufficient information to be able to describe and explain the behaviour of interest and to make accurate predictions about that behaviour at some future time t_1 given a state of the system in terms of those features at time t_0.

The ease with which two individuals will be able to communicate and learn from one another is dependent on how developed the learning strategies of one are at coping with the cognitive style of the other. It may be assumed that successful communication and learning will enhance each individual's strategies while a lack of success leaves strategies unchanged, and that any two individuals can communicate and learn from one another even if they do not share any common strategy space. Simple mechanisms can be defined for the interaction of a group of agents. That is, for any two agents the probability of their successfully communicating can be calculated and the outcome determined of an encounter based on a random number, as shown in Figure 7.2.

A number of agents each with randomly generated strategy spaces are assigned randomly to a number of groups.

7.5.1 Interactions

A variety of ways can be arranged for interactions between agents to occur:

- Each group member is allowed to interact with every other member of the group.
- Each group member makes some fixed number of interactions with randomly selected members of its group.

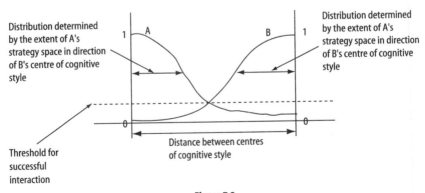

Figure 7.2

- Each group member is allowed to interact with a fixed subset of members of its group who are the only ones with which it communicates.
- Each group member is allowed to interact with each other member according to some probability.

Each approach reflects different "natural" constraints to be found in human group organisation. Regardless of the rules for interactions one needs to consider their effect on the individual and the group. It may be assumed that an interaction where learning takes place is inherently more satisfying than when it does not. A simple measure of satisfaction is then given by the ratio of successful interaction to total interactions. The satisfaction of the group can then be measured by the ratio of successful interactions for all members to the total interactions for all group members.

Movement between groups is similarly open to a number of treatments depending on the assumptions that are made about agent mobility and the cost of a move.

The simplest approach is to assume that an agent will randomly join another group if their satisfaction is less that the group satisfaction by an amount greater than the standard deviation for the group. In addition, a dissatisfied agent might randomly interact with members of another group and move or not depending on the outcome. This can be extended so that groups have a right of veto and so on. Individuals who are unacceptable to any established group are by default assigned to an excluded group.

7.6 Conclusion and Future Work

In summary, there are clear benefits in adopting this type of approach, as well as a need for further developments. In considering the purpose, the benefit of an agent-based approach can be seen as the ultimate interest remains in the discovery of the types of group structure and rules of interaction that lead to effective group dynamics.

In order to model this it is necessary to identify the simplest set of mechanisms that reproduce this behaviour and the minimum set of variables sufficient for measuring and predicting the likely behaviour of different configurations of those simple mechanisms. Simple random assignment of strategy spaces to agents results in some (intuitively) very unnatural outcomes; the additional constraints of such models impose additional assumptions that need to be clearly documented. The choice of conditions for change of group membership can be crucial. If changing groups is too easy the model is likely to thrash around for a long time without the development of stability. This is tied directly to how much a successful interaction improves the agents' learning strategies. If this is too optimistic any group will quickly coalesce and individual differences will disappear completely.

This promotion of a self-sustaining and regulating culture and structure that does not restrict the organisation's development is therefore its long-term success.

The dynamics of the model are so constructed that successful learning will always lead to an increase in learning strategy spaces and it will always be possible for individuals to learn from each other regardless of their respective strategy spaces. A more realistic future model would benefit from the inclusion of some inhibitory or negative effects, for instance where a failure to communicate reduces the probability of future cooperation.

While these points represent a problem for developing the agent-based model, they indicate how this approach can be used to identify useful research questions to be explored by more traditional approaches. These approaches will nurture the development of awareness and understanding, which enhance the creation of positive situations for work teams to evolve. The encouragement of the development of common strategy spaces for learning and cooperation is central to the creation of a dynamic and adaptable workforce.

Additional organisational benefits are achieved through the facilitation and migration of personnel and knowledge across the organisation, further enhancing the ability to embed knowledge within the organisation's structure. This enables an organisation to evolve and maximise its learning, and in turn reduce the effects of key personnel leaving.

Once suitable models have been developed it will become possible to ask more specific questions about how favourable group dynamics can be developed. Investigation of the effect of introducing training programmes to improve learning strategies or the effect of introducing highly skilled facilitators (with large learning strategy spaces) into sink-groups can be undertaken.

While this approach does not enable the identification of guaranteed successful structures it does enable the identification of inherently bad structures. The key to the viability of any organisation is the avoidance of circumstances that lead to non-viability. Inasmuch as it enables the avoidance of such states, the approach is very promising. Clearly, these ideas are still in their infancy and there are many difficulties to be resolved, not least in the development of rigor in the mapping of observed real-world phenomena to model constructs. Looking to the future and given the profound impact that the internet is having on the potential for group formation, the following factors need to be considered:

- the nature of interaction between members that it permits (e.g. groups pursuing common goals whose members' interaction may be entirely text based and asynchronous); and
- the difficulties that these interactions cause for traditional approaches to interpersonal relations (where interpersonal groups are defined by face-to-face interactions).

In conclusion, agent-based modelling provides a comprehensive tool set for exploring the inherent dynamics and sensitivity to conditions of any new theories that might be proposed.

Chapter **8**

The Importance of Individual Knowledge in Developing the Knowledge-Centric Organisation

Jonathan D. Pemberton and George H. Stonehouse

8.1 Knowledge Management and the Role of the Individual

In an uncertain economic and business environment, knowledge is "the one source of lasting competitive advantage" (Nonaka, 1991), with products and services essentially differentiated by knowledge and intellectual capital.

Furthermore, the knowledge and skills of its workforce, and the knowledge platform upon which these skills are based, govern, in part, the performance of a company (Senge, 1990). The development of the knowledge-centric organisation, a term discussed in more detail later in this chapter, essentially involves an organisation actively exploiting knowledge in relation to its operations, performance and success, resulting in superior competitive performance. Such knowledge might include technical prowess, creativity, personal and organisational know-how, original thinking, problem-solving expertise and competitor intelligence, for example.

Developing and leveraging this information is the crux of effective knowledge management, which is a dynamic process relying on the adoption, application and sharing of practices, with effective knowledge transfer being a catalyst throughout. Although organisational knowledge acts as a conduit through which improved decision making and greater responsiveness result, it is primarily developed from the knowledge of individuals within the organisation and as a consequence of social interaction (Sveiby, 1997; Stonehouse and Pemberton, 1999).

Technology figures prominently in the much of the discussion of knowledge management, but this perspective represents at best a partial, and at worst an inadequate, explanation of how knowledge is created and managed within organisations.

Invariably, both explicit and implicit knowledge begin as individual knowledge but, to improve performance substantially, are transformed into organisational knowledge through the processes of articulation and internalisation. In short, the conversion of individual ideas, know-how, creativity and problem-solving skills are necessary elements of developing organisational learning and building an effective knowledge management strategy.

More specifically, the transition of tacit individual knowledge to measurable and usable organisational knowledge signifies a major hurdle in the knowledge

The technological approach relies predominantly on the identification of explicit knowledge under the banner of intellectual capital, typically focusing on its quantification in a database, but failing to capture the true value of implicit individual knowledge that forms the backbone of an organisation's knowledge assets.	The sociotechnical perspective highlights the importance of the interplay between the social aspects of an organisation, typically human resources and culture, with the technological infrastructure, a means by which new knowledge assets can be created, shared and communicated to develop the knowledge-centric organisation, the focus of this chapter.

management process. In essence, individual knowledge only results in intellectual capital once it behaves as any other tangible resource and becomes organisational knowledge with the potential to enhance a company's competitive position.

In effect, the problems facing companies in their quest to capitalise on individual know-how and integrate it within a coherent knowledge management strategy centre on:

- identifying a metric or metrics for extracting and representing individual knowledge;
- developing mechanisms for translating individual knowledge into organisational knowledge through cultural shifts and managerial initiatives;
- encouraging individuals to contribute, rather than withhold, knowledge, emphasising the personal and organisational benefits of doing so.

8.2 Extraction and Measurement of Individual Knowledge

Of the above three categories, the first represents the most difficult issue to address. Devising a meaningful, prescriptive and all-embracing measure is essentially unrealistic, as individual knowledge is a complex amalgam of factors. Personality, motivation, intellectual capacity, experience and area of expertise, coupled with an awareness of what is knowledge and what is not, are potential determinants in this respect. Such awareness, and a position from which to control the dissemination of individual knowledge, also figure prominently.

The use of patents and licences is often a way in which organizations attempt to create competitive knowledge by harnessing individual knowledge to develop intellectual capital. However, such assessment invariably centres on a structured and scientific approach where knowledge can be "commodified" within measurable technical systems, frequently failing to take account of the social environment and human psyche and, ultimately, developing objective measures to often subjective elements (McAdam and McCreedy, 1999). Exceptions do exist, notably

Skandia, the Swedish insurance company, which has devised an Intellectual Capital Index based on human capital, as well as process, customer, and renewal and development capital (Lank, 1997). Other attempts to address the social and human aspects invariably result in prescriptive systems resulting in qualitative or quantitative benchmarks of which, as De Jager (1999) acknowledges, the former, typically based on leadership, technology, culture, measurement and process, serve only to generate discussion of knowledge management issues rather than developing effective strategies, with the latter being mechanistic and lacking universal credibility.

While the above approaches are genuine attempts to represent knowledge, the identification of a singular metric in the context of individual knowledge is, it is argued, not feasible. Equally, multiple benchmarks, while being more realistic, rely too heavily on organisational facets, failing to embrace personal characteristics and traits in the creation of individual knowledge and, consequently, make measurement difficult. Combined, these factors give limited scope for adopting technically orientated measurement mechanisms and arguments associated with the intellectual capital approach, particularly when applied to the interpretation and assessment of individual knowledge.

8.3 Structure and Infrastructure

Recognition that reliance on technically orientated measurement of individual knowledge is unlikely to capitalise fully on expertise within a company leads to a sociotechnical viewpoint of knowledge management that embraces cultural, organisational and managerial initiatives, in conjunction with technological support systems. This represents a more realistic means of empowering individuals and offers most scope for handling individual knowledge within an organisation.

In particular, the individual learning process and the acquisition of knowledge are undoubtedly accelerated and enhanced by the sharing of information and ideas, accompanied by an openness that encourages questioning, debate and discussion of existing and future practices (Appelbaum and Gallagher, 2000). Such a social environment serves as a platform upon which to test individual ideas and beliefs prior to their transformation into organisational knowledge. Thus, the organisation provides a cultural context, supported by a structure and infrastructure that both fosters and stimulates the learning of individuals and groups, and encourages the creation and sharing of knowledge (Pemberton and Stonehouse, 2000).

The ideas of structure and infrastructure are crucial elements here as they bring together the social and technical context of the organisation and ensure that appropriate resources and mechanisms are in place to enable knowledge transfer to take place.

Structures that promote learning and harness knowledge capabilities are characterised by a determination to encourage knowledge sharing within a company. Although no ideal model exists, the use of specialist and cross-functional groupings through network structures or through cross-functional project teams or task groups, preferably within a flat organisational structure, represents a conducive environment for achieving these goals. Equally, deployment of a matrix structure is an alternative means of accommodating these objectives, which while blurring lines of responsibility, assists the promotion of a holistic view of knowledge. Alternatively, cross-functional project teams or task groups can be established within a more conventional organisation structure.

Without doubt, organisational hierarchy poses a problem, impacting upon the social context, with different levels making it harder to create an environment that facilitates the building of knowledge, its diffusion, coordination and control, with the distortion of ideas and knowledge resulting as a consequence of multilayer transmission. In addition, hierarchy may hinder cross-functional and horizontal communication.

> Flatter organisational structures tend to better assist the coordination and control of knowledge, creating a social context that favours effective knowledge management.

> While there is no single structure that uniquely supports learning and knowledge transfer, empowerment of the individual, together with flat network structures that foster cross-functional communication and where functional barriers are low, appears to facilitate knowledge management more effectively.

While structure has a significant bearing on an organisation's ability to harness its knowledge assets, the infrastructure, comprising the systems and technology that underpin its activities and learning culture, is equally important. Developments in information and communications technology, for example networking and multimedia, have transformed the ability of both individuals and organisations to augment their intelligence by accelerated learning. The media and channels of communication that assist in the creation, storage, sharing and transfer of knowledge are integral elements of the knowledge-centric organisation, permitting organisational configurations that were previously inconceivable.

Continuing improvements in both hardware and software considerably enhance an organisation's capacity for developing and sharing knowledge. Arguably, the generation and sustainability of competitive advantage rely on organisations embracing new technologies designed to facilitate the handling and management of knowledge within an intelligent enterprise.

The difficulties associated with knowledge storage and communication should not be underestimated and the location of the knowledge base is of critical importance, particularly in relation to implicit or tacit knowledge (Grant, 1997). To alleviate such problems, decentralising to individuals possessing implicit knowledge or, alternatively, ensuring decisions that requiring such knowledge are referred to these experts, is a desirable model within the knowledge-centric organisation. Explicit knowledge presents fewer problems, being stored centrally and transmitted via information systems.

Ensuring that a company capitalises on its knowledge assets is clearly a function of its structure and infrastructure, but without an organisational culture that encourages and empowers individuals to communicate and share expertise, any potential competitive gain in relation to knowledge exploitation is severely diminished. The cultural dimension forms the basis of the remaining sections of this chapter.

8.4 Towards a Knowledge-centric Organisation

Cultural shift is inextricably linked with the notion of the learning organisation, "a powerful metaphor driving the development of knowledge management activities ... raising consciousness about the value of knowledge through reflection and learning and the latent potential of what the company could gain if learning were shared across the firm" (O'Dell, Wiig and Odem, 1999). Thus, developing a conducive environment designed to encourage the sharing and transfer of knowledge is a pivotal feature of the learning organisation and is an integral element of the sociotechnical approach to managing knowledge. Demarest (1997) argues that effective knowledge management should not only address the organisation's infrastructure and the learning that takes place therein, but also capitalise on internal social interchange. McAdam and McCreedy (1999) expand Demarest's model further, suggesting that knowledge management initiatives depend on recognising both employee emancipation and the business benefits accruing. Changing behaviour, both individual and cultural, represents a crucial element of organisational learning and knowledge management.

The consulting group KPMG identifies five phases through which companies pass in the process of developing a knowledge-based culture (Fig. 8.1). At each stage of the journey, better use of knowledge resources ensues, with the potential for superior performance (KPMG, 1997).

Figure 8.1 The knowledge journey.

Arguably, progression from knowledge chaos to knowledge awareness represents one of the most significant hurdles and impetus for change is largely a function of managerial vision, commitment and organisational structure. Once this step has been taken, further movement centres on developing the infrastructure and systems, often technology based, to facilitate knowledge interchange and allocating physical and financial resources to achieve this. However, progression to the final two stages invariably relies on creating a cultural environment that supports and optimises knowledge assets. Furthermore, without such initiatives, the opportunities for encouraging and nurturing individuals to share their knowledge within a company are significant barriers in the development of a coherent and effective

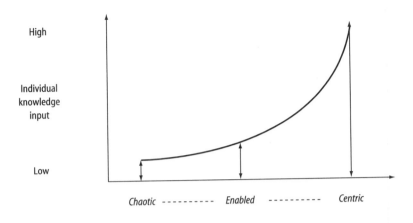

High

Individual
knowledge
input

Low

Chaotic ---------- *Enabled* ---------- *Centric*

Knowledge management stage

Figure 8.2 Individual knowledge and the knowledge journey.

knowledge management strategy (Skyrme and Amidon, 1997). Indeed, unless the culture exists to ensure that individual learning becomes organisational learning, the knowledge-centric organisation is unlikely to emerge. Figure 8.2 gives a visual representation of the role of individual knowledge in an organisation's knowledge management development, emphasising the higher weighted value of individual knowledge in the pursuit of a truly knowledge-centric organisation. Depicting the weighting as exponential reflects the critical role that individuals play in creating knowledge and the collective vision of all employees, not just managers, in moving from a knowledge-managed organisation to a truly knowledge-centric one.

Recognition of knowledge sharing and the importance of the individual in a sociotechnical context are now in evidence in a number of organisations. Chevron, for example, while implementing some of the "harder" elements of knowledge management through technology and systems, has also embraced and incorporated "softer" components representing behavioural and cultural shifts in an attempt to support learning and utilisation of best practices. The management of United Airlines has adopted a "walking around" approach to foster informal information exchange, resulting in a more fruitful use of human capital. Breaking down communication barriers, at all levels, acts as a catalyst in generating greater trust and creating a more productive environment.

Communication, often oral in nature, is an important element of knowledge transfer, but is highly dependent on individual ability and verbal eloquence, as well as the skills of the recipient in using this knowledge. Some companies have encouraged informal sharing of information between individuals without recourse to a corporate memory, the result of which is potentially "deeply creative and serendipitous" (O'Dell, Wiig and Odem, 1999). Others develop a sharing culture by the creation of teams, relationships and networks, with many formalising procedures based on structured guidelines.

8.5 Embracing the Sociotechnical Approach for Dealing with Individual Knowledge

A characteristic of individual knowledge is its often tacit nature (Spender, 1998). Examples include customer contact, where an employee establishes a close business relationship with a client, thereby deriving a picture of their needs, but never formally translating this mental information into measurable and explicit knowledge. The competitive application of knowledge is in future likely to centre on unravelling the implicit knowledge stored in an individual's head and disseminating it to parts of organisation for it to be used effectively, thereby resulting in organisational knowledge. However, organisational guidelines and knowledge management strategies are unlikely to help in this situation unless there is recognition by an individual that such information represents an asset to the organisation. In this sense, individual attributes, such as personality, motivation and intellect, are of paramount importance in leveraging individual know-how into tangible organisational knowledge.

Developing a knowledge-based culture and supportive work environment represents a pragmatic approach to the problem and various companies have introduced mechanisms for transforming implicit knowledge into explicit knowledge by creating a culture that encourages employees to record their knowledge.

- Andersen Consulting, Ford and Monsanto have developed regimes where employees produce written reports or video presentations, recorded with their companies' databases and intranets, and permitting others within their organisations to search and use this shared knowledge.

- Others, such as Hewlett-Packard, have used more formal mechanisms such as a community-based electronic discussion forum designed to transfer tacit knowledge into a repository. Here "tips tricks, insights and experiences" are captured using Lotus Notes, permitting local and remote access by employees around the world designed to bring together their decentralised workforce (Davenport, 1997).

- Microsoft has, since its inception, maintained advantages over the competition because of the knowledge and capabilities of its staff. Much time and effort has been invested in identifying knowledge competencies to great effect, resulting in increased communication between employees and an improved margin of advantage over competitors.

- British Petroleum developed a virtual teamwork project as a key element of its strategy to encourage communication and knowledge sharing amongst partners and employees. The use of coaching as a facilitating mechanism has produced significant improvements, accelerating progression along the learning curve and resulting in a significant return on investment.

- More informal approaches have also been adopted in some organisations. British hi-fi retailer Richer Sounds encourage employees to "go to the pub" for networking purposes, thereby loosening structures to enable knowledge, skills and experience to flow easily, with such encouragement even taking the form of small financial incentives. In a similar vein, ICL stimulates knowledge transfer using a Café *VIF* (Valuing ICL Knowledge) roadshow, operating from canteens and meeting points, serving complimentary coffee and croissants.

In the above examples, the development of a knowledge culture, either formal or informal, is seen as a central vehicle for capitalising on individual expertise and know-how. It should not be forgotten that management and leadership figure prominently in these initiatives, indicative of those organisations in the later stages of the knowledge journey. Managerial innovation is a key element in developing a knowledge-based culture but, it is argued, is ultimately merely a catalyst in the process.

> There is also a potential danger that as more organisations progress through the various stages of the knowledge journey, they do so by simply adopting and replicating the knowledge management strategies of "successful" organisations. Any attempt to enhance knowledge and learning is to be applauded, but superior performance relies heavily on the creativity, knowledge and motivation of individual staff.

Thus, while few disagree with the importance of developing a supportive culture and management, once in place, the ultimate challenge in keeping ahead of the competition centres on placing greater reliance on individual awareness and responsibility in relation to knowledge assets and sharing.

8.6 Empowering the Individual in the Knowledge-centric Organisation

The use of metrics in measuring individual contributions to organisational learning and knowledge management has been discussed earlier, but depends on creating objective measures in the context of predominantly subjective elements. Indeed, this technically orientated approach imposes a rigidity that can be counterproductive, with employees deliberately withholding information owing, in part, to fear and resistance of the systems in place designed to translate tacit knowledge into explicit knowledge (Bennett and Gabriel, 1999). Individual empowerment is unlikely to ensue under these circumstances.

Developing mechanisms for translating individual knowledge into organisational knowledge through cultural shifts and initiatives represents the most pragmatic approach to the problem. There is ample evidence, as presented in this chapter, to suggest that successful knowledge management strategies have resulted from the adoption and creation of such sociotechnical environments.

Yet, even when organisations are knowledge managed or knowledge centric, their commitment to knowledge transfer may not be shared by the workforce. In a recent survey by Cranfield School of Management and reported by KPMG (1998), while most respondents supported knowledge sharing, nearly half stated that there was too little time to share knowledge personally.

> The survey also revealed that the notion "knowledge is power" still persists and resistance to unravelling individual know-how for the benefit of the organisation should not be underestimated.

A truly knowledge-centric company should not concentrate solely on cultural changes instigated by management, but encourage individuals to contribute, rather than withhold, knowledge by emphasising the personal and organisational benefits of doing so. In essence, a top–down approach is merely the first stage in the process, complemented by a drive to empower individuals to recognise and share their knowledge.

Instilling in employees the importance of sharing knowledge is the first step in this process. A degree of trust must be fostered throughout an organisation, encouraging personal responsibility for knowledge dissemination. As Covey (1989) notes, "trust is the lifeblood of an organisation … the highest form of human motivation". The complex and implicit nature of individual knowledge dictates that the process cannot be micromanaged. Skandia was one of the first organisations to recognise this, placing great emphasis on individual responsibility, and has been successful largely as a consequence of a high trust culture. This is not (job) status dependent and is consistent with Hopper's view of an organisational platform where all employees have access to information and are encouraged to contribute to a knowledgeable enterprise (Hopper, 1990). The implication that knowledgeable employees benefit the organisation is prevalent throughout the argument.

Empowering individuals to accept responsibility must be handled sensitively and a fine balance is necessary. Quantifiable rewards, typically in the form of financial incentives, are an obvious route to take, but could be counterproductive if equated with the "knowledge is power" argument. Far from encouraging sharing, such a development could result in more competitive behaviour between co-workers, resulting in artificial withholding of knowledge, its release only occurring when it is in the (financial) interests of the individual. This approach can only really work if the incentive system is integrated within an appraisal regime where knowledge sharing is rewarded when visible benefits to the organisation accrue. In KPMG's survey, nearly one-third of companies were looking at initiatives to reward knowledge sharing, recognising that staff retention rates are improved and that their organisation is better placed to compete in the knowledge marketplace (KPMG, 1998).

While debate centres on the most effective way of leveraging knowledge stored in an individual's head to tangible practical organisational knowledge, the infrastructure must also be in place to support the transition from managed to individual responsibility. Where support systems are not in place, time and effort in knowledge transfer can be wasted by "reinventing the wheel". Technology, via e-mail, intranets, extranets and the internet, has a significant role to play here, and many of the examples cited in previous sections have emphasised its importance in nurturing a knowledge-based culture.

However, access to technology is not a panacea for success: employees must be trained to identify and use the technology as a knowledge-enabling tool.

Seemann and Cohen (1997) discuss the use of knowledge maps as one way of doing this, effectively acting as "corporate yellow pages" by detailing knowledge repositories and expertise within an organisation.

Much more pertinent is the issue of individual knowledge identification. Many employers and employees fail to recognise the value of tacit knowledge in the workplace. For employers, realisation may only occur on the departure of the employee, when replacements can no longer perform the job as effectively. For employees, failure to identify the skills and knowledge required in their job can lead to bad practices, poor performance, unnecessary repetition, and an inability to contextualise their worth and input within the environment and culture of the organisation. There is even some evidence to suggest that, in some cases, employees may recognise their individual know-how but are conditioned to believe that it is unimportant (Appelbaum and Gallagher, 2000).

Training and mentoring represents a key element of encouraging debate and sharing of knowledge, and can, if managed appropriately, help to retain employees by concentrating on personal growth and development, incentives equivalent to financial remuneration. Although training embraces a number of approaches and issues, extraction and transfer of individual knowledge can be stimulated by the use of employee groups and team working, both facilitating social interaction and creating an atmosphere of openness. Furthermore, Lee (1994) argues that frequency of communication between individuals is not a major determinant of enhancing information and knowledge transmission, but the quality of their relationships is a significant factor here. Once again, social interaction acts as a catalyst in empowering individuals and enhancing knowledge acquisition. The culture of an organisation surfaces again at this point, in the sense that the issue of individual knowledge and responsibility can only effectively be addressed where the environment supports and encourages all individuals to contribute in this respect.

The link between organisational culture and individual empowerment also arises when companies have previously operated in an environment where knowledge sharing has been discouraged, or new employees are not used to a knowledge-sharing regime. Breaking down such barriers should not be underestimated and movement in this area is likely to take several years.

The discussion of individual responsibility makes no distinction between job grades and levels. More senior personnel are often exposed to the knowledge politics of an organisation where personalities, egos, relationships, trust and competitive behaviour are visible to varying degrees. At this level, the issues discussed relating to individual responsibility may not be entirely appropriate, since recognition of individual knowledge is not necessarily the problem, but the control of it frequently is. Here, protection and withholding of expertise that could benefit the company is more common. Creation of incentives, a high-trust culture, as well as supportive organisational structure and infrastructure, may go some way to facilitating knowledge transfer, but personalities and vested interests will always persist. Only by ensuring that protection of knowledge is counterproductive for an individual can this be addressed.

In essence, the empowerment of the individual arises from the creation of a culture designed to support and encourage employees to recognise, share, communicate and create new knowledge. While the structure and infrastructure must clearly be in place, without the creation of a cultural environment that facilitates social interaction, organisations are likely to be little more than knowledge enabled and, at best, partially knowledge managed.

> Adopting a sociotechnical perspective, as opposed to a purely technological view of knowledge management, provides the setting in which individual knowledge is recognised and can be exploited for the benefit of the employee and organisation.

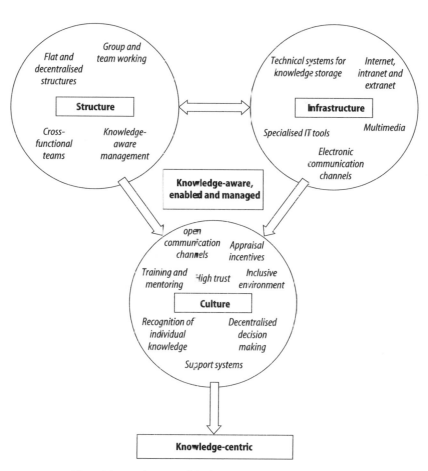

Figure 8.3 Key elements of the knowledge-centric organisation.

Figure 8.3 summaries the attributes required in developing the knowledge-centric organisation, emphasising not only the importance of the technical structure and infrastructure, but also the necessity for a cultural shift as part of the sociotechnical environment.

In summary, the development of the knowledge-centric organisation is dependent on a number of factors, and managers within these companies need to be aware of several issues, in particular:

- Technology alone does not create or sustain knowledge-based competitive advantage and merely acts as a knowledge enabler.
- Sociotechnical factors are crucial in facilitating knowledge creation by developing:
  - a culture that encourages trust, experimentation and sharing of individual and organisational knowledge;
  - flatter organisational structures that assist in developing a knowledge-sharing environment;
  - a technological infrastructure to facilitate interindividual, intraorganisational and interorganisational communication that cuts across internal and external barriers to support knowledge sharing;
  - informal mechanisms for communication and interaction between individuals, irrespective of job status, and designed to generate new knowledge in a more conducive and supportive environment;
  - surroundings that encourage creativity, but with appropriate reward systems that enhance job satisfaction and benefit both employee and employer, by increasing the rate at which individual knowledge is converted into competitively useful organisational knowledge.

8.7 The Way Forward

The realisation that an organisation's information and knowledge assets have the potential to influence its competitive performance is now visible in many companies, sectors and industries. In this sense, knowledge really is power. The issues and arguments presented in this chapter relate to the role of individual knowledge in this process, indicating that failure to address this critical element will severely inhibit an organisation's ability to emerge as truly knowledge centric and thereby reduce the potential for sustaining or gaining a competitive edge.

Paradoxically, the growing importance of individual knowledge within knowledge management hinges, ultimately, on ensuring that knowledge does not equate to power. The creation of a knowledge-based culture is a necessary prerequisite to ensure that individual know-how is extracted and used for the benefit of an organisation. However, such a culture, on its own, while improving organisational learning and knowledge, fails to capitalise fully on the expertise of individual employees. Knowledge transfer plays a pivotal role in this context, with the sharing and dissemination of individual knowledge vital to a forward-looking, knowledge-centric company.

Encouraging individuals to embrace the knowledge management paradigm relies on ensuring that tacit knowledge is first recognised and, secondly, communicated to colleagues to enhance organisational learning. The mechanisms for doing this are varied and revolve around reducing the personal, but increasing the organisational, value of this knowledge. Exactly how this is done is a fine balance of incentive and support, reliant on viewing individual knowledge not as a bargaining tool, but as a shared advantage for the benefit of all.

The use of quantifiable metrics for the measurement of individual knowledge, while acknowledged, is only a partial solution to the problem. While most companies would like to quantify their knowledge assets as part of a balance sheet and various approaches have been developed to address this, the use of objective measures can be counterproductive. Instead, the development of a knowledge-based culture within which individual knowledge and empowerment form an integral element of the sociotechnical environment represents a more balanced strategy. However, while there is evidence to suggest that several, typically larger international companies have embraced this approach, many organisations are barely knowledge aware.

For the latter, recognising the importance of developing a knowledge-based culture and its adoption, while enhancing organisational learning and knowledge, does not necessarily lead to superior performance. Instead, the exploitation and harnessing of individual knowledge, it is argued, have the potential to realise this goal. Reliance on trust, openness and individual responsibility, the main themes of the arguments proposed, is not without its pitfalls, but provided the cultural environment, structure, infrastructure and incentives are in place, the potential for advancement clearly exists, with individual empowerment representing an essential vehicle for enhancing an organisation's position and knowledge management prowess.

Part 3
Know-Who

Chapter 9

Managing Customer Knowledge: A Social Construction Perspective

Jimmy C.M. Huang and Shan L. Pan

9.1 Introduction

In recent years, there has been increasing research interest in the management of knowledge in relation to organisational efficiency (Grant 1996; Kogut and Zander, 1996) and competitive advantage (Matusik and Hill, 1998). This has included a particular focus on the anticipated significance of "knowledge-intensive" (Starbuck, 1992) sectors such as biotechnology, pharmaceuticals, information technology (IT) and the service industry (Pisano, 1994; Klavans and Deeds, 1997; Boisot and Griffiths, 1999). Relatively few studies have examined the dynamics of knowledge management in the retailing sector. To fill this gap, an in-depth case study of a knowledge-intensive organisation in the British retailing industry was conducted to gain much needed empirical evidence relating to knowledge management (Leidner, 1999).

Customer data collected from business transactions have long been used in the retailing industry as a basis for understanding consumers' shopping behaviour, particularly in chain stores (Harlam and Lodish, 1995; Messinger and Narasimhan, 1997; Flynn and Goldsmith, 1999). However, the process by which customer data are transformed into information and become strategically valuable knowledge remains something of an unknown "black box". This chapter examines this problem in relation to the experience of one of Britain's largest retailers, Boots The Chemists (BTC), and seeks to articulate useful lessons that can be applied to similar industrial settings.

In an attempt to understand this black box, the study adopts a social construction approach.

> The term "social construction" was first used by Berger and Luckmann (1967) to refer to the way in which social reality is shaped and constituted in everyday life through the interaction between the producers (individuals) and the produced (the social world).

A social construction approach can be considered as an extension and application of sociotechnical models, e.g. Bijker's Social Construction of Technology (SCOT) model (Bijker, Hughes and Pinch, 1997). Thus, the social construction perspective adopted in this study aims to provide a useful philosophical lens not only to understand the nature of organisational knowledge, but also to investigate processes of knowledge sharing and integration. It is clear from previous studies (e.g. Grant, 1996; Spender, 1996) that organisational knowledge is often perceived as a set of commodities or assets that have significant strategic value and can be transferred and utilised independently of their social context.

From a social construction perspective, organisational knowledge is a set of shared, consensual beliefs that are constructed through social interactions and embedded within the social context in which such knowledge is created (Nonaka and Takeuchi, 1995).

Hence, the study argues that only by understanding the dynamics of social interaction, the evolutionary process of knowledge and its social context can the underlying meaning of knowledge be externalised and understood.

At the centre of the social construction perspective is the belief that there is no 'real' or static knowledge and that knowledge is always embedded in social interactions within communities rather than being an asset that can be processed and disseminated. The social and technical debates related to this perspective suggest that the social embeddedness of technical systems needs to be understood as an enactment of social reality (Weick, 1995). This approach rejects any self-evident account of the effects of the material aspects of technologies, and sees such effects as a matter of interpretative action by people in their social context. Moreover, it regards the social and technical elements as a "seamless web", with no clear distinctions between the technical, social, economic and political elements of technological development (Bijker, Hughes and Pinch, 1987).

The social construction perspective, with its main objective of investigating the dynamics of the creation and development of social reality, provides a suitable theoretical stance to analyse processes of knowledge sharing and integration through the examination of the social interactions among organisational members. As Latour (1987) suggests, this involves opening up the black box. Hence, the main aim of this study is to find out how stabilised social relations are formed and re-formed in the context of managing customer and organisational knowledge. In this case, a social construction approach to understanding knowledge management activities means discovering how different sources of knowledge are synthesised throughout the ongoing interactions between relevant social groups that continuously stabilise and destabilise their social relations.

Three major sources of data were collected in order to portray the process of knowledge management within BTC: 18 members of staff from departments, such as information systems, marketing, space management, and stores, and the business process redesign team were interviewed during March and June 1999. On-site observation was also undertaken; and secondary data were collected from company intranet and internal documents. The paper is divided into the following sections. The background of the case study is presented and the business processes of managing customer data, information and organisational knowledge are discussed (in Section 9.2). Section 9.3 presents a discussion of the case study and its implications. Finally, Section 9.4 summarises the findings of the study.

9.2 Case Study

9.2.1 Company Background

The Boots Company is one of the UK's largest enterprises, with a sales turnover of more than £5 billion in 1998. BTC, one of the largest subsidiaries of the Boots Company, accounts for more than 70% of the company's workforce and sales turnover. As the largest retail chemist in the UK, BTC has more than 1300 stores located in high streets and out-of-town shopping areas across the UK and the Republic of Ireland. In the UK more than one in ten of all medical prescriptions issued is dispensed by BTC. BTC's UK stores are divided into 15 regional groupings. In addition, some functions, e.g. information systems, personnel, marketing and finance, are centralised, and there are three business units based on product categories: healthcare, beauty and leisure.

9.2.2 Knowledge Embedded Within Business Functions

Some of BTC's most vital knowledge is located in the three business units. This relates to the understanding of product categories, the identification of targeted customer groups for specific products, the methods of achieving sales targets, and details of suppliers and supplier relationships. In particular, from the perspective of BTC's stores, essential knowledge lies in the understanding of customers in their customer areas, the demand for various types of products, and the product ranges that satisfy the needs of customers. The critical knowledge for the marketing department includes the understanding of how products should be promoted, what resources are needed and what degree of efficiency a promotion programme can achieve.

From the viewpoint of the information systems function, knowledge is divided into two categories.

> First, there is technical knowledge, including the understanding of the technology used in the business and associated tools and techniques such as programming languages, computer operations, computer security and data management.

> Secondly, there is the knowledge of various business processes: for example, the knowledge of foreign currency markets (e.g. the Euro market) and their business implications is critical in developing computer programs for use by individual stores.

By contrast, the logistic staff rely heavily on their knowledge of how different suppliers operate, warehouse management, the arrangement of delivery routines, and the time needed to deliver products required by the stores efficiently and accurately.

9.2.3 The Traditional Approach to Managing Data, Information and Knowledge

In the past, BTC's approach to managing information and knowledge was often criticised by the company's employees for being too individualistic or lacking interactions across various business functions. Typically, customers' data were gathered from business transactions in stores and automatically forwarded to the head office. Using the computer program provided by the information systems department, data were then systematically analysed and distributed to various business functions according to their relevance. Information generated by the head office, such as that concerning sales volume and shopping behaviour trends, was disseminated to regional offices, which in turn distributed relevant information to their local stores (the end users). The stores then took the necessary actions based on the outcomes of their own analysis. This might involve, for example, adjusting in-store product combinations or organising special promotion programmes.

> Customer data flowed from the stores to the head office, and in return information flowed back to the local stores via the regional offices.

Such an operation was like a funnel system, with the head office acting as a valve to control the flow of data and information.

These procedures were often criticised by employees for their failure to promote knowledge sharing across different business function units. As one informant pointed out:

> "there is a lot of anecdotal evidence that there is no mechanism to share and disseminate knowledge across the region. A lot of local knowledge is generated by local retailers ... There is no mechanism for sharing that knowledge, which is a great shame."

9.2.4 Motivation and Goals

In response to growing external competition, slow profit growth and the need to improve cross-functional coordination, the BTC management identified and implemented some necessary changes in business processes. This included an initiative to reform the way in which BTC worked as a whole, and to improve the company's ability to respond to external environmental changes. To begin with, in 1998 an organisation-wide survey was conducted to gain an insight into employees' perceptions of the head office. One of the questions asked was: 'what animal can best describe the head office?' Most employees saw the head office as "a tortoise (slow but dependable, hibernates until Christmas)" or "a shire horse (traditional, English and good with children)". To enable the firm to act like a "tiger" or an "eagle", an organisation-wide change programme was launched in 1998. With a specific focus on the redesign of business processes, the programme aimed to transform BTC into a world-class retailer through the enhanced integration of knowledge from various sources, especially stores and customers, and across various business functions. The aim was

"to improve the quality of support we provide to our stores, to build effective relationships with store staff, to be more responsive to the needs of our customers, to introduce better ways of working and remove complexity from our business."

9.2.5 A New Approach

With organisational transformation in mind, the BTC management recognised the failings of the previous approach to managing information and knowledge. In particular, vital information and knowledge was often concealed by an individual business function, whereas ideally it should be shared cross-functionally. As a result, several initiatives were implemented by management to enhance the company's ability to manage its knowledge-sharing and knowledge-integration processes. Two specific initiatives, involving the rearrangement of the physical layout of the head office building, and the establishment of a space management department (knowledge brokers), are highlighted in the following sections. The primary objectives were to facilitate face-to-face interaction among members of staff and enhance knowledge sharing between the head office and regional offices and across various business units.

Rearranging the Head Office

A new head office building was designed and built to accommodate all business functions on one site. Several business functions that had previously been dispersed in the Nottingham city centre were gradually relocated to the new site, which was connected with other head office buildings from early 1999. This saved a lot of employees' valuable time because it overcame the problem of travelling between different sites to attend meetings. As one informant explained,

"I don't need to sit in the traffic for 40 minutes for a 30-minute meeting in the city centre."

With its open-space design, soft-colour interior and lobby café, the new head office is strikingly bright, pleasant and spacious. The rearrangement of floor space facilitates interaction between business functions and also encourages general socialising amongst members of staff.

> "you bump into each other when you pick up prints, do photocopies and make cups of tea. You say 'hi' and have a chat with them."

Introducing Knowledge Brokers

After the completion of the new head office, BTC took another initiative: to establish a central department that would bridge the head office and its 15 regional offices (known as "the regions" by BTC employees). The new department provides guidance on store space management and arbitrates the allocation of store space among the three business units according to the market growth of different product categories. In other words, the seven members of this department act as "knowledge brokers" (the term used by informants) in facilitating the sharing of knowledge generated by local stores and by the head office. As one of the members of the space management department pointed out,

The knowledge brokers work closely with the 15 regional offices to provide expertise in space management. Based on the integration of the local knowledge generated by stores and the consultants' space management expertise, product combination strategies for the stores are then formulated. At the same

> "we have roles to play in capturing, consolidating and disseminating all the best practices, what works well and what doesn't."

time, members of the department communicate back to the business units in the head office to enhance product performance and the efficiency of promotion strategies. Through the department's brokerage role, the distance between regional stores and the business units is reduced. Even more importantly, strategies at the head office and the regional level are further adjusted according to sales performance. As one of the space consultants observed:

> "in a local market, if the strategy doesn't seem to strike up, it doesn't increase the sale. There is an opportunity to communicate that back to the business units."

9.2.6 Problems Encountered

Despite the fact that the implementation of the two initiatives was generally successful, the implementation process was not without problems. For instance, members of one of the business units refused to participate and cooperate in the planning and redesign stages. Although this problem was later resolved after two crisis meetings mediated by top management, it meant that some rethinking had to take place. According to one informant,

> "If you come along and show them the facts and figures, and tell them that actually the world is changing and it is changing like this, intellectually they can see that, but in their hearts they are sort of feeling 'that is fine, but I still don't want to do it'. So you actually need to achieve buy-in on both levels. And a lot of the time you achieve it intellectually – that is quite easy to do; but emotional buy-in is hard to do."

9.2.7 Redirecting flows of Information and Knowledge

One of the most significant consequences of the implementation of the two initiatives was the impact on information and knowledge flows within the organisation. Despite the fact that the technologies used to collect and analyse customer data remained unchanged, the approaches to managing data, information and knowledge were greatly improved.

At the regional level, knowledge generated by local stores is now articulated and shared throughout BTC:

> "instead of having each business function working solo, new business processes have moved the organisation to work more cross-functionally than before."

> "they have their own local knowledge on what the products should be. So the head office gives local stores complete responsibility for the space they have in the stores."

With minimum requirements for displaying Boots' own products, local stores are given the flexibility to decide what other products to sell on the basis of their experience and the advice given by the space management consultants. Moreover, by having a centralised profit measurement applied to all types of store, the comparison of stores' performances has become transparent and more consistent. This system of measurement provides opportunities for knowledge brokers to identify and articulate the best practices from stores with outstanding performances, and to disseminate these valuable lessons to other stores.

At the level of head office, the centralised measurement is also applied to the three business units to determine how the different product categories perform in relation to the space that they occupy. The three business units work collectively with the marketing department to produce promotion plans based on the product knowledge possessed by the business units and the market intelligence collected by the marketing department. The business units work closely with the head office and the regional offices to coordinate store space. Moreover, the business units and the marketing department rely on stores to provide feedback on the effectiveness of promotion plans and strategies. It is clear that the implementation of new business processes led to the freeing up of information and knowledge previously concealed by each business function or region. This was achieved by the reduction of the physical distance between business functions, head office, regional offices and local stores, as well as by the introduction of knowledge brokers. The flow of information and knowledge in BTC has gradually shifted from a "funnel" process to a much more dynamic process of organisation-wide information and knowledge sharing.

9.3 Discussion

The purpose of this case study is to examine how knowledge is managed in a UK retailing company and, more specifically, to examine how customer data are transformed into information and then further developed into strategically valuable knowledge. Three important issues emerge from the study:

- the transformation of data, information and knowledge;
- the integration of departmental knowledge and the creation of organisational knowledge;
- knowledge sharing and integration as processes of social construction.

9.3.1 The Transformation of Data, Information and Knowledge

The transformation of data, information and knowledge plays a critical role in the management of organisational knowledge (Nonaka and Takeuchi, 1995) and hence in the determination of the organisation's competitive advantage (Teece, Pisano and Shuen, 1997; Nahapiet and Ghoshal, 1998). The case of BTC suggests that in the retailing sector, customer data collected through stores serve as one of the most important sources for understanding customers' shopping behaviour. However, such data have no commercial value unless they are technically analysed. This requires inputs from the marketing department and other business units in order to develop appropriate analytical programmes and software. In this way, customer data are transformed into useful information. This information is then further distributed across business functions, the head office, regional offices and local stores through mechanisms such as the intranet and written reports.

> It is also clear that information has no particular value until it is transformed into knowledge.

Once further inputs of experience and expertise are added to the information provided, organisational knowledge becomes available for utilisation (Madhavan and Grover, 1998). In terms of the transformation process from information to knowledge, the BTC case suggests that the information received by business functions becomes the foundation for decision making and strategy formulation, e.g. in the design of promotion plans and the arrangement of store space.

Vital lessons are articulated through a process of trial and error, and valuable knowledge is generated through the learning-by-doing process (Christensen, 1997).

The knowledge gained by each business function is further applied in the analysis of data and information, and in the making of decisions. Hence, it is clear that the strategic value of data and information can only be realised when these are transformed into knowledge. The case study also indicates that the accumulation of strategically valuable knowledge depends on the continuous transformation of data and information. However, it is also clear that the value of knowledge will not be maximised unless the knowledge embedded within each business function is integrated (Grant, 1996).

9.3.2 The Integration of Departmental Knowledge and the Creation of Organisational Knowledge

Lawrence and Lorsch (1967) argue that organisational efficiency resides in the differentiation and integration of organisational knowledge. The case study indicates that the knowledge possessed by each business function represents its own particular expertise, which is also complementary to the expertise of other business functions. The two critical conditions of knowledge integration, according to Tenkasi and Boland (1996), are mutual learning and perspective taking. Such conditions highlight the importance of knowledge acquisition (Huber, 1991) and the building of a shared, collective mental model (Senge, 1990). In this case, mutual learning represents the intellectual aspect of knowledge integration, and perspective taking represents the emotional aspect. More details related to these two aspects are provided in the following discussion.

The case study shows that mutual learning in BTC takes place not only among regional stores, but also between the regional stores and the head office. The sharing of best practices across regions as well as between the regional offices and the head office is a critical example that illustrates how knowledge is integrated by sharing and learning. The BTC case suggests that perspective taking depends on the social interaction and communication among members of staff from various business functions. By redesigning business processes and reallocating business functions physically, the organisation in this case was able to enhance cross-functional collaboration and communication. This facilitated the disclosure of the perspectives held by each function and further eased the process of building a shared, cross-functional perspective. The research findings show that both the intellectual and emotional dimensions of knowledge integration greatly influence the process by which organisational knowledge is created.

In the case of BTC, business functions share not only the information that they analyse together but also the knowledge articulated through common lessons and experiences. The social interaction and commu-

Nahapiet and Ghoshal (1998) suggest that organisational knowledge is created through processes of exchange and combination.

nication among business functions serves as a vehicle for exchanging ideas and best practices (Pisano, 1994); it makes previously embedded departmental knowledge available for other functions to acquire and share. Most importantly, it provides a foundation for combining different sources of knowledge as the trigger for creating new knowledge.

Furthermore, in BTC, created knowledge is further applied by members of staff and business functions to guide decision making and strategy formulation. For instance, business units and the marketing department use feedback from the regional stores as a basis for formulating and adjusting their sales strategies. Business processes and organisational routines are gradually modified in response to the input of new knowledge. In this way, organisational knowledge evolves and is constantly redefined.

9.3.3 Knowledge Sharing and Integration as Processes of Social Construction

The case study shows that the transformation process (from data to information and knowledge) relies on the application of the tacit knowledge possessed by each party to the task of systematically making sense of data and information (Boyce, 1995). Moreover, the data–information–knowledge transformation process is not just a technical issue, but also involves social collaboration among different business functions during the analysis of customer data.

The study thus concludes that the management of knowledge in an organisation cannot be studied from a technical or social perspective in isolation. For instance, in the case of a retailer such as BTC, the sophistication of IT and information systems in obtaining customer data is not sufficient to transform information into knowledge. Nor is social interaction among business functions with the support of IT sufficient to handle the amount of data generated by stores. Despite the fact that the accumulation of customer data and the development of market intelligence require sophisticated technologies, the processes by which data are transformed into information and by which information is used to create knowledge can be best understood and facilitated through the interplay of social and technical elements. In other words, the ability to synthesise various sources of knowledge throughout the ongoing interactions between relevant social groups, and the use of technology, resulting in the continuous stabilisation and destabilisation of groups' social relations, play a crucial role in managing knowledge management activities (Pan and Scarbrough, 1999).

The social construction perspective on knowledge management also requires management to take both intellectual and emotional elements into account.

The intellectual perspective on knowledge integration highlights the process by which knowledge should be synthesised.

For example, in the case of BTC the intellectual elements of the knowledge-integration process can be perceived on the one hand as a technical issue involving the various technologies used to transfer data, information and knowledge. On the other hand, the emotional perspective on the knowledge integration process can be described as "emotional alignment" (Lembke and Wilson, 1998). This refers to the conditions by which knowledge can be shared and integrated. In other words, effective emotional alignment is dependent on the achievement of emotional buy-in in relation to cross-functional knowledge sharing. The BTC case findings suggest that by reducing physical distance, face-to-face interactions are facilitated among members of staff, and this further contributes to collaboration across business functions. In particular, the introduction of a centralised department (including knowledge brokers) to coordinate knowledge-related activities between the head office and the regional offices played a vital role. The case study thus suggests that by sharing and integrating vital information and best practices, new organisational knowledge can be created.

9.4 Conclusion

Despite the popular enthusiasm for using sophisticated IT to manage knowledge residing in geographically dispersed sites (Ciborra and Suetens, 1996), insufficient attention has been given to the important lesson, illustrated in the present case study, that the management of knowledge requires a sociotechnical focus. The study has examined the experience of one major British retailer (BTC) in transforming its customer data into information and knowledge as a strategy for achieving profit maximisation. This case highlights the importance of reducing physical distance in order to facilitate face-to-face interaction and enhance cross-functional collaboration. It also illustrates the crucial role of knowledge brokers in identifying, articulating and disseminating best practices across the organisation. As a result of the implemented changes, the flow of information and knowledge has been redirected through an increase in cross-functional collaboration and the continuous sharing of lessons across the organisation.

This case illustrates that knowledge sharing and knowledge integration across the organisation depend not only on technological advancement but also on achieving emotional alignment.

It is thus essential for a retailer, or possibly other firms with similar organisational characteristics, to harness the ability to develop and maintain creative interdepartmental relationships when using customer data for the purpose of sharing and integrating strategically valuable knowledge.

Apart from offering empirical insights on managing customer and organisational knowledge, this study further emphasises the importance of using the social construction perspective as a means of understanding the nature of organisational knowledge. First, the socially embedded nature of organisational knowledge indicates that the latter is always shared and cannot always be accessed by its members (Moorman and Miner, 1997). The boundaries surrounding organisational subunits further limit the access of members to the knowledge possessed by other subunits. Secondly, the findings suggest that the social construction perspective provides a more appropriate approach to studying knowledge management processes than the information-processing school of thought. The latter emphasises the efficiency of information dissemination as a means of innovation success, but accordingly neglects the fact that the interpretation of information and even knowledge is not universal and unproblematic. By contrast, the social construction perspective, with its emphasis on the disclosure of different interpretations, takes into account the process by which a commonly acceptable interpretation can be achieved through negotiation and interaction (Pinch and Bijker, 1987).

In conclusion, from a social construction perspective, knowledge management is perceived as an ongoing process of social interaction between participating members as a means of disclosing paradigmatic differences to achieve a commonly acceptable interpretation and shared understanding of social reality.

Chapter **10**

Facilitating Learning and Knowledge
Creation in Community of Practice: A Case
Study in a Corporate Learning Environment

Jessi Qing Yi

10.1 Introduction

Competition in the current global market is becoming ever more intense. As companies seek new ways to leverage their resources to gain competitive advantage, there has been a growing awareness that knowledge that exists within a company is one of its most valuable assets (Nonaka and Takeuchi, 1995). Knowledge management has been increasingly recognised as an important activity for many large multinational companies (KPMG, 1998). Current literature in knowledge management and organisational learning shows that one of the major lines of thought emphasises human networks.

> Despite the advent of advanced information technologies, human resources still lie at the heart of knowledge creation and dissemination.

10.2 Research Background

Senge (1997), in his foreword for Arie de Geus' book *The Living Company*, pointed us towards seeing a company as a living being that "creates its own processes, just as the human body manufactures its own cells, which in turn compose its own organs and bodily systems." The metaphor of a company as a living being is used here by Senge to refer to how the informal organisation of any company comes into being. Senge draws attention to two issues that have been under heavy discussion recently in the area of knowledge management.

The first issue is that of informal organisations that are naturally formed among practitioners within and across the boundaries of formal organisations. Lave and Wenger (1990) first coined the term of "community of practice" (CoP) to describe such informal organisations.

The second issue is closely associated with the issue of informal organisation: what kind of learning would happen within such an entity? Brown and Duguid (1991) suggested that learning needs to be the bridge between daily work and innovation. But how would it happen? Stamps (1997) reported a case in Xerox where training personnel transformed the traditional training curriculum into one that facilitates the restructuring of the workplace so that workers can train other workers on the job. The question remains, however, of whether the transformational learning as described by Stamps could happen in an informal organisation such as a community.

10.3 Research Site

In the current heatwave of knowledge management, Motorola, Inc., among other large USA-based global corporations, has been exploring the use of different knowledge management approaches to improve its business performance. In early 1998, the company launched a corporate wide initiative, MOT,[1] which aims to improve its wireless systems availability at customer sites. To achieve their goals, the MOT program office identified a number of enablers. Two of these enablers are:

- to construct a training curriculum that helps company employees to develop their skills and knowledge in systems availability; and
- to establish communities of practice around different subject areas related to systems availability as a way to disseminate knowledge across the organisation in an effective and efficient manner.

This chapter reports on a case study constructed around the first experiment of CoP development in the context of the MOT initiative at Motorola. The company attempted to use this pilot as a test ground to gain an understanding of the effectiveness of learning and knowledge sharing in a CoP environment, and determining what it takes to develop a CoP. The pilot MOT CoP started in May 1999 and was implemented through August 1999.

10.4 Research Question

The focus of this case study is reflected in its research question:

In Motorola, how does a community of practice work to create values for both community members and the company?

More specifically, this study intended to address three variables that framed its boundary:

- Learning: How do CoP members learn in the web of social interaction? How does knowledge creation happen? What is the role of knowledge sharing and creation in members' learning process? Does learning occur at both individual and organisational levels?
- Processes: What is the learning and knowledge-sharing process that the CoP members go through? What is the support process that the CoP support team goes through during the development of the CoP?

- Value creation and exchange: What makes the CoP valuable to both its members and Motorola? What are its costs? How are the created values exchanged within and outside the CoP?

Based in Motorola, the primary unit of analysis for this study is the MOT pilot CoP, i.e. the SMART CoP,[2] wherein members from the company's engineering community learned and shared knowledge about the SMART system-modelling tool.

10.5 Literature Review

There has been research around community of practice that is naturally formed and exists as informal entity in the context of large organisation (Orr, 1990). Recently, there has also been discussion around learning communities, defined by some scholars as those that aim to increase and optimise both individual and collective knowledge in a community (Resnick and Williams Hall, 1998; Bielaczyc and Collins, 1999). Moreover, there has been research conducted in small and middle-sized companies to understand the significance of learning communities in the organisational context (Mandl and Reinmann-Rothmeier, 1999). The following is a brief overview of some important literature relevant to this study.

10.5.1 Environment for Learning and Knowledge Sharing

Community of Practice

On the meaning of CoP, Stamps (1997) speculated: "At the core of the new thinking is the notion that work and learning are social activities. As people work together, they not only learn from doing, they develop a shared sense of what has to happen to get the job done. ... It is in these groups where some of the most valuable and most innovative work-related learning occurs" (p. 36).

Wenger (1998) proposed a theory of learning based on social participation in groups. His theory explores the intersection of community, social practice, meaning, and identity. Wenger demonstrated a broad conceptual framework for thinking about learning as a process of social participation.

Knowledge Community

Botkin (1999) asserted that companies must build "knowledge communities", composed of "groups of people with a shared passion to create, use, and share new knowledge for tangible business purposes" (p. 6).

In the context of this study, the MOT pilot CoP shared some characteristics with both Wenger's concept of CoP and Botkin's definition of knowledge community. The pilot CoP was made up of a number of engineers from different business units within Motorola.

10.5.2 Key Learning and Knowledge Sharing Activities in a Community of Practice Environment

Action Learning

McGill and Beaty (1995) defined action learning as a continuous process of shared learning and reflection, supported by colleagues, with an intention of getting things done.

Transfer of Internal Knowledge and Best Practice

O'Dell and Grayson (1998) reported that the biggest barrier to internal transfer was ignorance on both ends of the transfer. "At most companies, particularly large ones, neither the 'source' nor the 'recipient' knew someone else had knowledge they required or would be interested in knowledge they had" (p. xi, Preface). Another big barrier to transfer was the lack of relationships between the source and the recipient of knowledge. One major purpose of the MOT CoP pilot was to leverage internal expertise across the company, and use organisational support to foster the development of social relationships among CoP members to maximise opportunity of internal knowledge dissemination.

Action learning and internal knowledge transfers are interrelated activities. They take place both within and beyond the boundary of a community, and consequently learning grows from the individual to the organisational level.

10.6 Sociotechnical Perspective: A Design for Community of Practice

In search of a holistic and systemic approach to structure this study, the author encountered the "sociotechnical perspective" that amalgamates the "dualism" of people and technology. In their coal-mining studies, Trist and Bamford (1951) claimed that the implementation of technical systems has to take into account social systems in order to succeed. Furthermore, Pasmore and Sherwood (1978) stated that sociotechnical system design is by nature organisational development, "techniques that typically involve the restructuring of work methods, rearrangement of technology, or the redesign of the organisational social structure" (p. 3). It seems that the main objective of this framework is to optimise the relationship between the social or human systems of the organisation, and the technology used by the organisation to increase workplace productivity.

At the basic level, it considers an organisation to be composed of two subsystems: a social subsystem and a technical subsystem (Pasmore and Sherwood, 1978). The social subsystem of an organisation refers to both the individual workers in the organisation

> The uniqueness of the sociotechnical framework lies in its broadened definition of technology. It views an organisation as an open system.

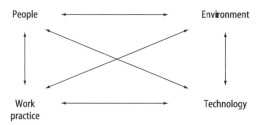

Figure 10.1 Sociotechnical system model (Goodrum, Dorsey and Schuven, 1993).

and the social attributes that determine the web of interactions among these individuals. It represents the personal traits of these organisational members such as attitudes, beliefs, capabilities and the relationships within and among various groups. By contrast, the technical subsystem of an organisation refers to the mechanisms and the processes that the organisational members use to transform inputs into outputs. Here, technology is referred to as the tools, techniques, devices, artifacts, methods, configurations, procedures and knowledge of the organisation.

Viewing the MOT pilot CoP as a bounded system, it was thought necessary to adopt a systems view when examining the processes that will be used in the community to facilitate learning and knowledge sharing. The sociotechnical perspective provides such a view, because it sees an organisation as comprised of people using technology to perform specific work practices in a particular environment. This framework is systemic since it considers that a change in one component may lead to changes in other components. The processes of the four components are interdependent and dialectic, and hence cannot be completely separated from each other (Goodrum, Dorsey and Schuven, 1993), (Fig. 10.1). The following is a discussion on the use of the sociotechnical perspective in the MOT pilot CoP.

10.6.1 Work Practice: Action Learning in the MOT Community of Practice

In the context of the MOT pilot CoP, the work practice refers to that of the action learning, knowledge sharing and creation. The action learning method was used as a learning process to drive the learning, sharing and collaboration activities in the pilot CoP.

10.6.2 People

Changes in work practice result in "concurrent changes in the nature of relationships and the patterns of formal and informal communication among the people involved" (Goodrum, Dorsey and Schuven, 1993, p. 12). When a CoP becomes part of working, learning and being, it requires a re-examination of the different roles that people play and their relationship in a CoP. From the experience of the pilot CoP, there were seven major roles: CoP member, subject matter expert (SME), live-session facilitator, online discussion moderator, system administrator, content editor and process consultant.

10.6.3 Environment

In the pilot CoP, since the change to a member's physical working setting was minimal, the value change was of far more importance. Such change requires people to value learning through reflection and action as an integral part of their daily work. Equally important to the value change was that of the reward and recognition system. However, such change went beyond the control and jurisdiction of the pilot MOT CoP project team, and thus was not implemented during the pilot. It requires the endorsement of senior management.

10.6.4 Technology

Technology, if used properly, can support people in the process of change. In this study technology refers to both hard technology (e.g. computers, networks) and soft technology (e.g. processes, tools). For the SMART CoP, the use of technology was designed to support learning, knowledge sharing and collaboration. The technology and tools used were:

- action learning templates (e.g. the member profile, action log, and action plan);
- intranet-based community infrastructure: electronic bulletin board, e-mail distribution list, online document repository and virtual meeting space using Microsoft NetMeeting;
- support tools: job aids for the use of tools.

The role of technology was to overcome differences in time and distance and to provide an unobtrusive learning environment for community members.

10.7 Research Methodology

During the fieldwork from spring to summer 1999, the author took the role of participant researcher and was a member of the pilot project team in order to obtain first-hand data.

Data from six sources were used:
- observation of all activities during the pilot;
- semi-structured interviews of CoP members at the beginning, during and the end of the pilot;
- documents related to the pilot;
- learning surveys of CoP members at the beginning and the end of the pilot;
- focus group meeting with CoP members at the end of the pilot;
- post-mortem with CoP members, the project team and senior management for the MOT initiative at the end of the pilot.

Data analysis was conducted in parallel with data collection, with the focus on identifying key themes that authenticate the pilot CoP as a live model. Validation was achieved by triangulation, member checking and peer debriefing. Member checking entailed asking CoP members to confirm the accuracy of their interviews, and presenting the research results to the CoP to gain their confirmation or refutal on the findings at the end of the pilot. Peer debriefing refers to sharing the findings and results with peers and colleagues to enhance the study's trustworthiness. Triangulation was achieved by using multiple data sources to form a complete story of the case.

10.8 Findings

Seventeen members were involved to various degrees in the pilot CoP:

- Two SMEs took part: one expert on the SMART[3] modelling tool that was the subject of learning for the pilot, and the other a modelling process expert.
- Nine members actively participated during the pilot.
- Three members participated at the beginning of the pilot and were not able to continue.
- Three members signed up to participate but attended no more than one CoP activity.

10.9 Major Themes

The major themes of the findings are organised under each of the four components of the study: learning, knowledge sharing, CoP learning process, and value creation and exchange.

10.9.1 Learning

Data from the baseline and post-pilot survey indicate an average increase in CoP members' knowledge on modelling (the content domain), as well as their skill and knowledge on the SMART modelling tool (the topic of learning for the pilot), after the pilot. As shown in Figure 10.2, while there was a slight increase with their background knowledge in modelling, the more substantial learning gain was on the members' knowledge and skill on the use of the SMART tool.

By cross-examining the CoP members' self-evaluation and the SMEs' comments, it was concluded that at the individual level, the pilot CoP members' learning outcome varied based on their background knowledge, their attempt to use the SMART tool during the pilot and the extent to which they used the tool in their projects. With diverse background knowledge and working context, they all learned to various degrees and for different purposes throughout the pilot. For example, just-in-time learning and application took place by those members who came into the CoP with a higher level of background knowledge in modelling. With a real project at hand, these four members were able to learn about the

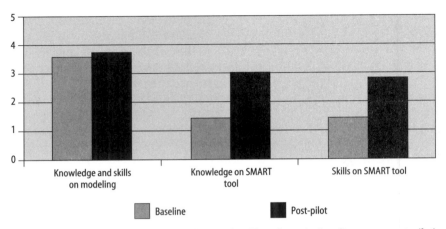

Figure 10.2 MOT Community of practice pilot members' learning gain (baseline versus post-pilot).

SMART tool quickly, and leverage the SME expertise in helping them to solve problems and make progress in their projects. In addition through helping other members, the SMEs were able to see different ways of applying their expertise and thus broadened their understanding of the utility of the tool.

Indicators that the CoP would lead to organisational learning began to emerge by the end of the pilot. The data indicated that learning in the pilot started to proliferate outside the boundary of the SMART CoP in the later stage of the pilot. Therefore, individual learning acquired by participants during the pilot benefited more people in the organisation. For example, one member reported that not only was he able to use the SMART tool in two projects during the pilot, but he also interacted with others in his organisation who were interested in learning to use the SMART tool for their work. He planned to become a SMART tool expert in the near future and had started to foster a community around the tool in his organisation. In the long run, more people in the company would be involved and benefit from their participation.

In summary, learning on both modelling and the SMART tool occurred to various degrees among the CoP members during the pilot. Although not clearly demonstrated by the end of the pilot, organisational learning around system modelling and the use of the SMART tool would have enormous potential within Motorola.

10.9.2 Knowledge Sharing and Collaboration

As one member put it, sharing knowledge enabled workers to know what others in the community were working on, and in the long run, it can substantially shorten the time it takes an individual to reach final conclusions.

The pilot CoP members believed that the benefit of sharing knowledge outweighs the cost of time and effort to do it.

However, knowledge sharing was limited in extent and scope. The pilot CoP experienced different states of knowledge flow during its process, starting from its initial inertia to its active state towards the end. Sometimes knowledge flowed well in the pilot CoP, other times not so well. There were also times when it did not flow at all. Knowledge sharing occurred more between SMEs and other CoP members than among members who came from different organisations within Motorola. As a result, the CoP members had diverse opinions on the effectiveness of knowledge sharing during the pilot.

Similarly, collaboration in the pilot was also limited. Among 13 active CoP members, four reported that they collaborated with either the tool SME or another member in developing a model. Because of a lack of time, face-to-face interaction and a critical mass in the CoP, another four members did not regard knowledge sharing or collaboration with others as part of their learning experience in the pilot.

In short, knowledge sharing and collaboration were limited by time constraints, lack of critical mass and momentum, or lack of need. Although some sharing and collaboration took place during the pilot, it was not enough to be regarded by the CoP members as an integral part of their learning experience.

10.9.3 Community of Practice Learning Process

The original CoP learning environment was designed based on the principles of action learning. Action learning involves a group of people working together for a concentrated period, with group effort focused on the issues of each individual. In the original design for the pilot CoP, there were four major elements: ground rules, roles, learning process and technologies (adopted from McGill and Beaty, 1995). A comparison between the actual uses of the action learning process in the pilot CoP and its original design is shown in Table 10.1.

While the CoP members provided valuable recommendations on how to improve the CoP learning process, data from various sources revealed an overall positive feedback for the pilot CoP learning process. Major findings include:

- The facilitation and other support provided by the project team enabled CoP learning activities to take place smoothly throughout the pilot.
- Expert resource was critical to the members' learning. As one member pointed out,
- Because of time constraints, the pilot was not able to take the CoP members through an entire cycle of action learning as described in its ideal process.

"... having someone else think about your specific problems helps."

Although the pilot CoP members reported a positive learning experience overall, the issues that emerged, such as the difficulties with the use of the technology, could hinder effective learning and knowledge sharing if they are not overcome in future developments of CoP in Motorola.

Table 10.1 Comparison of the designed and actual learning process in the Commonity of Practice (CoP) pilot

Elements in the action learning environment	Original design	Actual happening
1. Ground rules	Reflection is a key to learning from experience	Other ground rules were followed. Reflection was not an explicit learning activity during the pilot
2. Roles	Seven roles	All seven roles were used; the role of content editor was not able to exert its function fully owing to the complexity of the content
3. Learning process	Biweekly live sessions	Over the eight weeks of the pilot, seven sessions were conducted. During the first four sessions, the tool SME presented materials in the first hour, and the second office hour was used minimally for Q&A. The last three sessions were focused on three participants' sharing of their projects. Discussion took place among the tool SME, process SME and the CoP members. These three sessions lasted for about one and a half hours each
	Compass bulletin board	Used mainly for Q&A among members and SMEs. With the moderator's facilitation, half of the CoP members and both SMEs posted their bio. The action plan and action log were not used because not every member was able to work on their project during the pilot. It seemed that the CoP members were mostly still in the mode of learning, although three participants started to use what they learned in their projects
	Compass repository	It became a space for SMEs and members to store presentation materials and documents related to the CoP learning activities. Compilation of reusable knowledge nuggets did not happen during the pilot. However, most CoP members agreed that it was beneficial to organise the existing materials and also to compile a collection of cases based on the models built by CoP members
	Facilitation	The facilitator prompted the CoP members to apply what they learned in their projects, identify the topics for presentations based on their needs, provide feedback and share knowledge among themselves
4. Technology	Microsoft NetMeeting and Compass	Both were used as planned
	E-mail distribution list was not included in the original design	Facilitator and SMEs used an e-mail distribution list for announcements and coordinated logistics of CoP activities

SME: subject matter expert; Q&A: questions and answers.

10.9.4 Value Creation and Exchange

The major values created for members involved in the CoP pilot include the following.

- For some participants learning in the CoP was transferred into application on the job. According to one of these participants, his use of what he learned in work projects helped to reduce his cycle time to achieve results for his work. However, learning transfer did not happen for all the participants.
- Overall, the CoP members perceived learning about the SMART tool, modelling and the use of NetMeeting as value added to their work. Not only the CoP members, but also the SMEs benefited from learning in the pilot CoP. Although the use of NetMeeting created problems, people perceived it as a potential tool for collaboration at work and thus regarded it as valuable for them to learn to use it.
- Knowledge assets produced in the CoP learning process were of value to members. The CoP members recognised that the presentation materials, the models built by some members, and the questions and answers generated during the pilot have reusable value for themselves and for others who have similar interests. They also suggested the compilation of case studies to demonstrate examples of using SMART to solve different modelling problems. As one member stated, these knowledge assets "...will be a huge benefit for both CoP participants and other SMART users."
- There was some value exchange among members of CoP in the form of the support they gave to each other in their learning process. A member contemplated:
- Most members confirmed that others offered value to their learning in a general way.

> "We all learned from each other. For people at elementary level, or for those at advanced level, they all had different perspectives. Some simple questions you might think not critical, but when you got stuck, the fundamental knowledge is the most important.'

- For some members, individual and social networks around SMART and modelling were expanded. They established relationships with the experts and some other members in the CoP, and would be likely to make use of such relationships in the future.

While the pilot CoP demonstrated tangible benefits to the members, there was also evidence that it created potential value to Motorola. For example, members' learning in the CoP led to the enhancement of the organisation's capability to do modelling.

In addition, the pilot CoP laid a foundation for future internal transfer of best practice and collaboration, which will foster continuous improvement and innovation of work practice in Motorola in the long run. One CoP member explained:

> "The beauty of working together is like leapfrogging each other – we took them so far with our knowledge and then they will exceed us; later, we will build on their advancement and exceed them."

In summary, the CoP pilot has projected tangible as well as potential values for both individual members and the company. Despite various problems that people encountered in the process of the pilot and the frustration that these problems caused, they all provided their endorsement for the future development and application of this model in the company. The pilot indicated that with some enhancement, CoP could become an effective learning model that contributes to the achievement of business goals set by the MOT initiative.

10.10 Recommendations

This section presents some recommendations on the use of the CoP model based on the author's research and practice experiences.

10.11 Opportunities for Using the Community of Practice Model

Data from the pilot CoP case study suggest some opportunities to use CoP in Motorola. First, there is an opportunity to gain social network capital by developing CoPs around disciplines or functions that cross the boundaries of projects, product lines or business units. Examples of disciplines or functions are marketing, engineering and account management. These functions are part of each business unit, as shown in Figure 10.3.

Secondly, there is an opportunity to form CoPs across the boundaries of various functions to enhance internal dialog and collectively to serve customers well. In Figure 10.3, those points of connection along each horizontal line can be used to form a cross-functional CoP within a business unit. This effort will enhance dialog among people in different functional areas who are working on common products and expedite the speed of communicating customer feedback from the frontline to the design and manufacturing groups. Collectively, such a CoP will strengthen internal collaboration and enable people working on different parts of a product to understand problems better.

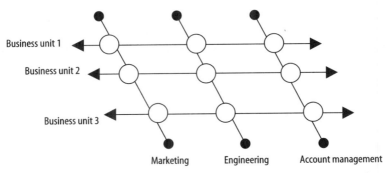

Figure 10.3 Opportunities for the development of communities of practice.[4]

Thirdly, there is also an opportunity to develop global CoPs in the engineering community to foster innovation and creativity across divisions, cultures and outlooks. Globalisation refers to crossing not only geographical boundaries, but also cultural and perceptive differences. In a global CoP, the focus should be not only on leveraging internal engineering resources to come up with better solutions, but more importantly, on fostering innovation by the use of the collective wisdom and market-sensing ability such a CoP would provide.

In summary, the CoP model needs to be used at strategically critical areas as part of a corporate-wide knowledge strategy to enable the achievement of certain business goals. Based on the learning in the CoP pilot, the author recommends three areas where CoPs need to be built: around functions or disciplines, across functions or disciplines, and in a global environment. The next section presents a CoP development model to describe strategies in developing CoPs.

10.12 Community of Practice Development Model

The CoP development model (Fig. 10.4) is conceptualised on the basis of two assumptions. First, a CoP is not a formal organisational structure; rather, it provides an environment where people from different parts of an organisation come together to pursue a shared enterprise. Hence, it coexists with the existing organisational structure (Wenger, 1999). Secondly, a CoP aims to integrate individual learning with their working process and to foster problem solving and innovation (Brown and Duguid, 1991). Ultimately, the organisation enhances its collective capability and capacity in learning and renewal.

The CoP development model (Fig. 10.4) is made up of three growing processes: the individual learning and working process, the CoP life cycle and the organisa-

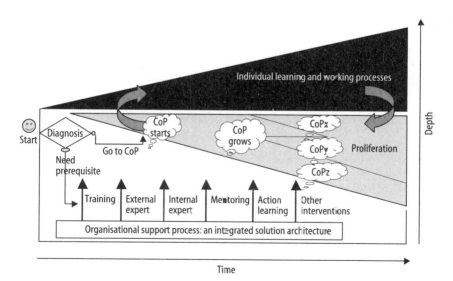

Figure 10.4 Community of practice (CoP) development model.

tional support process. These three processes are interrelated and should grow in relation to each other.

Before developing CoPs, an organisation needs first to identify strategically critical subject areas around which a CoP is to be developed. Secondly, it must identify groups or networks around the topic area that are already in existence so that one can use organisational support to strengthen or grow them into CoPs. Equally important is the need to secure resources and obtain management endorsement for the CoP development.

During the course of CoP development, it is important for the CoP manager or facilitator to market the CoP, and recruit or orient new members on an ongoing basis. According to the development model, over its life cycle a CoP will undergo three major stages: starting, growing and proliferation. The integration of individual learning and working processes will deepen as the CoP goes through various stages in its life cycle. Contrary to the growth of CoP and the integration of learning and working, the organisational support process in the forms of training, mentoring or other intervention should decrease in amount and depth as the CoP matures and becomes self-sustained. Lastly, ongoing evaluation of CoP development is necessary to ensure the quality of its activities.

Literature on CoPs point out that a community needs careful cultivation, which may take from several years to a lifetime. This depends on the number of members, the subject topic, the availability of resources and the critical nature of the business goals behind it. An estimate of 12 months may be a reasonable period for a small CoP of 20 members, who communicate via voice and computer networks and are working on a complex topic such as modelling, to grow to maturity.

A CoP might never die, but go through continuous self-renewal and evolution. Strong organisational support will be reduced to maintenance over time as a CoP matures. The future picture of an organisation with informal CoPs built along with its formal organisational structure is promising: faster communication, enhanced capability of problem solving and prevention through leveraging knowledge and learning, and most importantly, continuous innovating and self-renewal to be ahead of the customers and competitors. It requires the continuing exploration of ways of enhancing organisational learning and knowledge creation. A CoP has tremendous potential to help organisations to reach such a goal.

10.13 Conclusions

This study focuses on the issues of learning, processes, and value creation and exchange in order to answer the research question. Based on the data, the findings and the interpretations, the following conclusions were drawn.

10.13.1 Value Creation and Exchange

This study has concluded that, overall, the benefits of the CoP pilot at both individual and organisational levels surpassed the costs of time, effort, human resources and technology. At the individual level, value creation was manifested in the knowledge assets and social capital that the participants gained during the pilot CoP. Value exchange was achieved, although to a limited extent, when the participants provided support to each other during their learning process.

At the organisational level, the pilot CoP indicated its potential to enhance organisational capability, foster knowledge sharing and collaboration, expand organisational social networks, and transfer learning and internal best practice through continuous use of the CoP model in the company. Value exchange beyond the boundary of the SMART CoP also started to emerge by the end of the pilot when knowledge assets from the pilot CoP were disseminated to benefit more people in the company.

10.13.2 Learning

At the individual level, the increase in knowledge and skill in the subject of learning indicated that the participants acquired learning at various degrees in the pilot CoP. However, with their diverse background, experiences and learning needs, the pilot CoP was able to meet some participants' expectations, but not all. Such diversity reduced the effectiveness of learning in the pilot. However, organisational learning began to emerge, when learning in the pilot started to proliferate outside the pilot CoP in the later stages of the pilot.

Furthermore, owing to various constraints or lack of need, knowledge sharing and creation and collaboration took place within a limited scope in the pilot CoP. Although some knowledge sharing and collaboration took place, it was not enough to be regarded by the participants as an integral part of their learning experience.

10.13.3 Processes

The actual pilot CoP learning and knowledge sharing process was a combination of both synchronous and asynchronous sharing of expertise, learning of the subject matter and applying learning into work. The project team underwent a process to support the pilot CoP. Seven supporting roles were involved in the support of the pilot. The role of SME and that of facilitator were regarded as being most critical in the development of the pilot CoP.

Technology tools such as Microsoft NetMeeting, audio conferencing, and intranet-based document repositories and bulletin boards were used to enable the participants to learn and share across distance and time differences. Overall, the participants felt that the technology worked well during the pilot, despite the problems with NetMeeting. However, the use of technology could not overcome the barriers to sharing and collaboration created by the lack of face-to-face interaction during the pilot.

Although the participants had an overall positive learning experience, the process issues that emerged from the learning and sharing process, the use of technology, the support of the working environment and the support the project team provided to the participants hindered the effectiveness of learning and knowledge sharing in the pilot.

> With the conclusions on the three key variables in this study, the answer to this research question is that with proper facilitation, adequate resource support and well-designed learning activities, a CoP can provide an accelerating environment to cultivate knowledge sharing and creation, collective learning and collaboration that will add value through expanded capability and continuous growth at both individual and organisational levels.

Notes

1 MOT is used in this paper as a pseudonym to stand for the corporate initiative on systems availability.
2 "The MOT pilot CoP", "the SMART CoP", and "the CoP" are used interchangeably in this study.
3 SMART is used in this paper as a pseudonym to stand for the modelling tool discussed above.
4 Figure 10.3 is adopted from the learning map materials for the communications enterprise in Motorola. Credit is due to participant AM9, who identified this opportunity and shared this graphic representation during the research finding confirmation meeting.

Chapter 11
Information Technology and Knowledge Acquisition in Manufacturing Companies: A Scandinavian Perspective

Fredrik Ericsson and Anders Avdic

11.1 Introduction

Information technology (IT) can be used as an enabler for the acquisition and reuse of knowledge. The development of IT-based information systems for knowledge management is not an easy task to accomplish. Issues concerning the reuse and acquisition of knowledge, user participation in the development process, and considerations concerning control and the working environment, are of importance when developing IT-based information systems for knowledge management.

This chapter addresses these issues by answering the following question:

> How can an IT-based information system be designed so that it systemises knowledge in an organisational decision-support context, in order to avoid operational disturbances, in small to medium-sized manufacturing companies?

In order to design an IT-based information system, a specification that incorporates principles for collecting, classifying and evaluating knowledge and principles for usability has been formulated. Of these three factors, the principles for evaluation were found to be of primary importance, and therefore a measurement of operational disturbance relevance (ODR measure) is introduced to evaluate knowledge. The process of evaluation assumes that knowledge is classified: knowledge availability is an important concept and is related to the presumption that knowledge is possible to collect.

Operational disturbances have an impact on the organisation's ability to conduct business. This ability depends on how actions are coordinated in business and core processes. An operational disturbance occurs as a result of unsatisfactory variations in core processes. These variations have a negative outcome on business processes, which is the reason why it is relevant to manage knowledge of operational disturbances in order to maintain and increase the organisation's ability to conduct business. When formulating principles for collecting, classifying and evaluating knowledge, these variations act as a framework (Fig. 11.1).

The empirical research represented in this chapter has been conducted through a case study using interviews, conceptual analysis and prototyping. The unit of analysis is a Swedish small to medium-sized manufacturing company. Theories are related to the empirical findings to understand the findings on a general level.

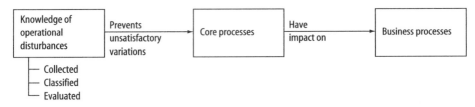

Figure 11.1 Framework used to formulate principles for collecting, classifying and evaluating knowledge.

Among the theories are knowledge acquisition in an organisational context, i.e. knowledge management and organisational learning (e.g. Argyris and Schön, 1996; Brooking, 1998; Swan, 1999), information systems theory (e.g. Mumford, 1979; Nurminen, 1988) and business action theory (e.g. Goldkuhl, 1996, 1998). The notion of organisational context is regarded as important in order to specify consequences for the organisation, people (members of the organisation), interorganisational relations and technology; that is, the organisation may be regarded as a sociotechnical system (e.g. Leavitt, 1970; Bjørn-Andersen and Hedberg, 1977; Mumford and Weir, 1979).

11.2 Managing Knowledge about Operational Disturbances Using Information Technology

This section is a clarification of the authors' view on organisational processes, and the applicability of principles, based on their empirical findings. It answers questions such as how IT enables knowledge management and what the prerequisites are in order to undertake a project for the development of IT-based information systems for knowledge management using principles outlined in this chapter.

An organisation can act as a customer and supplier towards external actors. Actions carried out according to these roles towards external actors define the interaction in the organisation's business processes. The same argument is valid for actions carried out between members of the organisation, but this kind of interaction is labelled core processes. A distinction is made between the organisation's business processes, where members of the organisation act on behalf of the organisation towards external actors, and core processes, where members of the organisation act towards other members of the organisation. An operational disturbance occurs when there are unsatisfactory variations in core processes. Unsatisfactory variations affect the organisation's ability to fulfil commitments to external actors and these commitments are a part of the organisation's business processes. In manufacturing companies, there is a very strong relationship between unsatisfactory variations in core processes (i.e. operational disturbances) and business processes.

Before developing IT-based information systems for knowledge management, it is essential to identify core and business processes. It is of equal importance that both current and potential information systems in those processes are identified.

Conceptual analyses that address actions undertaken both by people (i.e. members of the organisation) and by technology (i.e. information systems), can be used to disconnect ourselves from what is referred to as technological determinism (e.g. Katsioloudes, 1996) and some shortcomings identified by Swan (1999). The role that information systems play in the organisation is analysed from a usability point of view, which means that information systems are studied in an organisational context, and a parallel analysis is preferred to a sequential one. Thus, humans are not excluded from technology and vice versa. The authors have frequently used a conceptual modelling technique called action diagrams (see, for example, Goldkuhl, 1996, for notational rules for action diagrams) to re-create production and business processes. An action diagram is a technique which includes actions carried out by both humans and technology in a parallel mode.

Members of the organisation experience and solve different kinds of problems in their working environment. These experiences are crucial for manufacturing companies in order to fulfil obligations towards customers. To reuse crucial knowledge, experiences held by individuals must be made explicit and available to others, without losing the origin or context (e.g. Brooking, 1998). This is very important when designing information systems for reuse of crucial knowledge related to production.

IT-based information systems act as a medium for communication between the individual and the whole, as well as a repository containing knowledge held by the individual. The aims are to:

- collect people's knowledge in a container (in a metaphorical sense) without losing its origin;
- transform knowledge in such a way that it is easily distributed to those who require it. This is further elaborated in Sections 11.4 and 11.5;

and thereby make knowledge held by the individual available to the whole organisation, and enable others to share that knowledge. The main obstacle to overcome is to make people understand that information systems act as a medium for communicating knowledge between the individual and the whole. People's perception of IT-based information systems and the properties by which they characterise such systems as an artefact are very important. This is a strong reason why prototyping and user-centred design (Carey, 1990; Smith, 1991; Preece, 1994) are used as the primary methods for developing information systems. This is further elaborated in Sections 11.4 and 11.5.

11.3 Collecting, Classifying and Evaluating Knowledge Related to Production to Maintain Current Customer Relations

The principles of collecting, classifying and evaluating knowledge related to operational disturbances, in order to maintain and develop organisational performance, require answers to three interrelated questions:

- What do we consider to be relevant knowledge to collect?

- How do we classify relevant knowledge?
- How do we evaluate classified knowledge?

11.3.1 Collecting Knowledge

"Collecting knowledge" is related to the question: what do we consider to be relevant knowledge?

In business processes, there is an exchange of value between customer and supplier, which is undertaken in different actions carried out in business processes. In core processes, there is an exchange of value between members of the organisation. This exchange of value is undertaken in different actions carried our in core processes. By separating these kinds of action there are external and internal actions related to business and core processes. To determine whether this exchange between members of the organisation that is carried out in core processes is valuable, the consequences of this value on business processes are determined. In other words, how does this exchange affect the organisation's ability to conduct business? The main concern here is the exchange in terms of knowledge and how IT can make this exchange effective. This reduced uncertainty secures actions in business processes, for example by securing delivery of goods to customers. This research has focused on completion (i.e. supplier completes commitment by delivery of goods to customer). It is fair to say that a focus on fulfilment has a potential to create synergy effects. Amongst these effects are, for instance, an overall increased ability in conducting business and quality assurance.

Relevant knowledge is knowledge about operational disturbances that reduces uncertainty in core processes.

According to the argument above, the following principles can be extracted for determining whether knowledge is relevant to collect:

- Knowledge is required of operational disturbances that create unsatisfactory variations in core processes. Variations of interest are those that prevent the organisation fulfilling customer commitments.

This overall principle can further be described by the following principles:

- Knowledge of operational disturbances in core processes must be related to business processes. To determine whether knowledge is related, it must support actions carried out in business processes.
- There must be a relationship between actions carried out in core processes and business processes, where the former supports and secures the latter.
- Knowledge must support people's actions carried out in core processes to secure completion. This means that knowledge must be demand driven (i.e. actually used by people).

An essential feature in determining what knowledge is relevant to collect or not is business processes. They represent more a way of thinking about what consequences an operational disturbance has for the organisation's commitments towards its customers.

In practice, operational disturbances are often equal to a break in delivery (i.e. completion). However, this must not always be the case (e.g. see synergy effects).

In this case study research experiences have been identified concerning errors in production as a fruitful source of knowledge of operational disturbances.

11.3.2 Classifying Knowledge

"Classifying knowledge" is related to the question: how do we classify relevant knowledge?

This question is more practical than the first. It is relevant to classify knowledge to make the evaluation and distribution of knowledge from the individual to the whole as relevant as possible depending on the situation at hand. Knowledge is classified with respect to what is identified as relevant knowledge. This means that before classification one must know what knowledge there is to be classified. A prerequisite for classification is that core processes and business processes are made explicit (see Section 11.2).

Knowledge is classified with respect to core and business processes. In these processes a natural classification is sought that does not violate people's perceptions of how things are done. Figure 11.2 illustrates the classification identified in the case study research. The relation between core and business processes is implicit and is not illustrated in Figure 11.2 (see Fig. 11.1).

In the case study research, knowledge about operational disturbances that concern tools is very important to prevent unsatisfactory variation in production

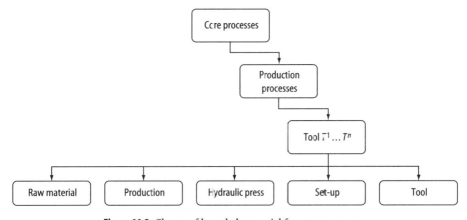

Figure 11.2 Classes of knowledge crucial for core processes.

and to secure delivery of goods. A tool is an item that is a prerequisite for producing an article (i.e. products) and it may be rigged on a hydraulic press to shape raw material such as steel into different articles. Tools cut or bend raw material and multidimensional tools perform multiple tasks. An error related to tools has different sources: A tool that fails in performance is related to one of the following sources: raw material, production, hydraulic press, setting up and the tool itself. In principle, a corresponding classification can be done of raw material, hydraulic presses, etc., as for tools illustrated in Figure 11.2. In other words, this knowledge related to these classes serves as input to an IT-based information system and an output to prevent operational disturbances. Tools have been divided into different categories, using the kind of operation that each tool performs as a variable (see $T^1 \ldots T^n$ in Figure 11.2).

According to the argument above, the following principles for classifying knowledge can be extracted:

- Knowledge of operational disturbances is classified into different categories by:
- identifying what kind of knowledge of operational disturbances is crucial;
- categorising knowledge in a systematic way, optimally by giving each kind of operational disturbance a category (i.e. operational disturbance categories);
- identifying where in production, and for whom, this knowledge is crucial (i.e. that benefits from having this kind of knowledge available).

This overall principle implies that the following criteria are met:

- Core processes and business processes are made explicit.
- Crucial knowledge is knowledge of operational disturbances that prevents the organisation from completing commitments to customers in business processes. This principle is close to the concept of knowledge relevancy in the principles for relevant knowledge.

With respect to the case study research, a principle can be formulated for classifying knowledge of operational disturbances that is highly case specific according to the above:

- Identify categories of tools.
- Identify categories of errors related to tools and sources of these errors.

11.3.3 Evaluating Knowledge

"Evaluating knowledge" is related to the question: how do we evaluate classified knowledge?

In order to distribute knowledge of operational disturbances to those who require it, principles for evaluation are required. A failing tool must be given some priority. In the case study research, consequences due to an error and its causes are realised by giving each error a different priority, where 1 represents the lowest and 4 the highest priority. Priority is a measure of how the organisation's

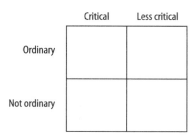

Figure 11.3 Principle for evaluation.

ability to fulfil commitments to customers is affected when an operational disturbance occurs. In the case study research, operational disturbances are represented by errors concerning tools. In principle, operational disturbances are given a value of relevance depending on how often they occur and what implications they have. Implications are related to what the consequences are when an operational disturbance occurs and priority is a measure of how critical these implications are for the organisation's ability to conduct business. Placing each operational disturbance in the matrix in Figure 11.3 according to its priority (critical and less critical) and frequency (ordinary and not ordinary) provides a way to sort operational disturbances.

A matrix like the one illustrated in Figure 11.3 is a rather simple way to illustrate the principle of knowledge relevance. With respect to the idea of relevance an operational disturbance that occurs is, in the case study research, related to different kinds of error on different kinds of tools. Depending on how often an error occurs, it is classified as ordinary or not ordinary. To judge the effects that an error has for production processes and business processes, it is classified as critical or less critical. When using this matrix the main focus is on operational disturbances that are placed in the upper left corner. Going beyond this simple view led to the development of the idea of relevance using a concept called the measurement of operational disturbance relevance (ODR measure). The aim with such a measurement is to distribute knowledge of operational disturbances according to what implications these have on the organisation's ability. This is done by considering the following:

- The frequency of how often an operational disturbance occurs for a unique tool is represented as a scale with ordinary and not ordinary at each end.

- The priority of the implication that an operational disturbance has is represented as a scale with critical and less critical at each end.

This is a further interpretation of the matrix in Figure 11.3. The result of this reasoning, using frequency and priority and multiplying these two figures for each category of operational disturbances, is introduced here as an ODR measure.

An ODR-measure diagram can be drawn from ODR measures and is illustrated in Figure 11.4. Principles for the ODR measure and diagram are explained in the following section.

In the case study research, knowledge of operational disturbances is knowledge about errors on tools. To evaluate this kind of critical knowledge it is classified into

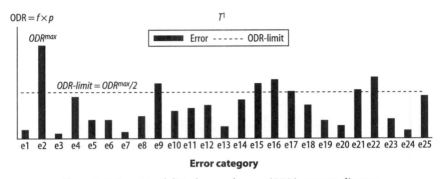

Figure 11.4 Operational disturbance relevance (ODR)-measure diagram.

different error and tool categories. A unique tool in one tool category can be subject to different error categories [e.g. tool (T^1) in tool category (TC^1) failed in operation because of error $(e^1, e^2 \dots e^n)$]. Under the assumption that errors (e) have occurred at a frequency (f) between 1 and 25 and are given a priority (p) between 1 and 4 for a unique tool (T^1), each error's ODR measure can be measured by multiplying frequency and priority $(f \times p)$. This gives a maximum ODR measure set to 100. An ODR-measure diagram (alt. error relevance diagram with respect to the case study research) under these assumptions is illustrated in Figure 11.4. The horizontal curve in Figure 11.4 represents an ODR limit for which errors are interesting, by dividing the maximum ODR measure for a unique tool (T^1) by two $(ODR^{max}/2)$. This limit is an estimated ODR factor, which excludes operational disturbances perceived as not relevant from the ODR^{max} point of view. This is set to 50 (the limit for relevance is given by a factor of 2 in the formula for ODR limit, but this need not always be the case). From the organisation's perspective this limit can be interpreted as a limit of tolerance. With respect to the matrix in Figure 11.3, this reasoning represents a 45-degree curve from the lower left to the upper right corner, as illustrated in Figure 11.5. The relevance for each error provides a way to sort errors. In Figure 11.4 the relevant errors for tool T^1 are e^2, e^{22}, e^{16}, e^{15} and e^9. These errors are placed on the left side of the 45-degree curve in Figure 11.5.

Evaluation according to the principles outlined above provides the opportunity to create a report containing the most relevant errors, source, cause and actions that prevent the error from occurring.

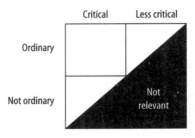

Figure 11.5 Principle for evaluation including relevance.

According to the argument above, the following principles can be extracted for evaluating knowledge:

- Evaluate knowledge to prevent the most unsatisfactory operational disturbances from occurring by:
  - giving knowledge of operational disturbances in each identified category a priority;
  - giving each category of operational disturbances an ODR measure.

This overall principle can further be described by the following principle:

- Evaluating knowledge is to sort knowledge depending on how crucial knowledge is in order to prevent operational disturbances and to fulfil commitments to customers.

It is assumed that there is a relation between critical knowledge of operational disturbances and business processes. This idea has been elaborated in the preceding sections and the assumption is not unlike when it comes to manufacturing companies, at least not in this case study.

With respect to the case study research a principle can be formulated for evaluating knowledge of operational disturbances that is highly case specific when it comes to giving knowledge in each identified operational disturbance category a priority:

- Give knowledge of different kinds of errors related to a unique tool a priority.

In this section principles have been formulated for collecting, classifying and evaluating knowledge about operational disturbances. Principles for evaluation were found to be the most important and an evaluation method for knowledge was developed by introducing the concept of the ODR measure. The following section shows how these principles have been applied in the case study research in the form of a prototype, an IT-based knowledge-management tool for the reuse of knowledge in a manufacturing company.

11.4 A Prototype for Reuse of Crucial Knowledge Related to Production of Goods in a Manufacturing Company

A prototype for the reuse of crucial knowledge related to the production of goods that meets the requirements outlined in Section 11.3 has been developed using Microsoft® Access 97. Information systems development involves organisational change. This change should be of an evolutionary mode to have a positive outcome. This prerequisite is met by involving those who are affected by the information system in the development

An evolutionary mode of change means understanding of the logic (i.e. how things are done) that an information system is developed to support, and what changes it brings about (i.e. how things are done in the future).

process. In other words, users and other actors are very important for an evolutionary mode of change. The prerequisite is also labelled user-centred design (Preece, 1994). Transparency is important in developing IT-based information systems, i.e. users represent a very important part of the development process. Usability is crucial for information systems to be used in a decision support context in a manufacturing company, and is considered by involving the user when developing graphical user interfaces, functionality and so on.

According to the above argument the following principles can be extracted for usability and information systems development and design:

- Development of IT-based information systems must have managerial support (see Section 11.5).
- Designing usable systems demands frequent involvement of users.

The development of IT-based information systems for knowledge management requires that the following principle is met:

- Identify the context that an IT-based information system for knowledge management is supposed to support.

For an information system to facilitate reuse of crucial knowledge, to collect and distribute knowledge to those who need it, requires a common interface (i.e. graphical user interface), a knowledge communication process and a knowledge store (Fig. 11.6). This prototype is designed to be used in a decision support context, limited to production processes where the decision is whether production should be initiated or not, and whether some actions must be undertaken in order to prevent operational disturbances and to secure a positive outcome for production and business processes.

Before an information system can support these kinds of decision a knowledge repository (i.e. database) is needed. In this prototype, users have the chance to

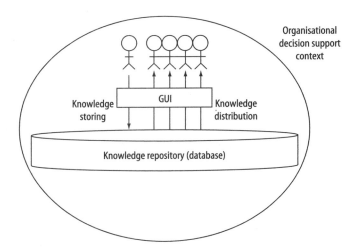

Figure 11.6 Properties of information systems for the reuse of knowledge. GUI: graphical user interface.

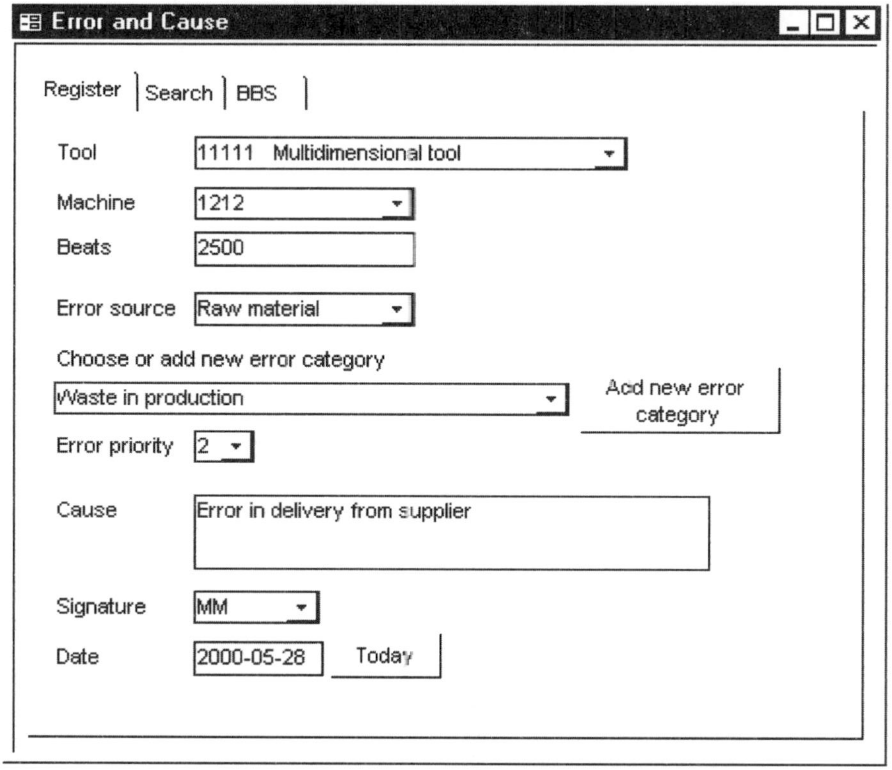

Error and Cause _ □ ×

Register | Search | BBS

Tool	11111 Multidimensional tool ▼
Machine	1212 ▼
Beats	2500
Error source	Raw material ▼

Choose or add new error category

Waste in production ▼   Add new error category

Error priority   2 ▼

Cause   Error in delivery from supplier

Signature   MM ▼

Date   2000-05-28   Today

Figure 11.7 Registering error for a multidimensional tool.

enter errors that appear in production. Figure 11.7 is a screenshot from the prototype, which illustrates an error concerning a multidimensional tool.

Errors entered into the system are related to a unique tool. The most important fields to fill out are the error source, error category, priority and cause. If the error category does not correspond to the error at hand, the user can add new ones. In principle, a unique error category related to a unique tool, source and category always has the same priority. Consequently, if such an operational disturbance already exists and new entries are added (i.e. same operational disturbance at a different point in time) priority is given. Entering errors is done according to the principles of collecting and classifying knowledge of operational disturbances. The evaluation of knowledge is realised by a search function. Figure 11.8 is a screenshot from the prototype, which illustrates a search on a multidimensional tool.

When the button "Create list" is pushed, the system creates an ODR-measure diagram (alt. error relevance diagram with respect to the case study research) and an error report (see Fig. 11.9 and Table 11.1).

Error category "Tool not correctly attached" has the highest relevance, followed by "Waste in production". The other two error categories are not relevant because they are below the limit of relevance. The corresponding error report, where each

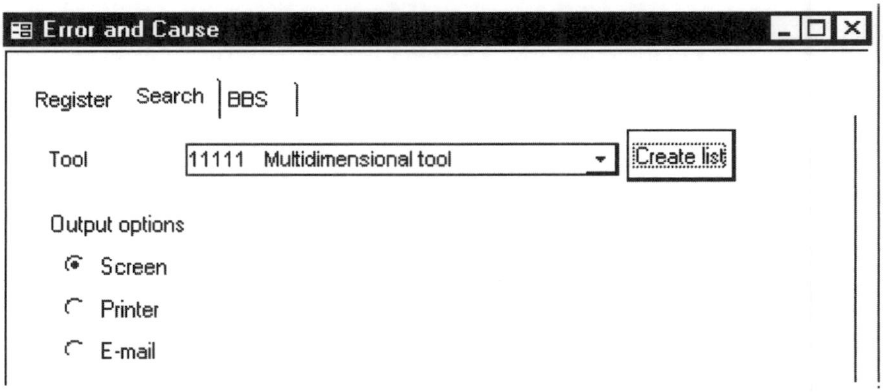

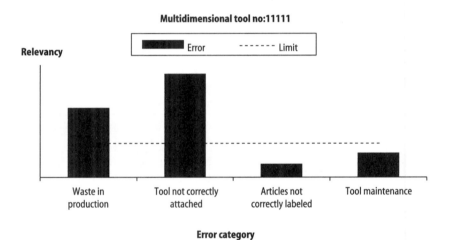

Figure 11.8 Creating an error report for a multidimensional tool.

Figure 11.9 Error relevance diagram (operational disturbance relevance-measure diagram) for a multidimensional tool.

error is sorted by relevance, is illustrated in Table 11.1. In the report, source and cause are described. The diagram and report serves as a summary of errors related to a unique tool and may be the only knowledge one needs to draw attention to sources of possible errors.

This example is a simplified version of an error report. Knowledge about actions can be added that corresponds to each error category: who is using the system; where to focus to prevent operational disturbances from occurring. In principle, the evaluation method sorts knowledge and reports and other demanded output from users from the system can be created as long as the output is related to the evaluation method.

Table 11.1 Error report for multidimensional tool

Multidimensional tool no:11111

Relevance	Category	Source	Cause
1	Tool not correctly attached	Set-up	Unable to start production
2	Waste in production	Raw material	Error in delivery from supplier

11.5 Information Technology and Knowledge Management from a Sociotechnical Perspective

The development of the IT-based knowledge reuse prototype can be characterised as a product of a sociotechnical approach, being dependent on both human and technical aspects. A key sociotechnical aspect is that the design process used in the development of the prototype is characterised by its participatory nature (Nurminen, 1988). The prototyping approach is participatory: in the development of the prototype, different groups are represented (IT experts, management and experts in the field). According to Bjørn-Andersen and Hedberg (1977) there are three different goals of user participation:

• gaining the acceptance of users;
• improvement in the quality of the system;
• a genuinely democratic effort to enhance the influence of individuals over that which concerns themselves.

The design process has been worked on in collaboration with the users. Initial interviews were held with the users and experts; when the prototype was ready to be presented, seminars were arranged to collect opinions and information. Mumford (1979) points to job satisfaction as a major objective for the systems design process. Systems design in this respect is really a matter of work design. In the design process, considerable efforts have also been made to take advantage of earlier attempts to systemise the causes and effects of manufacturing problems.

According to Leavitt's sociotechnical diamond (Fig. 11.10), the variables (structure, tasks, technology and people) are mutually interdependent: "... change in any one will most probably result in compensatory (or retaliatory) change in others"

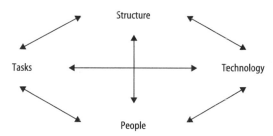

Figure 11.10 The Leavitt diamond.

(Leavitt, 1964, p. 363). Accordingly, a change in technology (e.g. an IT-based information system) affects people and their tasks and even the structure of the organisation in one way or another. This view of IT is quite different from, for example, a systems-theoretical perspective where IT is looked upon as a phenomenon more isolated from the rest of the organisation and where considerations of the effects on people, tasks and structure do not have the same importance.

However, not even a sociotechnical development process of a knowledge management system is without problems. Using a classification from Swan the following problem areas are therefore addressed:

- codification and tacit knowledge;
- exploration and exploitation (i.e. organisational learning);
- supply and demand.

In this paper tacit knowledge is defined as knowledge not articulated (Avdic, 1999). One explicit aim of the project has been to articulate tacit knowledge and make it explicit. This task is difficult, since professional activities are often based on personal and tacit knowledge. Swan suggests that attempts to codify tacit knowledge often produce knowledge that is either useless, difficult to verify, trivial, redundant, irrelevant to a wider audience, politically naive or inaccurate (Swan, 1999). It can be argued that this has not happened with the present prototype, perhaps because the systematic ordering of knowledge, not explicitly known to anybody, was a major goal of the project, rather than codifying the knowledge of experts.

Knowledge management is about managing and/or creating knowledge: "… exploitation of existing knowledge is only a small part of what constitutes effective knowledge management. Also crucial are processes of exploration, whereby new knowledge is created" (Swan, 1999, p. 7). Exploitation is refinement and extension of existing competencies, technologies, etc., whereas exploration is experimentation with new alternatives. An organisation's ability to learn and act decreases when it is characterised by too much exploitation or exploration. There is a need for balance between unorganised and organised action (e.g. March, 1991; Dogdson, 1993), where the former relates to exploration and the latter to exploitation. This can also be related to single-loop learning and double-loop learning (Argyris and Schön, 1996). The present prototype not only aims to stockpile workers' knowledge, but also aims to detect and identify problems to avoid operational disturbances and thereby secure deliveries in the future. This implies discovering patterns that have not been fully recognised by the workers. Another explicit aim of the project has been to integrate the knowledge reuse system with existing systems. This aim implies new possibilities to combine information from different sources and thereby produce a more complete basis for decisions about production.

Two different approaches to the design of IT-based knowledge-management tools are supply-driven and demand-driven design processes. The latter is normally preferable since the chances that the system will be used are greater when users themselves demand it. One risk with supply-driven processes is information overload. Two ways of addressing this problem are to minimise the output information from the IT system and to address problems that are relevant to the worker. A desirable effect of the system when it is implemented is that the workers' control over their immediate work environment will increase.

11.6 Conclusions

To design a system for the reuse and acquisition of crucial knowledge in a manufacturing environment, a specification consisting of principles for collecting, classifying and evaluating operational disturbances has been formulated. Evaluation relies on the idea of relevance. The relevance of a specific operational disturbance is decided with respect to frequency and priority. A knowledge evaluation method was developed by introducing the concept of the ODR measure.

This concept makes it possible to design an IT-based information system that systemises knowledge of errors, with respect to the authors' case study research, in an organisational decision-support context to avoid operational disturbances in a manufacturing company.

The principles for collecting, classifying and evaluating knowledge of operational disturbances are summarised in Table 11.2.

Table 11.2 Principles for how to design information technology-based information systems that systemise knowledge in order to avoid operational disturbances

Usability (ISD)	Development of IT-based information systems must have managerial support Designing usable systems demands frequent involvement of users
Collect	Collect knowledge about operational disturbances that creates unsatisfactory variations in core processes Variations of interest are those that prevent the organisation fulfilling commitments to customers
Classify	Classify knowledge of operational disturbances into different categories by: • identifying what kind of knowledge of operational disturbances is crucial; • categorising knowledge in a systematic way, optimally by giving each kind of operational disturbance a category of its own; • identifying where in production, and for whom, this knowledge is crucial (i.e. who benefits from having this kind of knowledge available)
Evaluate	Evaluate knowledge in order to prevent the most unsatisfactory operational disturbances from occurring by: • giving knowledge of operational disturbances in each identified category a priority • giving each category of operational disturbances an ODR measure

ISD: information system development; ODR: operational disturbance relevance.

Part 4
Know-How

Chapter 12
Methods for Knowledge Management Strategy Formulation: A Case Study

Christine Cuthbertson and John Farrington

12.1 Introduction

The organisation investigated in this case study is the Royal Naval School of Educational and Training Technology (RNSETT). RNSETT is the "lead school" for educational and training technology within the Royal Navy (RN) and provides policy, training, advice and consultancy to all RN organisations involved in training. The RNSETT Mission Statement is:

> "To identify, disseminate and assure Educational and Training Technology best practice throughout the Naval Service".

12.2 RNSETT

RNSETT is one of 21 training schools within the Naval Recruiting and Training Agency (NRTA) which was formed in 1995. The agency is owned by the Second Sea Lord and Commander-in-Chief Naval Home Command (2SL/CNH). The chief executive of the agency is Flag Officer Training and Recruiting (FOTR).

The chief executive of the RNSETT is Commander RNSETT (Cdr RNSETT). He manages the internal organisation through the executive board and provides the interface with the corporate headquarters.

In addition to Cdr RNSETT, the RNSETT's executive board consists of Staff Officer RNSETT (SO), Training Systems Group Officer (TSGO) and Training Media Group Officer (TMGO), each of whom leads a business group within the RNSETT. Further to his role as the chief executive of a RN establishment, Cdr RNSETT fills the role of Commander Training Technology (Cdr TT) within the FOTR organisation. In this capacity, he is responsible for providing advice on educational and training technology to FOTR.

The RNSETT is a relatively small organisation and only employs thirty people. Sixteen of these are military officers involved in all RNSETT business areas. Three military officers are currently on exchange from the Royal Australian Navy (RAN), the Army and Royal Air Force (RAF). The RN officers are all of the engineering training manager [E(TM)] or information systems [E(IS)] subspecialisation. They are all graduates and many have masters degrees in training technology. Having served from five to twenty-five years, the majority are experienced naval officers in the service and thus have a good understanding of the RNSETT business.

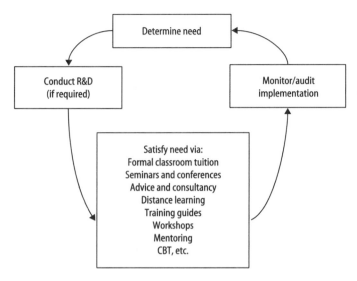

Figure 12.1 RNSETT business model. R&D: research and development; CBT: computer-based training.

The RNSETT's objectives are based upon the NRTA corporate objectives and are pursued through the RNSETT's business areas, broken down into sections, each with its own objectives. They are grouped to reflect the key strategy areas identified within the NRTA business plan. The five business areas are: train the trainer, advice and consultancy, training audits, research and development, and corporate development.

RNSETT's business model is shown in Figure 12.1. After determining that a customer's need exists, research and development (R&D) may be conducted to assess the latest industry best practices relevant to the problem situation. The need is then satisfied by a suitable business activity that may be updated by the R&D effort, such as advice and consultancy or formal tuition. This action is then monitored by mechanisms, such as training audits, to assess its impact.

12.3 The Problem Situation

The real-world situation perceived as being problematic within the RNSETT is the enforced loss of knowledgeable staff due to the RN's appointing cycle. There is a view expressed by the members of the RNSETT that this situation should be managed, and this study considers a knowledge management approach to bring about improvement. The routine of officers and ratings only being "in post" for two years is standard throughout the military. Although problematic, this approach brings some advantages. It ensures that the RN's personnel are broadly experienced in a number of areas. When these personnel become more senior, as leaders and managers, they can use this experience to appreciate the situation and be more effective problem solvers.

RNSETT is keen to ensure that knowledge is shared and retained, independent of personnel movements. A knowledge management approach appeared appropriate, and the study ultimately led to the development of a knowledge management strategy for RNSETT, intended to complement information, information management and information technology (IT) strategies.

12.4 Knowledge Management

RNSETT employs a staff of highly qualified training experts with a wealth of experience – both individually and as a whole – to provide formal courses, advice and consultancy, R&D and tailored training solutions to an ever more divergent range of customers. These services are provided across the navy and increasingly to the other armed services, related government departments, and the commercial and industrial sectors.

Knowledge management addresses many organisational knowledge issues. Even if some approaches may not be suitable, others will be. For example, the studies of Davenport *et al.* (1998) have shown that the maximum size of an organisation in which people know one another well enough to have a reliable grasp of collective organisational knowledge is two-hundred to three-hundred people. As RNSETT is a tenth of this size, it is not surprising that the employees know who the experts are in each particular area. This approach may therefore not seem suitable for RNSETT. However, for larger naval establishments, which employ several thousand personnel, this approach may well be suitable, and the recommendations from the study are intended to be, to some extent, generic.

> A knowledge management approach can be advantageous, but is it suitable for RNSETT?

The work of Starbuck (1992) supports the adoption of a knowledge management initiative within the RNSETT. RNSETT may be considered a KIF. Starbuck (1992) provides several considerations for classifying a firm as a KIF, two of which are appropriate to the RNSETT. First, a KIF may not be information intensive. "Some activities draw on extensive knowledge without processing large amounts of current information – management consulting, for example". Just as management consultancy draws upon extensive knowledge, so do the educational and training technology advice and consultancy services provided by the RNSETT across the navy. Secondly, one ought to weigh the emphasis on esoteric expertise instead of widely shared knowledge. "One should not label a firm as knowledge-intensive unless exceptional and valuable expertise dominates commonplace knowledge". The RNSETT possesses many specialised experts in areas as diverse as instructional techniques and computer-based training (CBT).

> Starbuck coins the term knowledge intensive to imitate economists' labelling of firms as capital intensive or labour intensive. A knowledge-intensive firm (KIF) therefore implies that knowledge has more importance than capital or labour inputs.

Although managing knowledge occurs anyway, knowledge management as a management initiative is an explicit and structured recognition that knowledge is the single most important asset within an organisation. Even though many companies are starting to adopt knowledge management practices, this is not a passing fad. It can bring sustainable competitive advantage, but its adoption is neither simple nor easy.

12.5 Methodology

Initially, soft systems methodology (SSM) was used to appreciate the problem situation and to provide a clearer focus to the knowledge practitioner for subsequent studies. An audit of RNSETT's knowledge was then conducted. This included consideration of previous studies and an assessment of RNSETT's existing and knowledge-creating activities. Finally, a method developed in the US firm JD Edwards was used to elicit recommendations for a suitable knowledge management system.

A knowledge management initiative should consider three key interacting components, namely people and culture, business processes, and technology. These three components interact and depend upon each other. A knowledge management study must therefore address each component in parallel, rather than in isolation. To tackle this complexity, the study is necessarily wide ranging and should consider the components as a whole, rather than in a series of reductionist stages. Consequently, it is believed that a systemic process of enquiry is a suitable and necessary approach in the initial stage of conducting a study into the production of a knowledge management strategy.

Senge (1990) argues that one must see "wholes" rather than "parts" to solve the root causes of organisational problems, instead of just tackling the symptoms.

"Systems thinking" is viewed as the cornerstone of the learning organisation. Indeed, Senge's "fifth discipline" is "systems thinking". As learning is an important part of knowledge building (as declared in the conceptual framework of enquiry), this reinforces the view that a systemic methodological approach is suitable and necessary in the initial stages of the study to tackle organisational complexity. Magalhães (1998) uses Boulding's hierarchy of systems to argue that "knowledge and learning in organisations are, first and foremost, attributes of complex systems". The initial study must therefore make sense of this complexity.

Further, as any knowledge management initiative will effect a change within people's environments, it will be viewed differently by different people. For example, some people may take the view that "knowledge is power" and that this will be eroded in a knowledge sharing culture. As Davenport and Prusak (1998) state, "knowledge management is a highly political undertaking. You'll have to tread lightly in giving access ... to knowledge to those who formerly lacked it. Or you will almost certainly run afoul of someone powerful to whom your knowledge management activities are threatening". Consequently, an initial investigation should account for people's different views and perspectives on knowledge management in order to improve its chance of success.

Finally, the conceptual model of a knowledge and learning system purports that "effective action" is a result of the knowledge process. It is shown that knowledge depends upon the interaction of people for its development. Human activity is therefore an important element within the management of knowledge. Indeed, as Wiig, de Hoog and van der Spek (1997) point out, knowledge management does not carry its name lightly: management implies that something has to be managed, and management further implies human involvement and activity.

12.6 Soft Systems Methodology

SSM was selected for the initial stages of the investigation. This decision was taken for a number of reasons. SSM takes the view that all problem situations have one thing in common, claim Checkland and Scholes (1990). They all feature human beings in social roles trying to take purposeful action. Further, SSM also accounts for differing views of the same situation. As it is not goal seeking, but rather attempts to seek accommodations by providing insight and illumination on the problem domain, differing beliefs and perspectives can be considered.

Finally, SSM's use of "system thinking" (see Checkland, 1981, for a detailed background) facilitates an organised way of making sense of messy situations. As Checkland and Scholes (1990) state, "the particular form which SSM takes (helped ... by its use of systems thinking) both enables it to be used descriptively to make sense of a complex situation ... and prescriptively to control ... 'chaos'". SSM is therefore suitable for the initial enquiry into RNSETT's knowledge 'situation'.

To elicit relevant tasks and issues in the RNSETT, interviews were conducted. The order in which they were conducted is important. A "top–down" interview approach affords several benefits. Senior officers highlight more general issues of concern, especially those with strategic implications. This helps the interviewer to grasp organisational issues at a high level, before descending into detail. Secondly, as time is spent with these people, it helps to give the interviewer authority when approaching their subordinates to discuss more detailed matters. Indeed, it is only courteous to approach senior officers before talking to their staff. This act of diplomacy in a very hierarchical organisation, such as the military, can be considered culturally sensible.

Who to interview also needs to be considered. In all but the smallest organisations, it is impractical to interview everyone. Selection of representatives from specific groups is therefore necessary. In the RNSETT, the heads of groups (HOGs) and representatives from each subgroup area were interviewed. These people were chosen after consultation with the RNSETT managers to determine who would provide a wide spread of experience, knowledge and opinions. As part of the initial project scope, only representative "knowledge workers" who are perceived to be involved in RNSETT's core business areas were interviewed. As knowledge workers are people who work with information, not all personnel within RNSETT can be considered to fit into this category. So, for example, whilst staff such as cleaners and storeworkers remain important to the effectiveness of the organisation, it does not rely on their knowledge to perform their core activities. Consequently, they were excluded from the initial study.

Four purposeful systems in the form of models of human activity systems were named, modelled and used to illuminate the problem situation. By comparing these models with perceptions of the parts of RNSETT being examined, they served to structure debate about change and to reach accommodations between different interests. Although many more systems could have been modelled, four were considered adequate for a number of reasons. First, the models that were developed provided sufficient insight into the problem situation. After a rich debate with RNSETT managers, a wider appreciation of perceived actions and disagreements relevant to losing knowledgeable staff was gained. Secondly, if additional complexity and lack of consensus were reached at a later stage in the project, more purposeful systems could have been modelled. At this stage, however, a conscious effort was made to progress with other methods.

Numerous "rich pictures" were used throughout the project in an attempt to represent the overall problem situation. Powerfully, they represented relationships, thoughts and opinions that otherwise would be difficult to structure in standard text. Further, the ability to draw logically a boundary around the area of concern helps to scope the project at the initial stages; one is able to question which relationships and entities are relevant and which are not. However, using this technique, difficulty was experienced in attempting to find a way to represent the whole of the problem situation in a satisfactory manner. With many differing viewpoints and a complex interaction of relationships, it is challenging to ascertain the major issues from those at a more detailed level. Consequently, it is helpful to draw a rich picture after each interview with a knowledge worker. Using a highlighter pen, recurring issues, concerns and relationships between individual rich pictures are more easily identified. These are then included in later, more global rich pictures. Ideally, this would not have been necessary. However, difficulty has been experienced in seeing the wood for the trees in order to form a mental model of the problem situation. Such an approach addressed this difficulty.

Successful interpretations of SSM take a multidimensional approach that maps between the real world and the systems thinking world. The analyses of the intervention, social system and political system were conducted in parallel and with reference to each other to identify and promote debate about issues and tasks. Throughout the use of SSM, these different strands continually evolved and matured until a clearer perception of the problem situation was developed. At this stage, when accommodations between all stakeholders were reached, it was time to progress to a suitable knowledge management method.

12.7 Moving On

The SSM study provided a clearer focus for the knowledge management practitioner of the necessary actions. However, any effort and action must also be aligned to the corporate objectives. Wiig (1995) recognises this:

"It is clearly not the role of knowledge professionals to establish the enterprise's strategy. However, to a larger degree than most other activities, knowledge management work affects its future capabilities, potentials and direction. Therefore, it is important to ascertain that the knowledge management work is in line with and provides strong support of the enterprise's missions and plans".

As a knowledge management strategy must address these missions and plans, suitable tools and techniques are required to identify the enterprise's key issues and aspirations.

It is apparent that knowledge management activities can be wide ranging and address many organisational activities. Further, these activities must consider the sociotechnical issues of people and culture, business process and technology issues in parallel. In attempting to do this, it can rapidly become a daunting prospect to attempt to solve all the organisation's ills in one large swoop. The knowledge practitioner rapidly becomes swamped in detail and can lose focus on what is really required. An organisationally systemic approach continues to be important, yet for the novice, the simpler task of initially focusing on just a few key issues will afford more likelihood of success.

Davenport and Prusak (1998) state, "to make headway ... it is generally advisable to do a number of things along multiple fronts – technical, organisational, cultural – rather than to focus on a single topic".

Davenport and Prusak (1998) have many years of experience observing initiatives in knowledge-intensive firms and provide advice for those starting a knowledge management project. They support the approach of focusing on a few key issues: "... in knowledge management, it is important to start small, actually accomplish something and then trumpet about what's been achieved". They go on to suggest that "knowledge management should start with a recognised business problem that relates to knowledge". The SSM-identified "knowledge problem situations" are therefore a sensible starting point for the knowledge management study. These must, however, be aligned with the corporate business objectives of the organisation.

The above requirements not only provide a direction for the project, but also provide factors to identify a suitable methodology. In addition, a previous study undertook a strengths, weaknesses, opportunities and threats (SWOT) analysis and identified critical success factors (CSFs) for the organisation as a whole. Armed with this information, the knowledge practitioner can focus the knowledge strategy towards the most important business activities. It may be considered appropriate to use this work as a quality-assurance measure to validate the current project's investigations into the business problems that are related to knowledge.

12.8 Knowledge Audit

Wiig (1995) defines a knowledge audit as: "Survey and characterisation of the status of knowledge in an organisation. Knowledge audit may refer to identifying specific knowledge assets such as patents and the degree to which these assets are used, enforced and safeguarded".

With considerable practical experience, Carl Frappaola (1999), an executive vice president of the Delphi Group, asserts that "the first step in any knowledge management initiative should be a knowledge audit".

The audit should look at current levels of knowledge usage and communication, the current state of corporate knowledge management, identification and clarification of knowledge management opportunities, and the perceived value of knowledge within the organisation. This work helps the knowledge practitioner to identify areas for improvement and opportunities to leverage knowledge.

Applehams, Globe and Laugero (1999) also believe that the purpose of an audit is to break knowledge management down into digestible, manageable projects without losing sight of the big picture. They support the argument that an audit is initially required to match knowledge management projects to business objectives.

Consequently, a knowledge audit is an essential front-end to the study. It should assess the business objectives, help to focus on a few key issues and identify recognised business problems. To do this for RNSETT the following methods were employed:

- Knowledge profiling uses an eight-level scale of proficiency which is used to identify the level of knowledge required by each knowledge worker to fulfil the organisation's objectives.
- A knowledge SWOT maps organisation goals against individual representative knowledge workers.
- Knowledge creation maps the existing knowledge to the required knowledge to identify disparities.
- The concept of the hypertext organisation considers developing an organisational structure that supports knowledge creation and retention.

12.8.1 Knowledge Profiling

To obtain the data, a knowledge profiling survey was given to each individual. The knowledge practitioner was available to answer any queries and ensure that the surveys were completed, and it was found that the presence of the investigator could encourage rich debate and afford valuable further information. In the RNSETT, each knowledge worker has a job description with a description of the skills and experience required to fulfil the post. Any training that is job specific and has been identified by the HOG to ensure that the person filling the post has the necessary skills and competencies to be effective in that position is included. However, requirements continually change and additional new training is required. Consequently, individual job descriptions do not reflect the latest requirements and hence need to be updated with staff skills and development data. By combining an updated job description with the individual knowledge profiles, a richer portrait of the skill sets and knowledge for each individual was obtained.

12.8.2 Knowledge SWOT

In the context of knowledge management, Wiig, de Hoog and van der Spek (1997) argue that SWOT can be used for analysing the knowledge "household" from the perspective of one or more of the organisational high-level goals. Consequently, it does not make sense to start a SWOT analysis of the knowledge without a clear definition of the organisational goal(s) against which to measure the SWOTs. In the RNSETT, the organisational goals and objectives are clearly defined and so can be used as the foundation for further analysis. However, as Wiig, de Hoog and van der Spek (1997) caution, "lumping too many goals together will confuse the analysis". Only RNSETT's key objectives were therefore analysed with SWOT.

Rather than conduct a typical SWOT analysis at the organisational level (which had already been done in the earlier study), Wiig, de Hoog and van der Spek (1997) recommend a candidate knowledge SWOT as more appropriate for a knowledge management study. Individual, representative knowledge workers are interviewed to ascertain their knowledge strengths and weaknesses, etc. This provides a greater amount of knowledge detail and, because a common frame of reference exists, recurring themes can then be combined to identify organisation-wide knowledge SWOTs. However, as argued above, these SWOTs need to be aligned with the key objectives within the organisation. Fortunately, as the RNSETT business objectives were used as attributes in the knowledge profiling activity, it is possible to identify these for each individual. It is then possible to analyse the key knowledge strengths, etc., that individuals need to meet their main business objective(s) and hence avoid a confused analysis.

12.8.3 Knowledge Creation

Part of the SSM study revealed that the existing knowledge within RNSETT is needed to solve future problems. In particular, there is a need to identify, capture, store, transfer and update the organisation's current know-how. However, in addition to the existing knowledge, knowledge creation is important to the RNSETT. Initiatives such as marketing and IG require new skills and knowledge. Corporate decisions must be made on whether new "train the trainer" courses are required. Further, assessment of the latest training media techniques and technologies is required to ensure that RNSETT's advice and best practice is up to date. In one form or another, all these activities need knowledge creation. However, the methods selected so far predominantly focus upon the existing knowledge within the organisation.

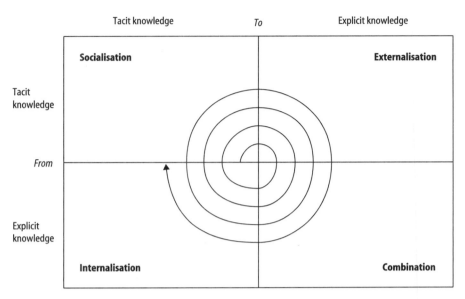

Figure 12.2 Knowledge Spiral from *The Knowledge-Creating Company: How Japanese Companies Create the Dynamics of Innovation* by Ikujiro Nonaka and Hirotaka Takeuchi, copyright © 1995 by Oxford University Press, Inc. Used by permission of Oxford University Press, Inc.

Nonaka and Takeuchi's (1995) influential work addresses this shortcoming. Their dynamic model of knowledge creation is anchored to the critical assumption that human knowledge is created and expanded through social interaction between tacit and explicit knowledge. Coining this interaction "knowledge conversion", they emphasise that the conversion is a social process between individuals and not confined within an individual.

Using Nonaka and Takeuchi's (1995) knowledge spiral, shown in Figure 12.2, it is possible to map appropriate RNSETT activities onto the four modes of knowledge conversion that are necessary for knowledge creation within the organisation. Consequently, it is possible to ascertain whether there are any gaps in knowledge conversion that would hinder the knowledge-creation process within the RNSETT.

12.8.4 The Hypertext Organisation

Identifying the gaps in the knowledge-conversion process is an important part of auditing RNSETT's knowledge. However, the efficiency of this conversion must also be considered. Nonaka and Takeuchi (1995) argue that a new organisational structure, referred to as a "hypertext" organisation, is required to create knowledge efficiently and continuously. The hypertext organisation is a synthesis of two traditional organisational structures: bureaucracy and task force. Each has its benefits, and a combination of the two is necessary for efficient knowledge creation.

A bureaucracy works well in conditions of stability, since it emphasises the control and predictability of specific functions. It is most suitable for efficiently conducting routine work on a large scale. However, it can also stifle individual initiative, lead to skirting of responsibility and encourage red tape. In contrast, a task force is a structure that is designed to address the weaknesses of bureaucracy. It is flexible, adaptable, dynamic and participative. It brings together representatives from a number of differing areas to form a team to achieve a certain goal. However, because of its temporary nature, new know-how created in the team is not easily transferred to other organisational members after the project is complete.

What is unique about a hypertext organisation is that three totally different layers, or contexts, coexist within the same organisation. At the top is the project-team layer. This is where multiple project teams engage in knowledge-creating activities. The team members are brought together from a number of different units across the business system and are assigned exclusively to a project team until the project is completed. In the middle is the business-system layer. This is where normal, routine operations are carried out. Since a bureaucratic structure is suitable for conducting routine work efficiently, this layer is shaped like a hierarchical pyramid. At the bottom is the knowledge-base layer. This layer does not exist as an actual organisational entity, but is embedded in corporate vision, organisational culture or technology.

The process of organisational knowledge creation is conceptualised by Nonaka and Takeuchi (1995) as a dynamic cycle of knowledge traversing easily and efficiently through these three layers. Consequently, mapping RNSETT onto Nonaka's hypertext structure determined whether knowledge is created efficiently and continuously. Ideally, the organisation should map onto the structure quite closely. Any shortcomings that are identified can then be addressed.

12.9 The Next Stage

The knowledge audit was used to identify areas for improvement and opportunities to leverage knowledge aligned to the business goals. The techniques selected to do this are the SWOT analysis and CSF from the information systems strategy, knowledge profiles, individual candidate SWOT and Nonaka's knowledge creation and hypertext organisation. The next logical stage in the production of a knowledge management strategy is to select an appropriate method to exploit or leverage knowledge opportunities whilst addressing any knowledge shortcomings.

However, the choice of suitable knowledge management methods is limited. Wiig, de Hoog and van der Spek (1997) reviewed the rapid growth in coverage of knowledge management books, conferences and seminars. Considering the middle ground occupied by methods and techniques (i.e. neither too general nor too specific), they realised that this area was not so well covered. The material predominantly continues to be either a high-level theoretical study of the topic or more specific case studies. Although valuable, they are of little direct help to the knowledge practitioner (especially an inexperienced one).

This does not mean that knowledge management methods do not exist. Many of the large management consultancy firms (KPMG, Arthur Andersen, etc.) are conducting successful knowledge management activities to a set formula. However, it is apparent that they are reluctant to release proprietary methods that are currently providing them with a competitive advantage. However, one firm that has published a practical managing knowledge method is JD Edwards.

12.10 Leveraging Knowledge with JD Edwards

Applehams, Globe and Laugero's (1999) JD Edwards' method is built upon the work of Nonaka and Takeuchi (1995) and Davenport and Prusak (1998). The organisation's business objectives and problems are identified during an initial knowledge audit. The method then guides the practitioner to start small by selecting a few key issues for further study, whilst recognising the equal importance of people, business process (content) and technology issues. Consequently, its use in the RNSETT is appropriate.

The method has three distinct stages: getting started; organising around knowledge and knowledge architecture.

Getting started helps the knowledge practitioner to understand the scale of the effort involved and essentially scopes the project. Knowledge audit and the profiling of key people are the key objectives. The need to focus on core business activities, or cycles, is also emphasised.

The method argues that knowledge management activities should begin with people and content before setting up a technical infrastructure. Organising around knowledge therefore focuses on putting together two diagrams that help the knowledge practitioner to determine important people and content in relation to business cycles and objectives:

- knowledge storyboard, which shows where the content is used in the business processes and cycles;
- knowledge network, which shows where the content resides within the organisation and who owns it (i.e. content centres).

The aim is to identify who needs what information, where and when, thereby avoiding the problem of 'infosmog'. Ultimately, it is to get the organisation to implement structures that organise around knowledge, with knowledge responsibilities assigned to individuals.

The knowledge architecture stage aims to bring it all together into a unified knowledge architecture. This is achieved by the translation of content centres into a networked organisation, including navigation strategies and other issues surrounding the deployment of people, content and technology. In particular, this stage focuses upon the use of technology as an enabler and the levels of management that need to exist within the organisation.

Davenport and Prusak's (1998) experience of knowledge management initiatives leads them to assert that "the roles of people in knowledge technologies are integral to their success". The roles of people are therefore a key factor in identifying the most appropriate types of knowledge technologies for an organisation. An even more critical differentiating factor is the level of knowledge required to use a particular technology successfully. Some knowledge tools require the user to be

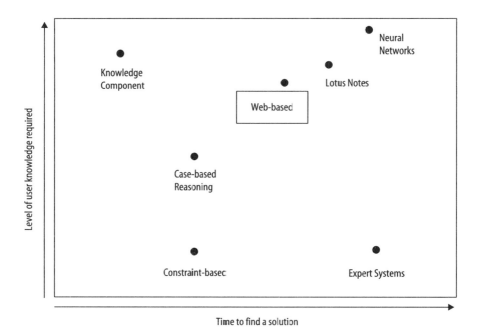

Figure 12.3 Key dimensions of knowledge management tools.

somewhat of an expert in a particular topic, whereas others assume that the user is a more passive participant in the knowledge process. The other key dimension is the time needed to find a knowledge management solution in a particular business application tool. Some knowledge–work environments allow time for search, synthesis and reflection; others, such as those involving customer enquiries, require near real-time performance. From their experience, Davenport and Prusak have mapped current technologies against these dimensions (Fig. 12.3).

The chart in Figure 12.3 can be applied to the RNSETT to assess whether web-based technologies are appropriate for the organisation. Consequently, the use of JD Edwards' method can be considered useful.

12.11 Conclusions

An account of methods used during the study has been provided. In order to defend their use, the reasons for their selection have also been provided. SSM was used to appreciate the problem situation and to provide a clearer direction for the knowledge practitioner. An audit of RNSETT's existing knowledge was then conducted to assess the organisation's existing and knowledge-creating activities. Finally, JD Edwards' method was used to address any shortcomings and leverage any knowledge opportunities that have been identified in the earlier part of the study.

To summarise, the initial stages of a knowledge management study should:

- use a systemic process of enquiry
- make sense of complex situations
- account for people's different viewpoints and beliefs
- address human involvement and activity.

Once this has been achieved, a knowledge management method should:

- consider the business objectives
- start small and focus on a few key issues
- start with a recognised business problem
- consider technical, cultural and organisational issues.

Chapter 13
Knowledge Creation and Management: The Case of Fortum Engineering Ltd

Abdul Samad Kazi, Jari Puttonen, Mika Sulkusalmi, Pekka Välikangas and Matti Hannus

13.1 Introduction

> Knowledge is an organisational capital that needs to be exploited to its full potential for value added business process delivery.

A clear understanding of what constitutes knowledge, knowledge management, knowledge processes (identification, collection, organisation, sharing, adaptation, usage and re-creation), and knowledge enablers (culture, technology, measurement, strategy and leadership) is essential. The aim is both to increase and to enable an individual to participate in decision making based on value-added information in addition to being in a position to exercise control over his or her work domain. This chapter advocates the appropriate use of technology for culture and social norms, which may be seen as a core need for knowledge management success. The coverage is primarily on knowledge know-how and, more so perhaps, minimal critical specification in terms of sociotechnical principles (Cherns, 1976, 1987).

The chapter starts with a clarification of what constitutes knowledge and goes on to describe its different forms and occurrences. Once the fundamentals are established, a brief mention of the knowledge life cycle is made and the role of different knowledge processes and enablers for knowledge management identified. The authors then introduce their palm tree model (Fig. 13.1) in an attempt to help the reader to visualise and then understand how knowledge is created, and furthermore, how the seeds of more knowledge are sown from the created knowledge. This model is presented from a sociotechnical viewpoint and is an illustration of how a learning organisation continues to learn and enhance its knowledge potential.

A case study of knowledge creation and management at Fortum Engineering Ltd (FE), a provider of engineering, procurement and construction (EPC) services to the energy sector, is presented to shed more light on the fundamentals of knowledge creation and management from a sociotechnical perspective. FE is part of the Fortum Group, a diversified group of companies, which is a lead player in the Nordic energy market. In a nutshell, FE's interest in knowledge creation and management is basically to "sort the wheat from the chaff and then to sieve out the real

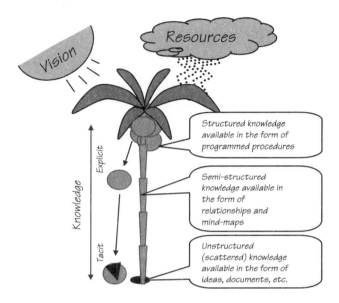

Figure 13.1 Palm tree model.

drops of wisdom" for the topic concerned. This wisdom is then to be used as an instrument contributing to both better decision making and value-added business process and product delivery.

As a concluding section, the reader is presented with "Guidelines for an adventure in growing knowledge coconuts". This contains a summary of the key lessons learned in addition to some practical hints and tips on how one may embark on a knowledge creation and management initiative from a sociotechnical perspective.

To stimulate some initial thoughts, Figure 13.1 shows an illustration of the palm tree model. As a first exercise, the reader is asked to bear this in mind and see how different pieces fit together through the course of discussion in this chapter. More details will be discussed in later sections.

13.2 What is Knowledge?

Before gaining any proper appreciation of knowledge creation or management it is essential to be able to understand what it is that we are trying to create and manage. As a first step, an attempt is made to identify what knowledge is. From a technical viewpoint, it may be safe to preclude that considering the well-known notion of information being "data plus meaning", knowledge may be said to be "information plus processing". While this may satisfy the need of the technocrat,

> Knowledge may be identified as, "the objects, concepts and relationships that are assumed to exist in some area of interest" (FOLDOC, 2000), and furthermore, knowledge "is a collection of facts and rules about some subject".

it leaves the "sociocrat" confused. This confusion may be resolved by referring to some more user-friendly dictionaries. Here, definitions of knowledge are likely to be more to our liking and understanding, in particular from a sociotechnical viewpoint: "the fact or condition of knowing something with familiarity gained through experience or association" (Meriam-Webster, 2000).

Gaining some confidence, one may now venture into the domain of the "knowledge community" to explore how it views knowledge. Here one finds some very explicit definitions:

- "the ideas or understandings which an entity possesses that are used to take effective action to achieve the entities' goals" (KNOWNET, 1999);
- "the capacity for effective action in a domain, where effectiveness is assessed by a community of fellow practitioners" (KBB, 1999).

While one can learn from the different viewpoints on knowledge presented, there is still some ambiguity as it is still difficult to pinpoint what knowledge is. There is a well-justified reason for this, as knowledge comes in two separate forms, explicit and tacit. Based on the definitions learned so far, an attempt is made to discern these forms of knowledge and understand what each one means.

13.2.1 Explicit Knowledge

Explicit knowledge may be defined as that form of knowledge which can be translated into certain rule-based logic (KBB, 1999; KNOWNET, 1999). A more formal definition would be that explicit knowledge is knowledge which "can be expressed in words and can be easily communicated and shared in the form of hard data, scientific formulae, codified procedures or universal principles" (Nonaka and Takeuchi, 1995). In simple terms, this form of knowledge is "programmable" (Davenport and De Long, 1997). Going further, explicit knowledge may be translated to constitute rules in the form of IF, THEN, AND, OR, etc. This is the form of knowledge that information technology (IT) people like to deal with, as it can, once appropriately translated, be embedded into IT systems to support business processes and perhaps in some cases go as far as allowing automated decision making.

For purposes of clarity, explicit knowledge could be said to constitute the "technical" part of the sociotechnical perspective of knowledge. This is for the simple reason that explicit knowledge may be translated to certain rules based on some semantics and logic, thereby making it transferable and usable through technology.

13.2.2 Tacit Knowledge

Tacit knowledge may be identified as knowledge that is very abstract and is not necessarily logic based (KBB, 1999; KNOWNET, 1999). Perhaps this is the "socioknowledge" that most people are accustomed to. One way of defining it is that tacit knowledge "is highly personal and hard to formalise. Subjective insights, intuitions and hunches fall in this category of knowledge" (Nonaka and Takeuchi, 1995). This knowledge usually comes from experience and is embedded in the minds of practitioners. A crude way to define some forms of tacit knowledge would be through the metaphor, "gut feeling". This form of knowledge is difficult to share, and if it is shared then the primary medium of sharing is through face-to-face interactions (Kazi, Hannus and Charoenngam, 1999).

For purposes of clarity, tacit knowledge could be said to constitute the "socio" part of the sociotechnical perspective of knowledge. This is for the simple reason that the only means for the transfer or use of tacit knowledge is through social cohesion and interaction.

13.3 I Know What Knowledge is; What Next?

Once the reader understands what constitutes knowledge, some basic questions emerge:

- How can I capture knowledge?
- How can I represent knowledge?
- How can I convert from one form of knowledge to the other?
- How can I share knowledge?

The answers to these questions form some core components of knowledge management. Before entering a discussion on knowledge management, however, it may be wise to address some of these questions, by exploring knowledge capture, representation, conversion and then sharing.

13.3.1 Knowledge Capture

Now that we know what knowledge is, the temptation arrives to capture it and then render it meaningful as an instrument for better decision making. The first and most important place to visit would be our own "knowledge workers" (experts who have knowledge) and attempt to capture from them both explicit and tacit knowledge. Two basic means exist for knowledge capture: person-to-person and person-to-computer. At this point a differentiation is made between the knowledge worker, as the one who provides the knowledge, and the knowledge seeker, as the one who seeks knowledge. From the viewpoint of explicit knowledge, both knowledge capture means may be used; first through some form of interaction between the knowledge seeker and the knowledge worker, and secondly by the knowledge worker feeding his or her knowledge into a computer and then the knowledge seeker retrieving this fed knowledge. For tacit knowledge, however, the most favourable mechanism would be through person-to-person interaction. This may be done at a personal level, or through workshops or conferences.

13.3.2 Knowledge Representation

Now that the knowledge has been obtained, it needs to be visualised or represented. First, knowledge "chunks" or "objects" need to be identified and then those relationships found that may be used to interconnect these chunks or objects. This would allow the knowledge to be structured and reconfigured to the needs of individual knowledge seekers. There are five basic ways in which knowledge may be represented (Murray, 1999):

- Conceptual indexing: this is synonymous with the traditional end-of-book index. Of value here is a heading–subheading type breakdown of knowledge and information for easy and quick access.
- Conceptual mapping: here ideas, topics, concepts, etc., and their relationships are represented in the form of a visual summary. Simple "mind mapping" typically falls into this category.
- Hypertext (hypermedia): more commonly known through the use of the internet, hypertext enables the user to jump across sources of knowledge and information. While not necessarily based on any explicit rule definitions, links are embedded at appropriate junctures to guide the knowledge seeker to the appropriate knowledge source.
- Information modelling: information modelling entails a model of the knowledge objects and the interrelationships between them. Information modelling is primarily used as a source for identifying the requirements and associated specifications for resolution of the issue at hand. A comprehensive information model paves the way for better semantic networks.
- Semantic networks: these are formed through an extensive analysis of different knowledge objects and their interrelationships. The output is basically in the form of some logical rules between items, for example, "IF A THEN B".

As may be noted from the five basic ways of knowledge representation, the level of detail and accuracy increases as one proceeds from conceptual indexing to semantic networks. For the time being, this may be viewed as simply a growth ladder through which unstructured knowledge is first structured and then made programmable.

13.3.3 Knowledge Conversion

It is always a tempting proposition to convert from one knowledge form to the other. In simple terms, how can tacit knowledge be converted to explicit knowledge? Furthermore, is it possible to extract some new knowledge (be it tacit) from explicit knowledge? Researchers agree that means have to be found to convert from one form of knowledge to the other (Skyrme, 1997; Abram Hawkes, 1999). Furthermore, within each form of knowledge, different conversion processes exist to transfer, for example, organisational knowledge to personal knowledge, and knowledge from one person to another. Four such knowledge-conversion processes exist (Skyrme, 1997):

- Tacit-to-tacit (socialisation): individuals acquire new knowledge directly from others.
- Tacit-to-explicit (externalisation): the articulation of knowledge into tangible form through dialogue.
- Explicit-to-explicit (combination): combining different forms of explicit knowledge, such as that is in documents or on databases.
- Explicit-to-tacit (internalisation): such as learning by doing, where individuals internalise knowledge from documents into their own knowledge.

13.3.4 Knowledge Sharing

In the past, there has always been some resistance to change as people view knowledge as an individual asset rather than an organisational one.

Once the knowledge has been captured, represented and converted, it needs to be shared efficiently. As an organisation gains in size, diversity and momentum, the competence in sharing knowledge will be a critical success factor. It is argued in some cases that effective knowledge sharing yields $2 + 2 = 6$ (Eckhouse, 1999). New business paradigms focus on the opposite, as attempts are made to consolidate individual knowledge and turn it into an organisational asset. This is then passed back to the individual in an attempt to enhance further his or her knowledge competence.

Assuming that all barriers resisting the sharing of knowledge have been broken down, the next step is to explore how to go about the process of sharing it. After all, "if we know what we know", then a highly effective workforce can result (Sieloff, 1999). This is possible only by knowing where the required knowledge exists and by having the means to enquire about it and access it: in short, to have the capability to share and receive knowledge. "The most effective tools seem to be electronic networks and E-mail, which easily transcend rigid organizational lines and promote the sharing of information that can bring suppliers, customers, and employees closer together" (Eckhouse, 1999). Face-to-face meetings, workshops, voice or videoconferences, text chats, sharing documents, etc., are other simple means of sharing knowledge.

13.4 Knowledge Management Basics

Now that some knowledge basics and fundamentals have been covered, it is time to jump on the bandwagon in the search and definition of knowledge management. The discussion will focus on a sociotechnical viewpoint. In general terms, knowledge management may be defined as the body of knowledge that deals with the management of both personal and organisational knowledge. While this has by now become a well-accepted fact (Nonaka and Takeuchi, 1995; APQC, 1996; Davenport and De Long, 1997; Skyrme, 1997; Bellinger, 1999), different communities of thought have interpreted and used this definition in different forms. Some view knowledge management as: "the ways to create, retain, share, account for, and leverage knowledge – at all levels, from the personal level, to the team level, the organisational level, the inter-organisational level, and the global level" (KNOWNET, 1999). While it is beyond the scope of this chapter to elaborate upon or challenge this and other interpretations, the authors present their own interpretations and the mental model developed by the American Productivity & Quality Center (APQC, 1996).

For all practical purposes, knowledge management may be defined or interpreted as a composite of:

- the capture, consolidation, dissemination and reuse of knowledge; and
- the translation of new best practices to tangible programmable processes to be automated through IT where possible.

Figure 13.2 is a simple graphical illustration of how things may be done. A knowledge worker decides which best practice to automate and share and makes this available to an IT system. Outputs are checked, verified, frequently updated and at times even deleted. The idea is to make available through an IT system information that is programmable and information that, although not yet programmable, is in a decent enough form for sharing (i.e. it has been experientially observed to be valid or conclusive).

The basic understanding here is that knowledge management is an important factor and enabler of better decision making as it enables the individual not only to participate more in an open decision-making environment, but also to be

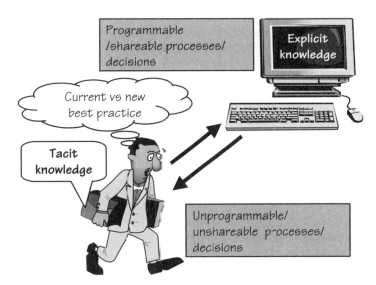

Figure 13.2 Managing knowledge.

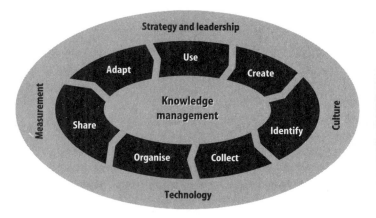

Figure 13.3 Knowledge management mental model (APQC, 1996).

equipped with better information and knowledge to improve his or her decision making. It would be wise at this point to draw up a basic mental model highlighting what needs to be done and how.

The knowledge management mental model (Fig. 13.3) offered by the American APQC (1996) shows the knowledge management life cycle through knowledge processes, and uses knowledge enablers as the driving forces for successful knowledge management.

The idea is really quite simple. For there to be a platform for knowledge management, a functional environment is needed that allows the sequential knowledge processes to interact with the other, and through these interactions complete the knowledge loop. Then come the knowledge enablers who, as the name implies, make the environment not only functional, but also operational. The main features of knowledge processes and enablers are as follows.

Knowledge processes:

- identify: methods and tools for the identification of best practices and reusable knowledge;
- collect: methods and tools for knowledge collection;
- organise: methods and tools for knowledge systematisation and consolidation;
- share: methods and tools for knowledge dissemination, search and retrieval;
- adapt: organisational guidelines for business processes, task descriptions and the organisation of information;
- use: methods and tools for knowledge reuse;
- create: methods and tools to re-create knowledge (new knowledge from existing knowledge).

Knowledge enablers:

- culture: key cultural enablers (incentives);

- technology: identification and deployment of enabling technologies and standards;
- measurement: performance indicators and metrics to monitor and control knowledge;
- strategy and leadership: vision, strategy and support for knowledge management.

As is evident from these lists, sociotechnical factors play a key role in knowledge management enablement.

13.5 Growing Knowledge Coconuts (Palm Tree Model)

Time and again, the authors have faced the question of how to create and manage knowledge. They have made many attempts to find an answer through different definitions and interpretations, but have come to a bottleneck. While the audience understands the basics and fundamentals, they find it hard to remember and exploit them. This has led to the formulation of the "palm tree model". The model uses a sociotechnical viewpoint to show how to enable learning in a learning organisation and how to capitalise on one's most valuable personal and corporate asset, knowledge.

The idea of the palm tree model (Fig. 13.1) is simple. The seeds are viewed as being the origins of knowledge. This is basically the tacit knowledge that needs to be structured for extra value-added business process delivery. Organisational vision acts as the sun and, when coupled with rain in the form of resources, the unstructured tacit knowledge is first semi-structured and then structured to yield explicit knowledge. This in turn yields knowledge "meat and milk" for use as programmed procedures. After digestion, the seeds are replanted to yield both new and better knowledge. As an example, based on the palm tree model, a starving monkey may manage to grow "knowledge coconuts" from "knowledge seeds". A cartoon is used to show this (Fig. 13.4).

The lesson to be learned from the cartoon is reasonably simple. The basic ingredient (tacit knowledge) is available in the form of either rules of thumb, gut feeling or even documents. Now some support and visionary guidance is needed from management to indicate the right direction first to collect these seeds of tacit knowledge, and then gradually to try to identify and where possible instil some structure in the form of relationships and rules. This could be as simple as providing pointers from one source of information or knowledge to the next, or even providing information on who to contact for more information. Once this has been accomplished, ways need to be found in which to use the structured (explicit) knowledge in existing and future applications to enable automation where possible and quick search and retrieval where not possible. Based on experience and knowledge sharing, people are bound to come up with yet newer and better seeds. Now all that is required is to repeat the process and maintain a presence on the knowledge "bullet train". Over time, opportunities will emerge for people to sell their knowledge competency if they so desire.

1. The sky is dark as our tacit knowledge is scattered in the form of seeds. Sharks (competitors) lurk for an opportunity to eat us in case we resort to eating seaweed! We need to find the means to survive.

2. Management vision (sun) and resources (rain) help to give life to the seeds and initial knowledge sprouts emerge. There is hope, we just need to be patient. Gaining awareness of our efforts, some sharks start to move away.

3. Management vision and resource support remain strong as the knowledge gains some structure. Competition (sharks) continues to disappear.

4. First knowledge coconuts (explicit knowledge) emerge. They provide knowledge meat and milk (programmed procedures). The sharks now leave.

5. The vision is still strong, but now there is no need for extra resources. More and more knowledge coconuts grow. Good coconuts are replanted to create new knowledge (new tacit knowledge from explicit knowledge). Equipped now even with a fishing rod, we scare off all competition (sharks).

6. A strong vision prevails, as our knowledge coconuts have now become a product and competence. We see ships bringing in opportunities. Our initiative is now self-supporting and can be used to support and finance future initiatives. Of course, at the same time, we try to catch any wandering sharks.

Figure 13.4 From Knowledge Seeds to Coconut Sales.

13.6 Case Study: From Knowledge Seeds to Knowledge Coconuts

So far, this chapter has covered the basic terminology and concepts of knowledge and knowledge management. It has even shown how a monkey can go from starvation to being a successful salesperson of knowledge coconuts. Now it is time to show how this lesson can be applied in a real-life situation. This section presents a case study showing how Fortum Engineering Ltd (FE) is growing and eating knowledge coconuts that they have grown from their own seeds.

One of the key success factors for an engineering company is the ability to share and, where possible, formalise its tacit knowledge in a meaningful form. This is then to be used by both its knowledge workers and seekers, in addition to being stored and used within the company's own expert applications for power plant design. The core underlying purpose is

This is possible through a mix of both purely technical and sociotechnical considerations.

"first [to] sieve the wheat from the chaff and then to sieve out the real drops of wisdom relevant for the topic under concern".

The basic functionality of FE's knowledge creation environment (KCE) is based on data mining to capture, classify and transfer information into an appropriate level in the knowledge hierarchy. From these different levels of knowledge, the information is captured through rule definitions (based on data content and information source correlations) and then made available to the concerned persons when so desired and also to FE's expert application for power plant design.

Rather than dwell on technical details (to be addressed in a different publication), this study starts with the underlying motivation that provided the guidance, and then provides some mappings to illustrate where FE's KCE efforts fall, first within the knowledge management (mental) model (Fig. 13.3) and then within the palm tree model (Fig. 13.1).

13.6.1 The Underlying Motivation and Vision

In engineering business operations, the principal asset is the knowledge that is accumulated through experience and can be made available for reuse and exploitation. While the explicit knowledge captured and nurtured is relatively easily recognised based on business operations, organisational hierarchies and documented procedures, the tacit knowledge is encapsulated in the minds of knowledge workers through experience, and personal interactions and communications. Thus, the tacit knowledge is hard to make first available and then usable in a tangible form. It is expected that this tacit knowledge alone will serve as an essential instrument towards a competitive edge in engineering, where the value of abstract products, such as information related to a particular topic, is expected to gain wide markets in different sectors.

Since explicit knowledge is in one way a descriptor of industrial best practices, it is not too long before it is duplicated by other companies and a competitive edge is then shared. The case for tacit knowledge is totally different, and is very difficult for the competitor to replicate and exploit. This is the area where FE believes it can create some competitive leverage, if it can encapsulate its tacit knowledge and make it available in a meaningful form to its knowledge workers and seekers.

Currently, the tacit knowledge (seeds of knowledge) is still largely undefined and hence leads to a case-by-case dependency on the intellectuals possessing it. As a first step, the aim of the KCE will be first to solicit this tacit knowledge and then to establish some reliability by presenting it in a tangible and usable form. This, in turn, would minimise the case-by-case dependency and provide better value to both the user and the customer.

The foreseeable vision includes the identification of new effective organisational models that support unofficial or unidentified linkages recognised by the KCE and the development of expert systems that at least partially convert the gathered tacit knowledge to explicit knowledge.

The development of FE's KCE is part of larger development activities whose focus is on the tendering phase of large EPC deliveries. FE's KCE is expected to support these efforts by way of improving cost estimation prior to tendering, and technical innovations during conceptual and basic design stages, which in turn can lead to shorter delivery times.

Now that an idea has been gained of what the KCE is in essence all about, the following sections explore how it fits into the context of the knowledge management mental model (Fig. 13.3). The findings are presented in the form of answers to a series of questions on knowledge processes and knowledge enablers. The reasons for this approach are explained later.

13.6.2 Knowledge Processes

How is Knowledge Identified?

FE's involvement is primarily with one-of-a-kind products, and hence direct replication of knowledge from one product or project to the next is not simple. Knowledge is primarily identified by the concerned knowledge worker based on lessons learned from the product or project and assimilation through experience. Of course, this knowledge needs to be checked later and verified by other specialists before being made available to the knowledge seeker.

How is Knowledge Collected?

Knowledge is collected through three means: face-to-face interviews, fill-in forms and web-based applications. Knowledge workers and seekers browse the main KCE database and report any inconsistencies or redundancies. Based on assigned access rights, the knowledge workers make corrections as required. Furthermore, once a piece of knowledge has been used or implemented, the outcomes of the usage are verified.

How is Knowledge Organised?

Knowledge, based on its content and status (scattered, semi-structured or structured), is set in its appropriate level (empiric, constraint or synthesis). The knowledge is further categorised based on its applicability domain as being configuration dependency knowledge, supportive requirement knowledge, connectivity relation knowledge or product life-cycle knowledge. Relational mappings between different knowledge objects are provided using hyperlinkable mind-maps.

How is Knowledge Shared?

Knowledge is primarily shared through the browsing of a web-based application which has different users with different access rights. Telephone conversations and e-mails are also facilitated as the KCE provides pointers to those knowledge workers who have the relevant information and knowledge.

How is Knowledge Adapted to Existing Products and Processes?

Since existing process and work flows are mainly based on the exploitation of explicit knowledge, new tools and associated organisational models are required to support the use of experiential (tacit) knowledge. FE is now in the process of testing the deployment of an expert system as an alternative to articulate the circulation and exploitation of tacit knowledge. The underlying idea is that the rules that are built into the expert system are based on experiences gathered from the knowledge workers and seekers. In turn, the use of the expert system will advise the knowledge user on how to proceed and where to find the required knowledge.

How is Knowledge Used?

The importance of tacit knowledge is extremely high during the tendering process where the amount of available explicit knowledge is limited, and yet major decisions need to be made. This is a common characteristic of the construction and EPC industry where the products are often of a one-of-a-kind type. Tacit knowledge can be used directly from within the KCE database where it is stored. This form of use requires that the classification system offers possibilities to search problem-specific product or project-specific knowledge from the KCE. FE's aim is that a relevant part of tacit knowledge can be taken into use by developing expert systems where the dependencies and rules are based on, and reflect the experiences of the organisation.

How is New Knowledge Created from Existing Knowledge?

Experiences with the exploitation of explicit knowledge and consideration of existing tacit knowledge over time lead towards more experiential observations and hence tacit knowledge. Interviews and audits are then used as a means to create new knowledge by combining the experiential observations of different knowledge workers. The dependencies and constraints providing some structure to the new tacit knowledge can be identified only by communication amongst specialists (knowledge workers) from different disciplines. This new knowledge and associated relational mappings can then be stored in the KCE database. While the new knowledge created through mappings between different levels of information and knowledge contains some risks leading to incorrect conclusions, this can be relatively well controlled once the specialists regularly review the KCE database and the outcomes achieved based on the use of its content.

13.6.3 Knowledge Enablers

How Does Technology Enable the Knowledge Creation Environment?

Technology is a key element in the value-added delivery of the KCE, as it provides quick access to structured knowledge in a representative format of an individual's own choice. While it may be seen only as a tool, its value and importance should not be undermined, it is a key instrument for every knowledge worker and seeker, initially in the form of a knowledge storage and search facility, and later as an instrument to automate knowledge-based procedures and applications. The final stage to be realised is the use of technology as a generator of new knowledge. The main methods, tools and technologies to be used in the KCE include mind-mapping, web-based applications, Java, relational database management systems, etc.

What Influence does Organisational Culture Have on the Implementation and Enablement of the Knowledge Creation Environment?

The challenge here is to encourage individuals who are used to working in a hierarchical organisation to reveal and share their personal intellect (tacit knowledge). As such, there may exist some resistance, especially when an individual is requested to post even those lessons that he or she has learned through failures. It is hence necessary to ensure that both the knowledge worker and seeker understand the importance and associated benefits that the KCE will provide for both the content of their own work and the business targets of the organisation. In short, they need to realise that it is a win–win situation at both a personal and an organisational level.

How is Knowledge Measured and what Impact does this Have on the Knowledge Creation Environment?

To ensure the quality and value of the knowledge provided by the KCE, there needs to be in place a regular "check and balance" system in the form of some performance indicators and metrics. Measurements are basically done in the form of interviews, audits, user feedback, internal seminars, workshops, etc., while at the same knowledge workers regularly review the existing knowledge to ensure its correctness and seek opportunities for creating yet newer knowledge based on this review. Knowledge of frequency of use of a particular piece of knowledge would, for example, enable this piece of knowledge to be provided by default without the knowledge seeker needing to dig it out. Furthermore, extra effort could be expended in searching for the possibilities of new knowledge that may be under creation based on the usage of this knowledge.

How does the Strategy and Leadership of Fortum Engineering Support the Knowledge Creation Environment?

Knowledge-based expert application development is understood to be an important asset and is encouraged by senior management. There is also a clear understanding that it is a long, step-by-step process. The KCE will be one of the main backbones in this process. One of FE's targets is to be an important player in the EPC business of power plants. The nature of engineering business emphasises the value of tacit knowledge exploitation to gain a competitive edge and on that basis the possibilities to be offered by the KCE are both well understood and appreciated. Senior management recognises that the development of the KCE is a process requiring persistence over a long time-span of development and implementation. It does, however, expect continuous results on a step-by-step basis both to support the present business targets and to provide motivation to potential users in the form of a sequential learning and using environment that will then become a natural part of the users' work environment. The long-term expectation is that this development work will introduce new alternatives to enhance the returns on current working flows and business practices.

The next section discusses how these findings can be mapped to the palm tree model (Fig. 13.1).

13.6.4 Fortum Engineering's Palm Tree

It is relatively easy to map FE's KCE to the palm tree model, as shown in Figure 13.5.

The evolution of explicit knowledge from initially scattered tacit knowledge is clear through an evolutionary process of knowledge structuring and organisation. Management vision and support for development help to nourish and strengthen

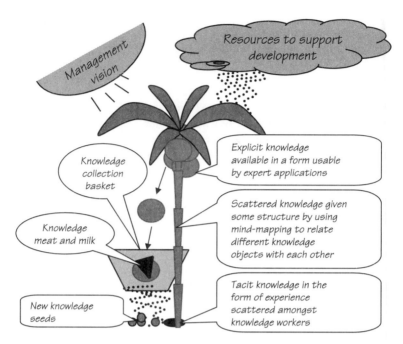

Figure 13.5 Fortum Engineering's palm tree.

this evolution. One addition is a knowledge collection basket (the KCE database) that is used to store the knowledge and the results of its exploitation. A sieve has also been added to filter out new knowledge seeds from the existing knowledge.

More information addressing both the social and technical aspects of the KCE development at FE will become available through future publications as more results are obtained from these experiences.

13.7 Guidelines for an Adventure in Growing Knowledge Coconuts

It is always tempting to try and jump on the bandwagon once a new paradigm or buzzword hits the market. Improper embarkation on a journey that has no clear disembarkation leads to nothing less than catastrophe, as was the initial case when everyone wanted to re-engineer "everything". Hence, the best advice is patience, followed by preparation, and then implementation to harvest successfully the knowledge coconuts from the scattered seeds of knowledge. Based on previous sections and in particular the knowledge management mental model and its counterpart palm tree model, the reader is redirected to the questions used to decipher and then map FE's KCE to the knowledge management mental model. These questions need to be answered once one embarks on a knowledge coconut-growing adventure. The following basic steps (with a focus on sociotechnical aspects) are recommended.

1. It is important to understand what is meant by knowledge and knowledge management. It is necessary to be able to identify how it will add value to business processes. This may be a selling point to top management to obtain the required support and resources to undertake the initiative.

2. All knowledge enablers must be in place before the process starts. Although initially unclear, for example, some measurement instruments should be in place to monitor progress and maintain coherence with the objectives.

3. The knowledge seeds are already available. They just need to be retrieved from the users of the system. This requires the users to be made to believe that the knowledge creation and management effort will yield both personal and organisational gains.

4. Step by step, each knowledge process should be developed, tested and then implemented. These steps should not be attempted simultaneously, as then the process may not work. Patience is the key here.

5. Once all processes are in place and enabled through the enablers, the first coconut will bear meat and milk. Now the process can be repeated, to keep on creating new coconuts based on the lessons and experience learned.

As a concluding statement, the word "LOVE" is intended to help readers on the path to success:

> **L:** Knowledge should be thoroughly **L**earned and understood.
>
> **O:** Clear and measurable **O**bjectives should be set. Progress should be measured periodically and must comply with these **O**bjectives at all times.
>
> **V:** Patience is key: the **V**alue of the effort will only be ascertained when the users accept and believe in it. This alone will be enough for **V**alue-added business process delivery.
>
> **E:** Once the initial objectives have been accomplished it is important not to stop. Using **E**xperience of both successes and failures can make a system more **E**fficient.

Chapter 14

Knowledge Requirement System (KRS): An Approach to Improving and Understanding Requirements

W. Al-Karaghouli, G. Fitzgerald and S. Alshawi

14.1 Introduction

This chapter describes a knowledge requirement system (KRS), which is an approach to determining the requirements of information technology (IT)-enabled business systems. KRS is the outcome of a research study conducted in the retail sector that identified serious problems, including a knowledge and communication gap between developers and the business that has proved a significant barrier to the successful development of information systems.

> It is argued that the requirements process is a sociotechnical process that relates to human–human interaction in the form of communication and understanding of the customer needs between customers and system developers, it is not a human–machine relationship.

The view adopted in KRS is that requirements emerge from a process of learning in which they are elicited, prioritised, negotiated, evaluated and documented.

Requirements evolve over time and cannot be elicited as a snapshot. This necessitates managing the evolution of requirements and aligning requirements to organisational change.

In any business, effective IT systems require detailed and specific requirements that need to be acquired through intensive and rich communications between the different stakeholders (Sanghera, 1999). Unfortunately, the determination of requirements and the development of specifications are frequently not seen in this way but simply as things to be established and finished with as quickly as possible. Any inherent problems and misunderstandings are thus only discovered late in the development process, often only at implementation, at which stage they require immediate modification. The result is that the system is often regarded as a failure.

14.2 The Culture Gap

The view of two cultures, that of IT and the business, is evident in many organisations. The culture of system developers is typically technically orientated and is based on an understanding of technical issues (Price Waterhouse, 1991, 1992; Kavanagh, 1998). In systems development this is reflected in a focus on issues such as the functionality of the system, its performance, the response rate and the type of programming language that should be used (Sturt, 2000; Flood, 2000). By contrast, the business culture and focus is rather different and is more concerned with business issues and the system as support for business and management processes. Many of the technical terms and issues, particularly when expressed in IT jargon, mean little and are frequently misunderstood by the business side, and the implications are often missed completely. These two cultures have been identified by many authors, including Nuseibeh (1996), Sommerville (1992), Cavell (1999), Griffin (1998) and Sabbagh (1999). However, going beyond this, two elements to the gap, a knowledge gap and an understanding gap, exist between the customer and the software developer.

This is the knowledge gap.	$\longrightarrow$	The customer's knowledge is mainly "business" knowledge with limited IT knowledge, whereas the developer's knowledge is "technical" knowledge with limited business knowledge.

This gap is probably a result of the different backgrounds, experiences and working environments of the parties, with each side talking a slightly different language. Further, an understanding gap is identified, which is to some extent a result of the knowledge gap, but is a whole set of differing understandings, meanings, assumptions and values (see Figs 14.1 and 14.2) (Parsons 1986).

"The business culture typically views the IT department as a cost centre rather than an investment and contributor to the success of the organisation. As a result customers and developers have different expectations of each other and particularly of any system to be developed which is not just about following rules and procedures but must take into account these differing cultures" (Howard, 1999).

It is argued that the view of two cultures is in evidence in most organisations, although it is true that some organisations have made efforts to overcome these different and conflicting cultures, usually by trying to mix the participants in seamless teams and by co-location of the two parties when developing systems. However, although this can help, the differences are still deep seated and not easily resolved. For the purposes of this chapter it will be assumed that there are two separate groups of people involved. First, the business users and customers of the system, which will be called the "customer", and secondly the developers of the system, which will include business analysts, systems analysts, programmers, software engineers, network specialists, security specialists, etc., which will be called

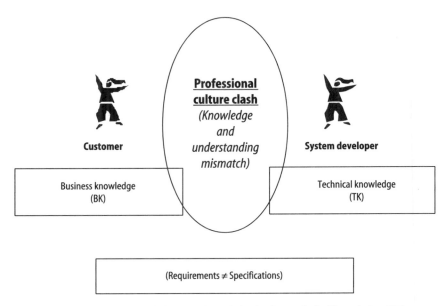

Figure 14.1 A culture clash: business knowledge (BK) vs technical knowledge (TK).

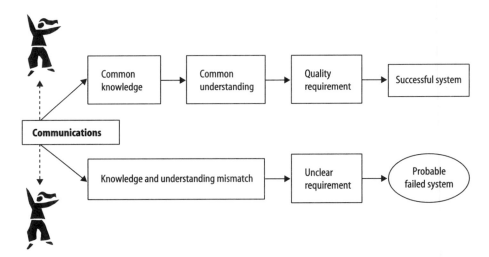

Figure 14.2 Requirement is a sociotechnical process (human–human).

"developers". Usually the developers are the internal IT department, although increasingly a third party organisation, such as an outsourcing vendor or consultancy company, may be used. This can exacerbate the communication problems owing to the physical separation of the organisations. For convenience this chapter will talk about the two sides, but this terminology should not indicate that there is only one of each or that they are not a diverse set of people. Nevertheless, it is crucial for systems to be successful that the problems created as a result of these different cultures are minimised.

Intensive and sustained communications between the customer and the system developer lead to a clearer understanding of the requirements and are likely to result in a better and more usable system for the customer (Lipnack and Stamps, 1997). The situation is also likely to be improved if the requirements are right first time, i.e. before any development is undertaken (Lee, Trauth and Farwell, 1995). This is not to say that requirements are always out there, waiting to be discovered. Often the notion of a full set of requirements existing in the minds of the customers is just not true. Frequently, customers have to learn and evolve their understanding of the requirements as part of the elicitation process, particularly in complex and new application areas.

> The determination of clear and adequate understanding of the requirements is a sociotechnical process and human communications and interaction are important ingredients in determining effective requirements.

High and unrealistic expectations of a system before development are well-known problems and can contribute to disenchantment with the system when it is implemented. Customers can be too enthusiastic about technology and hopelessly overestimate the technology's capacity to change their world (Mirl, 1998). This is an important issue which can lead to system failures (Duffy, 1993; Norman, 1998) and some recent examples of system failures in the UK seem to support the assertion that managing expectations is an important part of the requirements elicitation process (Groom, 2000; Ranger, 2000; Kelly, 2000). If both parties initially agree practical requirements and understand what the system is going to do when it is built, then their expectation will match the system performance. However, if both parties fail to discuss and evolve the requirements then this kind of mismatch of expectations is a possibility.

KRS is proposed as an approach to determining the requirements of IT-enabled business systems that addresses the problems and issues described above, particularly the knowledge and understanding gaps between developers and the business customers that have proved such a significant barrier in the past.

14.3 Research Basis of the Knowledge Requirement System

KRS was developed from a number of sources, including a research study of retail organisations in the UK and their use of IT, undertaken by the authors. The retail sector was chosen because of its dependency on IT and because it typically suffers from a legacy of varied developments of hardware and software (Cavell, 1999; List, 1999).

The study consisted of questionnaires and interviews in the sector. Two types of questionnaire were designed to study the prerequirement stage. The first questionnaire was targeted at senior personnel in IT development and the second questionnaire was sent to the different business departments (internal customers), such as the accounting and marketing departments. In total, 114 retail organisations (22 "retailers: food" and 92 "retailers: general") were surveyed. Each participating retail organisation was sent two questionnaires for the relevant department to collect quantitative and qualitative data. This was followed up by telephone interviews and some detailed face-to-face interviews and discussions in companies with individuals working within both the business and the IT departments concerning their requirements determination process. In addition, two case studies of major retail organisations were conducted in the second phase of the research.

It is not the purpose of this chapter to discuss the full findings from this study. However, it can be stated that in general the replies received from the business side and the IT side were significantly different, with the customers and the developers in many retail organisations having very different views concerning requirements and the requirements determination process. Further, there were clear instances of accusations made between the parties, indicating the degree of misunderstanding between customers and developers. The indications are that the responses support the hypothesis that there is a knowledge gap and an understanding gap between the two parties (see also Al-Karaghouli, AlShawi and Fitzgerald, 1999; Al-Karaghouli, Elstob and AlShawi, 2000).

14.4 The Knowledge Requirement System (KRS)

The knowledge requirement system is proposed as an approach to overcoming the problem of inadequate understanding of requirements. It combines both management science and computer science techniques (Louis Harris, 1974; Anderson, Sweeney and Williams, 1995), but its overall approach is sociotechnical, dealing with the social (human) interactions between customers and developers (Bostrom and Heinen, 1977a, b; Mumford, 1983, 1984, 1985; Pasmore, 1988). Earlier in this chapter, the importance of communications in determining requirements was stressed, and KRS, it is argued, provides a means of achieving the necessary level of communication that helps to overcome the problems of the culture gap discussed above.

> The process of customer requirements elicitation involves human–human communications with the aim of achieving a better understanding within organisations and helping to elaborate requirements that lead to systems that better meet the requirements and expectations of the stakeholders (Mumford, 1995a, b).

The overall approach is aimed at generating the knowledge and understanding needed by both the customer and the software developers to enable the development of a sound, agreed, and fully effective project requirements definition (Kotonya and Sommerville, 1998). This process is sometimes called customer requirements engineering (CRE) and is the process of determining a complete, correct and clear specification of a future software-intensive system from the incomplete, inconsistent and ambiguous statements of need from stakeholders as diverse as end-users, managers and members of the public. Whereas conventional software engineering approaches focus on models and languages to express system specifications, there has been a recent shift towards a focus on customer requirements engineering processes (CREPs) (Kotonya and Sommerville, 1998), and KRS adopts just such a focus.

Figure 14.3 illustrates the overall structure of KRS. The key principle that drives the approach is the belief that both sides must work together to generate knowledge and understanding of one another's worlds and that both have a lot of learning to do.

The authors believe that the only way to achieve good requirements definition is through partnership and mutual understanding. KRS provides a framework for achieving this.

> The authors reject the view that the customer already knows fully exactly what they want of the system, and also reject the view that the software developer knows fully about the customer's business and what is needed of the system.

KRS is a knowledge capture and a knowledge management system: a set of processes that creates the base of knowledge between the two parties (customer and system developer) for organising and matching requirements. This learning process also contributes to the creation of the learning or knowledge organisation, with the two parties interacting and leaning from each other (Weerakkody and Hinton, 1999; Guns and Anandsen, 1996). KRS captures this knowledge and understanding and thus can be regarded as a knowledge management system (Skyrme, 1998; Collins, 2000).

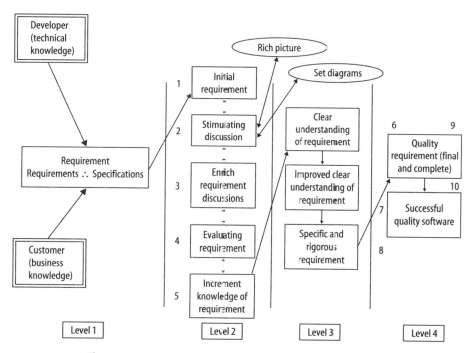

Figure 14.3 Structure of the knowledge requirement system (KRS).

KRS consists of four major levels and a total of ten processes within these levels. This chapter deals only with the first three levels. Level 1 is the overview of the relationship between the parties with the objective of developing the requirements and detailed specifications for an IT-enabled business system of some kind. This is broken down into the detail of levels 2, 3 and 4, i.e. the ten stages. A key feature is that the requirements determination and specification process is not a single step but a series of increasingly detailed refinements or evolutions. In the initial stages it is about stimulating, enriching and evaluating discussion before a more formal specification is even attempted. Typically, this changes the initial concepts and thoughts such that a radically different set of requirements may evolve. At each level a series of techniques is used. At level 2 these may include brainstorming, rich pictures, fishbone diagrams (Ishikawa, 1983), set diagrams, scenarios, joint application design (JAD) workshops, etc. The techniques for levels 3 and 4 are more formal and traditional.

KRS adopts the idea that it is best to spend time and effort in the early stages of the development process and improve the understanding and knowledge of both customers and developers in establishing and teasing out the requirements before progressing. KRS addresses only the first (requirements) stage, rather than the whole system development life cycle (see Fig. 14.3). Thus, KRS is not a full methodology or approach to systems development and is not intended to replace any existing methodology. On the contrary, KRS is aimed at complementing and enhancing existing approaches. Clearly, it would most easily complement an approach with a similar qualitative, soft or sociotechnical philosophy. However, it may actually be most effective in enhancing a hard approach because, in such cases, the need for better requirements analysis is greater, but the application of KRS may be more difficult to achieve in these circumstances, since the developers using a hard approach are unlikely to be so attuned or sympathetic to soft methods.

In this chapter we concentrate on discussing stages 2 and 3 via the associated techniques of rich pictures and set diagrams. It is hoped that these different techniques will help to illustrate the concepts of KRS at this level and particularly address the mismatch or gap identified between the customer and developer identified above.

KRS advises the use of a facilitator to drive the approach because of the notion of two separate sides. A facilitator is an independent person who guides the process and helps to overcome the various barriers that are in the way (sometimes deliberately put in the way) and any problems that occur. The facilitator may also arbitrate at times, but ideally should help the parties to agree rather than imposing anything. The facilitator is also responsible for the more mundane elements such as involving the right people, arranging meetings and setting agendas. Facilitators need to be independent, so as not to be seen as part of one side or the other, and not be tainted by any internal politics or bias.

The presence of a facilitator should be borne in mind in the discussion of the use of the two techniques below.

14.5 The Knowledge Requirement System as a Sociotechnical Process

KRS is a sociotechnical process, defining as it does the role played by the two parties, i.e. it works by the customer and system developer engaging in human–human communication. The requirement process is the most important stage in developing the product where the two parties express their knowledge and understanding of the future proposed product. It is conceived as a social constructivist approach (Barnes, 1974; Colins, 1982, 1983) where technological artefacts are open to sociological analysis, not just in their usage but also in their design and technical content. In KRS this implies that the elicitation of requirements emphasises the social interpretation and meaning rather than just the technical elements in the attempt to bind business knowledge and technical knowledge and establish a mutual understanding.

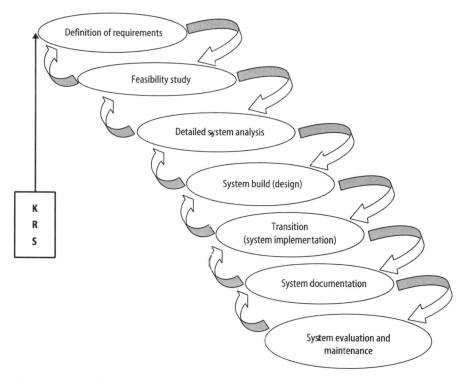

Figure 14.4 Contribution of the knowledge requirement system (KRS) to the system development life cycle approach.

14.6 The Knowledge Requirement System in Practice

This section illustrates the early stages of KRS by describing an example of the use of two techniques that have been used. As mentioned above, other techniques may be used in KRS but these are two that hopefully illustrate the nature of the approach.

14.6.1 Rich Pictures

When the level of misunderstanding between the various parties is deep seated and there are serious conflicts of goals, values, perceptions and expectations, the approach that the authors have used successfully in the past is soft systems methodology (SSM) and in particular the use of rich pictures (Checkland and Scholes, 1997). Bustard *et al.* (1995) showed that SSM can be combined successfully with other requirements analysis methods. SSM is particularly appropriate for complex situations where fundamental underlying differences of opinions and perceptions are encountered. It addresses aspects that are typically not well addressed by most other analysis approaches and methods. It is not the purpose of this chapter to describe SSM or rich pictures in detail, but simply to indicate their use in KRS.

Frequently, deep-seated problems are found in a mismatch of structure and process elements, and the rich picture helps to illustrate this. However, the rich picture is simply a diagram, and the real benefit is in the discussion and understanding that its construction reveals. The rich picture should contain "soft" elements, such as people's values, concerns and perceptions.

> A rich picture is a caricature of an organisation or problem area that helps to illustrate what it is about. The rich picture should be self-explanatory and easy to understand. A rich picture is constructed by looking for elements of structure and process in the problem situation, and then representing them in the diagram.

Example of the use of Rich Pictures in the Retail Sector

Figure 14.5 was the result of discussions with retail personnel (customers and developers). It shows some of the different issues that were going through the minds of the participants when discussing the initial requirements of a new system.

The participants found rich pictures easy to use despite not having any prior experience. They also found that rich pictures made each side think about the other's perceptions and recognise some fundamental problems that needed to be resolved before moving on to more detailed requirements identification. They did

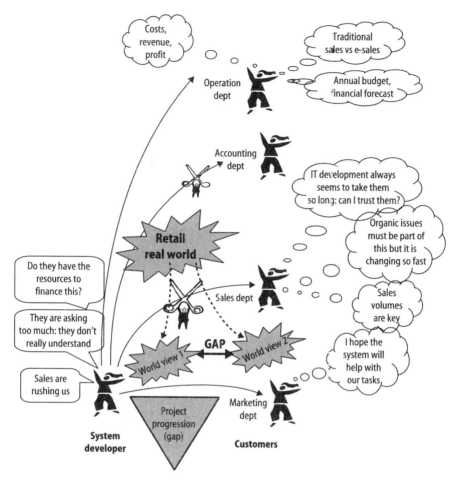

Figure 14.5 Rich picture of the initial situation.

comment on the time it took to reach any kind of agreement, but in the end both parties were happy that it proved beneficial.

14.6.2 Set Diagrams

The second technique within KRS that is illustrated here is the use of the set diagram (or Venn diagram) and how it can be applied to the understanding of customer requirements and the minimisation of the gap. The use of set diagrams is part of KRS and is ideally applied at level 3, after the use of rich pictures and other techniques at level 2, i.e. when the outline requirements and fundamental mismatches have been resolved.

Set diagrams have been used successfully for some time in management science (Anderson, Sweeney and Williams, 1995), as well as in their traditional areas of

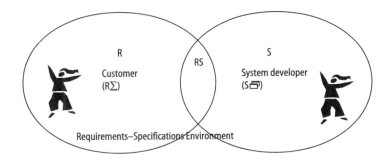

Requirement (Customer) • Specification (System developer)

Figure 14.6 Initial overlapping of customer requirements and system developer specifications.

logic and mathematics. It may seem strange that a mathematical technique is used in KRS, but set diagrams are used mainly for their graphical representation to drive the requirements understanding process. They have been found to be highly effective as a graphical or pictorial technique for illustrating gaps in understanding that exist at the requirements stage. The diagrams essentially illustrate the degree of overlap between the two parties in their understanding of requirements. They are extremely easy to understand and can be manipulated by both sides to make particular points. For example, by renegotiating the overlaps it is easy to indicate how good or bad current agreements are on particular matters. Although the set diagram has quantitative antecedents it is used as part of KRS in the context of a sociotechnical approach and applied as a driver of a sociotechnical process.

Example of the use of Set Diagrams in the Retail Sector

The example shown in Figure 14.6 is based on the research study and discussions with two of the participating organisations. One was a well-known high-street retailer and the other was the retail arm of a larger financial institution, both based in London. The example relates to the perceived need to enter the internet world and to have a web-based information and sales channel for the companies' existing products. Beyond this the case is simplified and does not reflect the detail of the organisations or their actual requirements. It is purely illustrative of the situation and the processes.

The two circles of the set diagram represent different areas of knowledge and understanding; one represents the understanding of the system developers, the other the customer. The matching or common understanding of the requirement is where the two circles overlap (RS).

The diagram (Figure 14.6) clearly illustrates that in this case the customer and the developer have different perceptions and understandings of what the system is to deliver and what it will be like, as the area of overlap is very small.

Customer Requirements

In the set diagram of Figure 14.6, (R) denotes the set of all possible customer requirements space, which contains the individual (fragments) business requirement as subsets viewed by the customer.

R contains a set of individual requirements, e.g. we would like to offer an e-commerce facility for our external customers, the image required for this business is one of trust, the new system must be operational by the end of the year, the system must be easy for internal and external customers to use, the system must provide quick response for customers, the system must be totally secure, the system must provide enough information for customers so that they do not place an additional burden on the existing helpline, a maximum of eight people (from the business side) will be available to support the development of the new system, the new system needs to fit very closely with the existing business processes, and the system should attract additional customers, not just be a different channel for existing customers.

System Developer Specifications

S denotes the set of all possible system developer specifications space, which contains the individual (fragments) suggested specification design as subsets viewed by the developer.

S contains a set of individual specification elements, e.g. an electronic retail channel is required, the development of the system is a major new undertaking for the ITS department, the time scale is extremely tight, the skills required are in short supply, the development environment will be Unix, a mirror environment will be required, absolute security is impossible, the development language will be Java and C++, response times depend on factors outside our control, and the system can use the existing processing systems for the underlying functions which will shortcut the development time.

In this case the common understanding (overlap) is relatively small. The common factors are that they are both talking about an internet channel and that the existing processes will be used which will obviously make them a close fit to the new system. The non-overlapping sector is represented by $R\Sigma$ and $S\boxminus$. For example, the customers want the system to be totally secure, whereas the developers are indicating that they believe total security to be impossible and are talking about a mirror system. This clearly shows an area of mismatch or misunderstanding (possibly on both sides) and in set diagram terms there is no mapping between the two sets in terms of security. Another example of a mismatch is that the clients want the system to attract new customers but this does not seem to have been taken on board in any way by the developers. Maybe it is difficult for them to achieve, but the fact that they have ignored this is likely to lead to unfulfilled expectations at the very least. Overall, there is a far greater degree of mismatch than match of requirements (or at this stage understanding and perceptions) between the two parties.

Whilst the diagram is only illustrative, it is nevertheless powerful in its ability to convey the size of the gap. In use, the specific elements, i.e. the Rs and Ss, would be fully defined and possibly written on the diagram in the appropriate places. However, this makes the diagrams rather messy and unwieldy so it has not been included here. When the elements of the gap are discussed in detail and agreements have been thrashed out the participants can redraw the diagrams with the overlap becoming larger as understanding develops. The point is that the diagram clearly represents the current level of agreed areas of understanding and misunderstanding between the two sides at any stage.

In KRS the focus is now on these gaps. There are some potential matches, for example, both parties have defined something relating to the implementation date. However, the customer has specified a date but this is not agreed by the systems developers, they simply state that the deadline is tight (S3) and this certainly does not indicate a meeting of minds as to the likely implementation date. In fact, were this to remain the state of affairs the project would probably be at a high risk of not meeting the deadline simply because the two sides have not really come to a serious agreement on the issue. Having this highlighted early on is obviously beneficial. Similarly, there is the issue of response rates, which both sides have mentioned, but at this stage there is little common ground, with different assumptions being made. Clearly, a mapping does not really exist and more dialogue and negotiation is required.

By contrast the customer requirement concerning the image of trust, is not really even on the agenda of the developers, as there is no corresponding element in their set. Thus, the developers do not seem to have taken any of the implications of these requirements on board. Equally, certain specification statements do not reflect any immediately identifiable requirement of the customer, again indicating a need for further clarification and discussion. A second stage or iteration would now be entered and attempts to resolve the mismatches made.

At the end of the second stage hopefully there is a far greater degree of overlap and in this case there is a greater convergence of the requirements and specification achieved. The issue of time-scale has been resolved as a result of its having been highlighted in the first stage. The customer has understood some of the limitations and concerns of the developers, and delayed the deadline by two months. Thus, as a result of discussion, negotiation and improved understanding on both sides the content of the requirement changed. On the developer side the issues of resources and project management were addressed, and it was agreed to buy in new skills. The sides were now in general agreement over time-scales and response rates were agreed. The customer agreed to match competitor systems and the developers agreed to identify and benchmark them. Similarly, the assumptions concerning security were discussed and agreed. The customer was persuaded that total security was unrealistic but agreed to specific measures that reflected best practice in the sector and the channel.

The new mapping diagram (Fig. 14.7), shows the agreed mappings after the second stage. The diagram helped the parties to focus on those instances that were not mapped in each set. These are then reviewed, discussed and negotiated as to what they mean, why they are there, and the implications for either side. Ideally, a

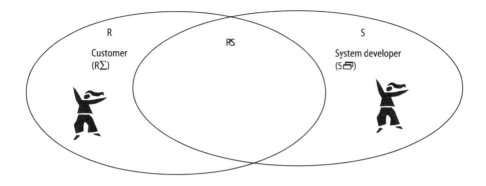

Requirements–Specifications Environment

Requirement (Customer) • Specification (System developer)

Figure 14.7 Greater overlapping of customer requirements and system developer specifications.

third stage or iteration of discussions is undertaken with the objective of mapping all the elements in each set.

In this case, there are still several instances in both sets that have not been agreed and mapped. For example, the issue of "the image of trust" has still not been resolved. It might be that there is nothing on the specification side that can be done to address this. If this is the case then this should be recorded and the requirement instance removed from the diagram. Everybody would now be clear that this is not something that the new system can directly deliver and there are no false expectations. Equally, there are some specification instances that are not mapped, for example the one concerning development in Java and C++. If there is no requirement that maps directly to this then again it should be removed. This would make it clear that there is no requirement that leads to the use of Java and C++, that some other languages could alternatively be used and that this is purely a technical decision. The customer should be made aware of the benefits and limitations of using these development languages. In other words, dialogue and negotiation ensue. It might be that the use of Java and C++ is mapped directly to some requirement. Either way the developers have to be very specific about the reasons for doing things in a particular way and explain them to the customer so that they understand the implications, and vice versa. As part of KRS the agreements are documented along with the reasoning behind the decisions, which forms part of the knowledge management system.

Compromise and trade-offs are inherent in resolving and illuminating differing perceptions, and although the technique proposed is the use of set diagrams it is really the negotiation and dialogue that is key: the diagrams simply drive the associated sociotechnical process.

14.7 Conclusion

This chapter has described some of the problems of inadequate determination and understanding of requirements and identified the culture gap as a fundamental element. KRS is proposed as an approach to help to overcome these problems and achieve a better understanding between developers and customers. KRS has been developed based on a number of theoretical antecedents and honed in a research study in the retail sector in the UK. KRS provides an environment and framework for helping to achieve this better work, but ultimately it is about different sides being prepared to come together and engage for the common good. KRS is not a methodology of systems development in its own right but an approach that can be integrated into existing methods. In this chapter, KRS has been described, and the use of two of the associated diagramming techniques illustrated, using examples taken from a study of the retail sector to provide a practical illustration of the approach.

One of the key philosophical underpinnings of KRS is its sociotechnical approach and one of its key features is that customers and system developers need to face up to the complexity of the requirements process: both parties must deal with each other and learn to work better together.

Chapter 15

Managing Tacit Knowledge in Knowledge-Intensive Firms: is There a Role for Technology?

Elayne Coakes, Gill Sugden, Steve Russell, Jason-Phillip Camilleri and Anton Bradburn

15.1 Introduction

This chapter looks at two international and multisite management consultancies and contrasts how knowledge management initiatives in two organisations were organised and developed.

First, the background to the meaning of tacit knowledge and the potential role of technology for knowledge management are considered. Then a brief discussion of how the research was undertaken is presented. Case histories of two organisations are discussed and contrasted.

15.2 Knowledge and Tacit Knowledge

For several years studies have discussed, under the general heading of knowledge management, the nature of knowledge in organisations and organisational ability to harness and manage knowledge. It is important to clarify the present approaches to some of the commonly used terminology before analysing any specific case studies exploring aspects of tacit knowledge management.

Kant's view, quoted by Nonaka and Tageuchi (1995, p. 24), that "Though all our knowledge begins with experience, it does not follow that it all arises out of experience", makes a good beginning to the discussion.

Some of this knowledge is based on acquisition of facts in a way that is well described by the French verb *savoir*, to know, as in to be factually certain. However, Kant must also mean that we are constantly involved in a process of adaptation of our personal knowledge bases as we increase our experiential knowledge; this is described in French by the verb *connaitre*, to know, as in to understand. More recently, Davenport and Prusak (1998a) defined knowledge as intangible: "It originates and is applied in the minds of knowers".

Both views can perhaps be equated with what Joseph Badaracco (1991) referred to as two different types of knowledge: embedded and migratory. Migratory knowledge can be passed on by the individual or move out of the organisation very quickly. It is usually codified in some form, and thus is easily transferable.

Embedded knowledge is embedded in the psyche of the individual or the culture of an organisation, in norms, attitudes, relationships among individuals and groups, and decision-making routines. Hildreth, Kimble and Wright (2000) also use the terms hard and soft knowledge, with soft knowledge likened to tacit knowledge. Soft knowledge comprises experience and work knowledge, and resides only within individuals. For a discussion of the frameworks of knowledge see Coakes and Sugden (2000b).

Nonaka and Tageuchi (1995) progressed the argument for two types of knowledge, using the terms tacit and explicit knowledge. They invented the concept of the knowledge-creating company, relying on a dynamic flow of tacit and explicit knowledge constantly re-creating and reinventing itself.

Explicit knowledge is generally considered to be facts that can be precisely and formally articulated and that can be easily codifed, documented, transferred and shared, perhaps similar to Badarracco's migratory knowledge. It is tacit knowledge that presents organisations with the greatest challenge since it is subconsciously understood or applied and therefore becomes difficult to articulate; it is developed from direct action and experience and only externalised and shared through conversations and story-telling.

According to Platts and Yeung (2000), tacit knowledge is "knowledge-in-action", indicating that tacit knowledge is what has not been articulated. This distinguishes it from explicit knowledge, which is readily accessible from within the organisational domain.

> "Tacit knowledge is not available as a text and may conveniently be regarded as residing in the heads of those working in a particular organisational context. It involves intangible factors embedded in personal beliefs, experiences, and values" (Pan and Scarbrough, 1999, p. 362).

According to Davenport and Prusak (1998a), it is in the "knowers" minds where "experience" and "information" are "incorporated" and "evaluated" through interpretation and reflection within a given context, and whilst information can stand alone, knowledge cannot.

While the potential value of tacit knowledge is generally agreed, a corresponding lack in the ability of organisations to collect, store and harness the value of the experiences of their employees has been observed (Geisler, 1999) and it is the problems surrounding these issues that were investigated through the two case studies discussed below.

15.3 Potential Role of Technology in Knowledge Management

When knowledge management became a popular topic for discussion it seemed to be in danger of being hijacked by the information technology (IT) community and turned into a vehicle for the marketing of new IT systems. In short, knowledge management may become another label for information management rather than a genuinely innovative attempt to increase the knowledge of the whole organisation. Although technology does have an important role to play in this field, it is an enabling role – a necessary, but not the only, condition for the effectiveness of knowledge management systems" (Davenport, 1996). Davenport continues by discussing the limits of technology which in themselves illustrate the "pain associated with previous recipes that over-emphasised technology and under-emphasised people – notably business process re-engineering (BPR – now called "The fad that forgot people").

Scarbrough, Swan and Preston (1999) complain that the presence of human resource management is being marginalised in the knowledge management process by information systems professionals. Defining knowledge management as "any process or practice of creating, acquiring, capturing, sharing and using knowledge, wherever it resides, to enhance learning and performance in organisations", they argue from this proposition that information systems are on the supply side of knowledge and that organisations have overlooked the demand side.

Pan and Scarbrough (1999) claim that knowledge management is generally concerned with the conversion of tacit knowledge into explicit knowledge, and this explicit knowledge is usually based on information technologies. Blumentitt and Johnston (1999) go on to state that knowledge can be created, captured and encouraged to flow around organisations. Knowledge creation, capture and flow can be facilitated by knowledge management applications in the form of systems such as corporate intranets and software such as Lotus Notes. There is evidence to support this view in the two case studies discussed in this chapter. However, although the example is often cited of intranets being examples of an organisational move towards knowledge management this may be considered a questionable view and there needs to be more evidence that an intranet provides better than a computerised version of organisational documents that set out structure rules and regulations, that is information about the organisation. This argument is supported by Blumentitt and Johnston (1999), who state that tacit, or soft, knowledge only resides in intelligent systems, by which the authors mean that the repositories of such knowledge are individuals.

Knowledge management tools may be useful to share and disseminate information, or explicit knowledge, but the extent to which they can achieve real sharing of tacit knowledge and experience, and the fostering of a learning organisation, is debatable. They are primarily management tools for the manipulation and control of knowledge assets. By contrast, tacit knowledge, which may comprise anything from the latent expertise and skills of employees to subjective insights, opinions and intuition, is firmly embedded in social networks and communities.

Support for this view comes from other sources where it is first argued that knowledge cannot be automated and contended secondly that the push to increase investment in IT for activities such as knowledge engineering is a scam (Angell, 1998). Angell outlines how human intelligence and knowledge are developed, rejecting the idea that computers can be programmed to reproduce this. Some organisations hold a vision of leveraging knowledge

> This view sees computer technology as being limited in its capabilities, pointing out that while the technology may have achieved some improvements in the form and delivery of information, only human beings have the skills to process information and deal with its complexity and ambiguity.

through the use of information technology (McDermott, 1999), but many have found that it is hard to achieve in practice. This, it is suggested, is because many organisations use information management tools and concepts to design knowledge management systems without recognising the characteristics of knowledge, or focusing on the elements of knowing, thinking and community.

The authors have not found any evidence in their own literature search that supports the view of the IT function's alleged claims to the knowledge management territory. They have found, however, that the evidence in the literature is ambivalent. At least as much has been written about the contribution that IT can make to knowledge management as about the attempts of the IT community to monopolise it. Daniels *et al.* (1999) recognise the importance of knowledge workers in business success and look at some IT tools for managing a company's intellectual capital. They consider how databases, groupware and document management software can help with the knowledge base and how knowledge management software can assist in actually making use of such a repository.

The argument for knowledge management tools is still a strong one. These tools may be able to support and encourage tacit knowledge and learning but only, it seems, if managers already nurture a learning environment and if they have a vision of how any given system can be used to support the aspirations of capturing tacit knowledge.

15.4 How the Research was Carried out

This section looks at what happens when attempts to explicate a formal system of knowledge management take place. Will the introduction of discipline, where previous *ad hoc* informality existed, trigger not only structural but also cultural adjustments? Or is the converse true? Does a change in the organisational culture lead to pressure to explicate a formal knowledge managing initiative? Are the players in the formalisation of the knowledge management initiative aware of the need for hybrid solutions of people and technology?

These questions are answered through exploring the case studies of two consultancy companies, Halogen and Delta. First, the way in which the research was carried out is discussed, followed by details of the findings.

15.5 Case Study 1 – Halogen: Methods

In this organisation, to discover how a business manages its tacit knowledge, a series of semi-structured interviews was conducted, as well as a three month period of work allowing participant observation and full involvement in the firm's activities (from working to socialising). During this process it was necessary to arrange interview times with people to gain their full attention and for the interview to be most productive. Many knowledge issues can be highly political and emotive, even in a self-critical, "learning" organisation such as Halogen. The interviews were, therefore, conducted in a variety of locations. Some were opportunistic and others held in conventional meeting rooms in and around the Hamburg, Stockholm and London offices. This also allowed a cultural perspective of the company to be seen. In total, twenty-five interviews were conducted at Halogen over a three month period. The results were transposed into stories, told from the point of view of the interviewees. The semi-structured interviews were based on a questionnaire which was compiled during the first two weeks at Halogen. The questionnaire had five parts and the questions were deliberately wide ranging to gain as much information and understanding of the company as possible. The broad nature of the questions was an attempt to prevent interviewees expressing preconceived ideas.

15.6 Case History 1 – Halogen

Halogen is a management consulting company and also a web design agency, formed five years ago. The company is the vision of several veterans of the Scandinavian banking market's early entry into electronic commerce. Some of the founders of Halogen also founded the early e-media agencies which took hold in Scandinavia two to three years ahead of the rest of Europe. The vision was to achieve what none of these agencies had been able to. They wanted to provide a full service, including consultation on business strategy and, if required, the full scope, design and implementation of an internet solution, to clients who envisaged entering electronic business. Halogen's vision is an organisation based on best practice and good business, providing a complete, unbiased solution for these companies.

Halogen is housed in seven offices situated in five countries in northern Europe. The company has more than 300 staff, including about 40 in London, and is prepared to double in size over the next year. Halogen's diverse business propositions require people from varied backgrounds to fulfil them. It evolved from the merger of a contemporary yet very formal and traditional strategy consulting company and a website design and production agency. Thus, Halogen has a full range of strategists, designers, marketers, software developers and platform experts. Halogen defines itself by three areas: strategy, communications and technology (see The director's story, Russell, 2000). These themes embody what the company undertakes for its clients. Employees work within one of these three competencies. This reflects not only their individual role but also how they and their role fit within Halogen's overall vision. This three-pronged model is part of the communications plan which instils the vision of Halogen as a dynamic and multifaceted organisation. "Everyone [in the company] will know their role in the production of the end result, including the client" (The director's story, Russell, 2000).

One of the best ways to transfer knowledge in a business is to "hire smart people and let them talk to one another" (Davenport and Prusak, 1998a). Naturally, Halogen attempts to hire good people who are able to do their jobs well. People are also employed because they share the vision of what the company is trying to achieve. The recruitment process is embodied in the information architect's need to "know how people think" (The information architect's story, Russell, 2000). It is relatively easy for employees to understand Halogen's vision and feel part of it in the way that Krogh (1998) describes, since it is a small company and the employees are bright, enthusiastic, articulate and embracing of people. There is a danger that as Halogen grows, the importance of communicating the company vision will be lost in the general noise of pitch and production. This noise is evident in the director's comment about his employees not being able to "look after long-term efficiency when so much is being asked of them in the short term" (The director's story, Russell, 2000). A loss of communication is already apparent between some offices (The strategist's story, Russell, 2000).

There is a culture of sharing knowledge at Halogen coming from the top. Using the words of a director at Halogen,

Managers realise that the way to be effective is to provide an environment in which a sharing culture can grow: "What is it that my people need to know about today and how can I facilitate this?" (The director's story, Russell, 2000).

"Everyone is responsible for knowledge in this company".

In Halogen all employees are expected to be catalysts in the way that Krogh (1998) describes. There is a general feeling at Halogen that everyone should have a part in managing knowledge. People are keen to share what they think might be useful and find time to converse where necessary. There is an awareness that the active facilitation of meetings "is important to capture the best from the creative process" (The art director's story, Russell, 2000). The employees are mainly young and there is a culture in which asking questions or asking for help is acceptable. There are titles such as information journalist, chief knowledge officer and even chief visionary officer. These titles reflect that knowledge management is a formal part of some people's roles. However, through lack of vision, sometimes these roles are unclear and work becomes uncoordinated.

Many knowledge enabling problems manifest themselves at a personal level and having regular dialogue in the form of a mentor system allows problems to be aired early.

Each employee at Halogen has a mentor who acts as a guiding figure. The mentor is not the line manager but another experienced person. The system of mentoring allows communication in all directions and aids the effective management of people's expectations. This can assist when employees claim to "not know what is going on around them" (The developer's story, Russell, 2000). Owing to the nature of their expertise, some employees become completely absorbed in their work. Mentoring gives such people an open opportunity for conversation when they have a problem to air.

Many people felt that locating journals and other reference material in a suitable place both on the servers and in a physical library would help the efficient retrieval of

A first impression of what knowledge means to people at Halogen is filing, both electronic and paper.

research. This feeling was exacerbated by the "lack of any data storage system" (The project manager's story, Russell, 2000). Many people felt that they could store their own work so that they could find it again, but realised that its real value would be lost if colleagues throughout the company could not also make use of their work. The fact that there is a realisation that their work is valuable and that there could be a system for retrieval and reuse of recently transformed tacit knowledge means that they feel partly responsible for how the design is effected. All people are expected to be "mobile knowledge activists" and have a part in improving the situation (The director's story, Russell, 2000). In addition to the problem of storage and retrieval of documents is the development of a structure for the storage system. Such a structure is entirely proprietary for whom it is designed. The database schema proposed for a document management system is therefore as much an expression of the tacit knowledge in the mind of the designer as the documents within the database are expressions of the research and thoughts that went into their creation.

You cannot "mobilise" people if you do not know whom to approach. Knowing "who knows what" is a new and growing problem in the company. Until recently, Halogen was small, and thus sharing of knowledge and experience was relatively easy. With more offices, many more people and no efficient system, a way of capturing has been devised which will be facilitated by technology. Without a system "it is possible to literally feel the inertia, almost tangibly, in the company" (The project manager's story, Russell, 2000). In this case the system devised is a simple database accessed through the intranet. It will hold details of all people's work experience and skills. This will allow a seamless redirection of expertise to prevent employees from constantly "reinventing the wheel" and permits the allocation of work to appropriate people.

In their book *The Cluetrain Manifesto* (2000), Levine, Resnick and Higgins believe that the internet is a medium that has "transcended the borders of businesses". They argue that the internet is the most powerful enabler of conversation since "we stopped shopping at the bazaar" and recognise that whilst the internet is driven by technology, "its voice is unmistakably human". If the people in a company such as Halogen, itself in the business of communication, wish to communicate with people outside the business, then the internet is the desired medium. There are visionaries at Halogen who grasp that the natural propagation of ideas is best served by having space on the web to fulfil this purpose. The concept of a gallery on the web for "incubating the seeds of ideas" (The information architect's story, Russell, 2000), both internal and external, will encourage dialogue which transcends the boundaries of the office. Although the place to which he was referring was not necessarily physical, the web lends itself to an environment of this kind. It promotes a "network of interactions, determined by the care and trust of participants" (Krogh, Ichijo and Nonaka, 2000). This is the "ultimate conversation" which Levine, Resnick and Higgins (2000) are describing. A forum of this nature is already happening in a few companies, but only in part (see websites at KPMG and Razorfish). There are sites dedicated to knowledge sharing which encourage the pursuit of

The Japanese philosopher Kitaro Nishida proposed a knowledge sharing concept called "ba", which roughly translates to "place".

excellence and allow the development of concepts by question and answer. In the engineer's story, Russell (2000) uses "these online forums to find out what is being developed at the very front edge of our discipline".

Software developers require rapid answers to problems. They also "know things that other people don't know they know" (The developer's story, Russell, 2000). Providing the people with whom you are in contact use the same system (there are no industry-wide standards, yet) an employee can see at any time whether a colleague is at their desk (logged on) and can ask questions which instantly appear on their colleague's monitor. A dialogue can be initiated and propagated across the room or across the continent. The colleague can arrange not to be disturbed and manage the potential torrent of messages in many ways. Some use has been made of the many communication systems available on the internet. There is no policy at Halogen to determine how employees communicate. It is a reflection of the open and determined attitude of many of the people at Halogen that they find out who is communicating through which program (The developer's story, Russell, 2000).

In addition to chat rooms and e-mail there are other forums for sharing knowledge publicly. Although there is little reason to use all of these media at Halogen some use is made of public files (or newsgroups). In their simplest form the public files, which are sorted by subject, allow people to upload interesting documents or share opinions and discussion without sending group e-mail. Thus, technology offers many opportunities for enabling knowledge globally.

The London office is situated in amongst the art dealers' showrooms of St James' in Piccadilly. The other countries' offices are similarly positioned in inspiring environments. Considerable expense has been committed to providing a suitable work environment (The art director's story). Apart from pleasing and contemporary interior design and decoration, the area is organised so that each person has ample space to do his or her own work. When the need arises there are numerous lobbies and rooms for meetings and team functions such as the planning of creative work. There are also spaces to eat lunch and have coffee, and the front reception area has a large work surface where flowers and newspapers are set during the day but which can double as a bar when required. The environment gives people the opportunity to communicate effectively and comfortably. It is one that inspires creativity and innovation. Correct design of the office environment has created a context that promotes conversation and enjoyable, productive work.

In the same way that the British Army benefits from "after action review" (AAR), Halogen's project managers hold post-project debriefings to learn where the practices and processes being used are either serving or failing the company. At Halogen a process captures all the documentation used in the project and allows discussion of "what went right and what went wrong" (The project manager's story, Russell, 2000). Creation of "learning histories" (Greco, 1999) is an activity that many companies have found useful. The process at Halogen is still in an early form but the benefits are visible now.

Perhaps because it is small and in spite of the paradox described above, a company such as Halogen is able to carry out, with at least some success, knowledge enabling activities. It should not be surprising that the most quoted story is that of the director. Many of the activities suggested need leadership. They are "things that leaders, and only leaders, can do" (Evans and Wurster, 2000). Leadership is where many companies may fail and an interesting case for further development.

15.7 Case Study 2 – Delta: Methods

In this organisation the researcher had been an employee of the firm's in-house technology department, ultimately becoming manager of technology, before this research began.

Qualitative analysis of individual semi-structured interviews elicited, from knowledge professionals and related support personnel, an articulated understanding and appreciation of the initiative. A case-study approach was used to analyse the phenomenon of formalising a system of knowledge management. The collection of interview data was augmented through an examination of the firm's relevant documentation, such as existed for the Lotus Notes' databases and e-mail memoranda regarding the knowledge management initiative. A significant challenge with this particular case study was one of research bias due to this researcher's prior employment as manager of technology.

A careful blend of methodologies influenced the actual processes used for selection of case, interpretation of material and presentation of findings. In determining the method, the following qualitative techniques each played a part:

- predefined dimensions for the selection based on perceptions and background of the topic;
- representativeness of a particularly typical knowledge-intensive organisation seeking formalisation of a knowledge management system;
- convenience due to the relative accessibility to and familiarity with the organisation (Flick, 1998).

Selecting who to interview was done through adherence to a formal technique, that of Corpus Construction (Bauer and Aarts, 2000). A cyclical process of interviewee selection was used, and saturation was reached when the inclusion of new strata no longer contributed to additional representations. Those best able to discuss the subject were those initially involved in the drive to formalise an explicit knowledge management system and subsequently in the decision to deploy the chosen system. It was found that organisational knowledge was divided along the same lines as organisational business offerings, each with its own individual responsibility for a particular area. The objective of the selection was to typify satisfactorily the varieties of representations available from the entire population of approximately 120 employees. In total, eight interviewees were selected.

15.8 Case History 2 – Delta

Delta Consulting Group (Delta) is a management and consulting firm with offices in New York and San Francisco. Delta (acquired in summer 2000 by Mercer

Consulting Group and renamed Mercer Delta Consulting) has worked closely since its formation, in 1980, with more than 150 Fortune 500 chief executive officers (CEOs) and other senior executives on the design and execution of large-scale organisational change. The organisation was founded by David A. Nadler, a leading organisational psychologist.

Delta's approach to management consulting combines two perspectives:

- understanding organisations in strategic terms as economic enterprises; and
- understanding organisations as complex systems of human behaviour.

The firm, which has been growing at a steady, accelerated rate since the mid-1990s, hires, almost exclusively, consultants with PhDs, with an average of ten years' experience in their respective fields. Currently, there are close to 70 consultants in a company of 120 people. The knowledge-intensive "products" delivered through consulting are Delta's stock-in-trade, comprising its "manufactured" inventory of intellectual capital, logically the equivalent of the entire portfolio of intellectual property it possesses.

Delta's initiatives dealing with knowledge were not considered in the confinement of departmental boundaries. Instead, intellectual capital was seen as something that concerned everyone and required several types of resources. In order for a knowledge management initiative to be effective, the correct technological ingredients must exist as both an enabler and a repository of organisational knowledge. This must also coincide with the people's cultural desire to be participants. This is how the two separate attempts to provide an organisational repository of intellectual capital ultimately merged, forming a unified approach towards knowledge management within Delta.

The time-frame under investigation ran from early 1993 until mid-2000.

"In 1993 ... the state of knowledge management was (first of all we were on the Mac, that's important) somewhere between 6 and 8 standard presentations up on the server in a folder. Then the informal thing was that you talk to research which at that time was David Wagner, then MarcoPolo came in sometime second half of 1994 ... until July 99 when we rolled out the full Lotus Notes Knowledge Exchange with 600 documents in there all coded, and put it on everyone's laptop and let it rip" (Rick Hardin:5:20, Camilleri, 2000).

At this knowledge processing organisation there were clearly two levels of approach leading to the formalisation of an explicit knowledge management system. It was revealed from the initial analysis of the interviews that the two different levels of approach had been occurring in parallel rather than in harmony, for a number of years. This seemed puzzling as those concerned with knowledge at this organisation should have been able to harmonise such efforts to facilitate knowledge exchange. The consultants employed at Delta had certainly understood the need to have a knowledge management system, as some of them were leading authorities on the subject. The entire organisation was in business to trade its shared knowledge. Delta was a classic scenario of the "cobbler's own children having no shoes" (Bill Pasmore:3:22, Camilleri 2000). The cobbler, however, recognised that his children were barefoot!

At one level a quite abstract discussion of what knowledge meant to Delta and how best to harness it had begun in 1993 and coincided with the hire of Rick Hardin. Rick was charged by the firm's Chief Executive Officer (David A. Nadler) to head up a knowledge board responsible for the firm's strategy for the handling of its intellectual capital. The knowledge board recognised the need to facilitate sharing of the firm's intellectual property through the appropriate enabling technologies, but a proposal for a knowledge management initiative did not materialise from these discussions. It was late 1998 before a design for a knowledge management system occurred, despite the knowledge board's best attempts.

Knowledge management "informally begun (sic) as a low level administrative task, that of a librarian whose sole manager was Kate" (Carlos Rivero:2:33, Camilleri, 2000). Around the same time as the formation of the knowledge board a single person, KL, took a more practical approach. KL was at the time responsible for the organisation's resource centre, home to materials such as publications, documents and the small internal library. This was not her only responsibility, as she eventually became the informal point of contact for accessing the electronic documents that comprised the firm's intellectual property. Through her own resourcefulness to facilitate the ever-increasing requests for the same documents, a precursor to the current knowledge management system was installed. The product was an off-the-shelf document management system called MarcoPolo. MarcoPolo served many people satisfactorily for several years. The only person who actually used it, however, was KL.

Technologically, there were issues that prevented the widespread adoption by users of MarcoPolo. The single most significant factor was that it was unbearably slow when used from the road, connecting via a laptop modem. The people that could benefit the most from the repository of documents were the consultants, the majority of whom worked on site for the client. A tool that did not function well remotely was not welcome. Even doubling of connection speeds, which improved remote searches, was no match for the level of discomfort experienced waiting for a PowerPoint presentation to download.

Apart from the purely technical difficulties experienced during remote connectivity, there was another issue. MarcoPolo's user interface was entirely different from that of any other application used at Delta. This required a commitment of precious consultant time to learn yet another application, which in general was resisted by the consultants.

"There are people that have had this since the 80s ... yea, we might wanted to have blown it up again when the web came along" (Rick Hardin:39:36, Camilleri, 2000).

A clear-cut message from all the interviewees was that knowledge management was nothing new. Rather, it was viewed as simply necessary for the good of the business. The two distinct levels of approach to knowledge management eventually merged. The most astonishing finding was that crucial technological developments coincided with cultural change towards the role of what was termed the "corporate citizen" (Bill Pasmore:20:22, Camilleri, 2000).

Eventually, in 1998, a Lotus Notes database was introduced, specifically designed as a vehicle for Delta's knowledge management. It would be used as a knowledge repository for what the firm considered its codified intellectual capital. Major technical issues were not experienced, primarily because Lotus Notes was familiar to the firm. It had been used as Delta's e-mail system since 1997. Most of the prior technical issues experienced with MarcoPolo were by default solved by across-the-board developments in technology, such as Lotus Notes' own graphical user interface moving to the more common look and feel of a web browser. Remote connectivity became a non-issue through the use of replication, a process by which each consultant kept a copy of the database locally on his or her laptop. Today, participation in the system of knowledge management is flourishing. It is slowly becoming another customary function of work, very much in the way people are expected to use e-mail.

At the very early stages of the firm's unified knowledge management initiative in 1998, the most explicit intellectual capital that was most readily identified consisted of an ever-increasing array of electronic documents. A focused initiative to capture intellectual capital, in the form of reusable documents, became the primary concern of the knowledge management initiative. Early on in the examination, identification and categorisation of this intellectual capital were concentrated in the company's "vault" of electronic documents, these being documentation of client deliverables such as Microsoft PowerPoint presentations and Microsoft Word documents. One interviewee made a very striking comment concerning the constituents of the organisation and its culture. Rajan Srikanth (55:02, Camilleri, 2000) proposed that Delta's value proposition to its clients does not allow for any inexperienced consultants, and that this factor stifled many attempts to foster the learning behaviours desired by the knowledge board. Each class of new consultants went through a three month integration period of intensive learning, and that was it. After integration, immediate client engagement was expected. At the time of the original knowledge board there was a very restrictive attitude towards client discourse among the consultants, as it was apparent that no one wanted to appear to be learning at their client's expense. This conflicted with newly hired consultants' eagerness to participate in the transfer of knowledge. The sought-after innovatory knowledge management system, coupled with its novelty, created the right climate for use. The result was an overwhelming attitude that learning was beneficial to consultants and clients alike.

It is fair to recognise the significant length of time (years) during which discussion on the topic took place before a formalised course of action emerged. Most of the interviewees focused on the constraints relating to the allocation of dedicated resources. The initiative was demanding, in both human and technological terms, requiring the devotion of considerable time by specific people, such as a Lotus Notes application developer. In addition, for a significant length of time, the preconditions for the deployment of the necessary resources remained elusive. The people involved in the design of the system demonstrated an understanding of how learning took place well before department directors universally accepted the level of resource commitment required. A more structured approach began to develop through the assignment of new knowledge-orientated roles, such as the role of knowledge manager. A distinction was made between the new position of knowledge manager and the existing library/resource centre administrator. In fact, both roles coexisted, further differentiating between documents considered to contain knowledge and all other documents. People were encourage to think in terms of metadata necessary to provide greater value to their work.

15.9 Conclusion

This view is clearly evidenced in Halogen and Delta's culture, as shown in the case study material. Another

> In the article "Working Knowledge", Davenport and Prusak (1998b) proclaim, "Now knowledge is everybody's job".

factor that links the two firms is the human resource strategy: in both cases they hire the best and the brightest who appear to share their cultural norms.

Both firms have developed their knowledge management initiatives supported by technology whilst acknowledging that technology primarily manages filing and document retrieval. This is primarily the management of explicit rather than tacit knowledge. Halogen, however, is also exploiting technology to encourage that sharing of tacit knowledge through discussion groups and the virtual "ba".

The two case studies also emphasise the need for the culture for knowledge sharing to predominate in the organisation and that a suitable physical environment is provided such as in Halogen's "inspiring" locations. This physical provision facilitates informal conversations and the general sharing of implicit and tacit understanding and wisdom. In addition, a prerequisite of knowledge is that it is known by someone, i.e. it "resides in an individual's mind" (Marchand *et al.*, 2000). Here it is also suggested by Halogen that organisations should approach the gathering and sharing of experience by applying the techniques of debriefing and mentoring, with the value of mentoring residing in conserving and transferring knowledge based on experience.

Chapter 16
Conclusion

Elayne Coakes, Dianne Willis and Steve Clarke

This conclusion takes an overview of the book's four sections, and reviews what has been added to the body of knowledge from the sociotechnical point of view.

> The sociotechnical approach, focusing on the joint optimisation of people and technology with a clear ethical principle, is clearly explained in the introductory chapter.

The sociotechnical paradigm is presented, and Cherns' principles discussed, looking in particular at the change of focus and interpretation between 1976 and 1987 with the divergence of the North American and Scandinavian views. The idea that knowledge management efforts have been focused on codifying, archiving and retrieving information is discussed, and this idea is revisited many times in the following chapters. The chapter then develops a sociotechnical view of knowledge management, drawing on the four-component sociotechnical model and arguing for a fifth component, the environment in which an organisation operates. The chapter concludes by explaining Cherns' principles in terms of knowledge management. This table gives a sociotechnical structure for the analysis of knowledge management and leads to a six-step approach for alignment for knowledge management. The theme of alignment of organisational culture, structure, management, reward system and infrastructure is often revisited in later chapters in the book. The chapter provides an excellent vehicle for the discussion of sociotechnical principles and knowledge management.

Having set the scene by clearly identifying the sociotechnical perspective on knowledge management, the book divides into four major parts covering the content of knowledge: know-why, know-what, know-who and know-how. Each section,

> Much of the emphasis of the book is on answering the question "what is knowledge management?" Is it a human or a technical process? Is there an accepted sociotechnical approach?

and indeed each chapter, adds to the sociotechnical perspective in some way and also expands the field of knowledge. Each chapter has something to offer on this subject in the themes, premises and models of knowledge which are developed and presented. Much of the work is firmly anchored in practice and is drawn from practical experience of how companies actually manage their knowledge. One of the really positive aspects of this book is the international perspective, which enables us to look at what is happening in a much more globalised dimension.

The first section deals with "know-why", and covers a range of international perspectives. Binney is concerned with building and implementing knowledge management systems in Australia. His previous work had led to the development of a knowledge management spectrum. This initial theoretical work has been built on and adapted, based on the need for a human dimension to the work. One of his major points is the need for balance or alignment between knowledge management technology, knowledge management applications, and knowledge management organisational change initiatives: a sociotechnical approach. His work investigates whether the human factor should lead the design and build of knowledge management systems. He posits that system level changes need to be balanced with a focus on what makes individuals use knowledge management applications. Binney concludes from his work that the human side is overlooked and underexplored in current knowledge management literature. He reiterates the view that there is a higher level of adoption when users are able to personalise the system. This insight gives an indication of the importance of this book to the field by bringing the human aspects to the forefront. It is helpful that Binney is able to draw on personal experience to reinforce what he is saying about the lack of emphasis on human aspects. The chapter addresses knowledge management "how" questions via the knowledge management spectrum, which consists of transactional knowledge management, analytical knowledge management, asset management knowledge management, process-based knowledge management, developmental knowledge management and innovation and creation knowledge management.

> Binney's case that "building of the technological mousetrap" is insufficient reinforces his call for further emphasis on the human element.

Goldkuhl and Braf offer a Scandinavian view. Sociotechnical principles are perhaps more well known in this part of the world, partly because of the work done in this field in the 1950s and by the Scandinavian industrial democracy studies, and it is interesting to see how these principles are applied in a knowledge management setting. A major premise for the authors is that organisations need to recognise and value knowledge. Their identification of this as a problem area relates to the idea that asset management must not be allowed to become mechanistic. They define organisational ability as consisting of individual knowledge, institutionalised shared knowledge, artefact functionality, and linguistic and pictorial descriptions of ability. Alignment between these points is key. Once again reinforcing the points made earlier in the book, alignment is a key requisite for effective knowledge management. Binney stressed the alignment between technology, applications and organisational change initiatives. Goldkuhl and Braf also stress this need for alignment between the constituent parts of their analysis; indeed, they refer to the need for congruence between constituents to enable leverage of potential ability. They develop the need for a combined approach developing human knowledge, intersubjective institutions, technical artefacts and linguistic descriptions as needed to achieve a sociotechnical balance. They conclude that knowledge management cannot be seen in isolation; rather, it requires a contextual approach recognising the relationship between knowledge and the other parts of the organisation.

So far, themes of the role of the individual and their knowledge and alignment of parts of the system are being raised as key to good knowledge management.

Scholtz brings a South African perspective to the question. Her work takes a slightly different approach in that she is considering a "knowledge business", i.e. that of a university. Her contention is that universities are an extreme type of organisational form focused on the creation, dissemination and evaluation of knowledge. This can be seen to link back to the sociotechnical framework in that it is looking to some extent at autonomous work groups that coordinate knowledge rather than at a specific structured management process. She points out that in a university setting knowledge has traditionally resided with the individual, individuals in universities will undertake research and become experts in various fields, and it is likely that they will be the only expert in that area within their organisation. Like Binney, she recognises the importance of discovering why people actually use information rather than focusing on the technology per se. Her conclusion relates to the fact that individual knowledge generation should aid organisational learning, especially within the context of a university; however, she recognises that this is problematic.

> Her question relates to how we exploit this knowledge base, given that this type of knowledge is often jealously guarded. She links the lack of knowledge management projects within a university to the individual rather than social nature of knowledge creation. Having acknowledged that knowledge workers need a different style of management, she draws on a seven-step model (get, use, learn, contribute, assess, build, sustain and digest) to produce a strategic overview of knowledge management processes.

The final contribution in this section is by Yoo and Ifvarsson, who bring an American perspective. Their work looks at why organisations invest in information systems to enhance the creation and sharing of knowledge, in that this provides a mechanistic or technological solution to a problem that is evidently not best suited to this type of response (see comments by Coakes). Their chapter examines why this is the case. They pose the question: "how do we know what knowledge resides within an individual organisation?" Their approach is to look at an organisation as a sociotechnical system having social structures, social actors, goals and technology. They stress the need for a balance between social and technical aspects, which has been the recurring sociotechnical theme. They take this analysis one stage further by asking the question is knowledge an object or is it socially constructed? From a sociotechnical standpoint, one would argue for social construction, but does it depend on the type of knowledge? Another question that they address which is revisited later in the book is the idea that knowledge may be more than the sum of individual knowledge; there may be organisational knowledge which is something outside individual knowledge. In seeking to analyse this question, the authors present a model of knowledge dynamics which takes a sociotechnical subsystems approach to dealing with knowledge management. This model leads them to the conclusion that organisations are dynamic and emergent and that static systems for capturing knowledge will not fit.

This section, then, has looked in depth at the knowledge management question of "why". It has provided a truly international flavour and proposed a series of models dealing with the issues raised. Each chapter has investigated the sociotechnical perspective and added to the existing body of knowledge.

The next section deals with the "know-what" concept in knowledge management. Both chapters in this section present a very individual view of knowledge management, which happens to be centred on the UK. Phillips and Patrick's chapter takes a view which focuses on personality types and how these affect the development of optimal knowledge. The clustering of personality types provides a number of challenges for generic knowledge management solutions. Their standpoint is that there needs to be a good fit between the people and the technology, which yet again reinforces the need for a sociotechnical approach. They also concentrate on the fact that the relationship between the individual and the group is important and this will correlate with the original analysis of personality type. Much of their work takes a psychological view looking at the need to develop common strategy spaces for learning and cooperation to develop a dynamic and adaptable workforce. This concentration on the individual and his or her role in knowledge evolution leads to the development of a model to ascertain which organisational structures will facilitate optimising knowledge and which will detract from the ability to do this. Since much of their work focuses on groups and group interaction, they emphasise the effect that the internet will have on this process, given the potential for much wider and more culturally diverse groups using the technology as a facilitator. This is an interesting question for sociotechnical thinking, in that the internet and its effects remain as yet a largely unexplored arena with a potential for extensive change in working relationships and agent-based modelling.

Pemberton and Stonehouse look at the skills and knowledge of the individuals who make up the workforce and how these affect company performance. Social interaction in the building of knowledge is also explored. Once more, the value of the correct balance between the human and technical parts of the process is noted as being of paramount importance. They argue that the profile of technology in the discussion of knowledge management represents a partial or inadequate explanation of how knowledge is created in organisations. They define explicit and implicit knowledge, saying that both start as individual knowledge but are transformed into organisational knowledge. (This transformation is revisited in the chapter by Kazi and co-workers in the final section.) Their analysis leads them to the conclusion that the technically orientated measurement of individual knowledge is unlikely to capitalise on expertise, as has been previously argued by Scholtz. They feel that a more human approach using a sociotechnical basis is far more likely to lead to successful results. They reiterate that access to the technology is not a panacea for success (see Binney and the "technological mousetrap") and that a balanced or more closely aligned approach is far more likely to be successful.

> The way forward is the creation of a knowledge-based culture using knowledge transfer to capitalise on the expertise of individuals.

Once again, the theme of this section has been the idea of the individual and the individual's knowledge being the starting point for successful knowledge management. The authors are in agreement that a purely technological solution is not likely to be successful and what is needed is a sociotechnical systems approach.

The third section addresses the "know-who" question. Here the discussion returns to an international perspective, comparing the UK, the USA and Sweden in their approaches to this question. This section applies practical case-study methods to look at real-life experiences in Boots, Motorola and Swedish manufacturing companies. From the matches between this section and the theoretical perspectives presented earlier, conclusions can be drawn about the need for further analysis and examination of existing and possible future knowledge management systems.

The chapter by Huang and Pan is based around a case study undertaken at Boots The Chemists, a large pharmaceutical company in the UK. They have chosen to examine in more depth the dynamics of knowledge management. They challenge the view that organisational knowledge is a set of commodities or assets that have significant strategic value and can be transferred and utilised independently of social context. Sociotechnical thinking would lead us to conclude that knowledge is embedded in social context, leading to the conclusion that the social and technical elements need to be aligned. They ask the question: what knowledge is needed in pursuing company aims of getting closer to the customer? Similarly, in other chapters, Binney and Scholtz have been concerned with questioning what users need from the system. Huang and Pan identify that given common organisational structures, knowledge could possibly be concealed by an individual business function. A vital factor from their analysis is the need to share knowledge cross-functionally. As a means to achieving this end, they consider "knowledge brokers" and their roles in disseminating good practice. Perhaps this role can be likened to that of a champion or hero innovator within a business in that they have roles in capturing, consolidating and disseminating which particular practices work. Their study shows that the use of these knowledge brokers has a significant impact on information and knowledge flows within the organisation, culminating in a more cross-functional approach. This improved flow will facilitate the transfer of knowledge to an organisational basis. They also conclude that the management of knowledge requires a sociotechnical focus to facilitate face-to-face communication and interaction instead of using technological mechanisms. They see knowledge management as an ongoing process of social interaction, supported but not dictated by technology.

Yi's work was undertaken with Motorola, a large car-component manufacturer, looking at a community of practice. A community of practice is an informal organisation that forms naturally within and across the boundaries of formal organisations. In terms of knowledge generation, human resources are seen as being at the heart of knowledge creation and dissemination, and human networks are seen as being of paramount importance. The focus is on the type of learning that is taking place within these informal organisations. Transformational learning is identified as a key and Yi looks at how this can happen in the informal set-up that characterises a community of practice. Another question addressed is that of how a community of practice creates value for members of the community and hence for the company. Analysis revolves around the organisation as an open system and adopts

The benefits of knowledge sharing outweigh the time and effort involved in doing this and a community of practice model needs to be used in strategically critical business areas as part of a corporate-wide knowledge strategy. A key to the success of the whole process is support, which enables the learning to take place.

a systems approach, which in turn leads to a sociotechnical approach with a dualism between the role of people and that of the technology. The community of practice development model addresses three processes: the individual learning and working processes, the community of practice life cycle, and the organisational support process. In order to facilitate the success of the model, it is acknowledged that expert resource is critical, and if this is forthcoming, then the social and individual networks will be expanded to the benefit of all those involved and the company.

Ericsson and Avdic's work looks at Scandinavian companies involved in manufacturing. The chapter considers information technology (IT) as an enabler for the acquisition and reuse of knowledge. They consider an IT-based information system as a medium of communication as well as a repository of knowledge. They are looking at how to achieve a goal where all individual knowledge is made available to the whole organisation. The method they propose is to use a three-step approach: collect, classify and evaluate. For the model to work, it is essential that core and business processes are explicit, and it is in this area that problems may occur, as not all knowledge is explicit: much is tacit and difficult to make explicit. The authors feel that an IT-based knowledge reuse prototype characterises a sociotechnical approach in that it deals with dependency on both the human and the technical aspects. They point out that participation, one of the cornerstones of good sociotechnical design, is a key factor in achieving success. They conclude that to design a system for reuse and acquisition of crucial knowledge in a manufacturing environment, principles need to be formulated that allow an IT-based information system which systemises knowledge of errors to avoid operational disturbances.

The final section deals with the "know-how" question. Here the discussion returns to a mainly UK-based approach, but with a contrasting aspect from Finland. Again, the work is based on case study, lending weight to the arguments produced.

Cuthbertson and Farrington's study relates to the UK Royal Navy. The culture in the UK armed forces is that job rotation takes place on a regular basis. In the case of the Royal Navy, it happens every two years. This leads to the potential for a great loss of accumulated knowledge. The authors are concerned with how to capture this knowledge and what type of strategy is most likely to lead to the required result. There is a prevalent culture in the Royal Navy, as the armed forces tend to attract particular personality types (which links back to the earlier work of Phillips and Patrick). Taking a soft systems approach, they progress to a knowledge audit and the development of a knowledge architecture. They conclude that the roles of people in the "know" technologies are integral to their success. Their methodology revolves around the use of a systemic process of enquiry. Their main precept is that if systems are to be effective, they must address human involvement: a strong sociotechnical argument.

Kazi, Puttonen, Sulkusalmi, Välikangas and Hannus worked with Fortum Engineering Ltd in Finland. Their premise is that organisational capital needs to be fully exploited to add value. An understanding of all aspects and constituents of knowledge is essential. They concentrate initially on a clarification of knowledge, of explicit and tacit knowledge and the relationship between them. They view explicit knowledge as the technical part of the system, with tacit knowledge forming the social part. The case study provides a vehicle for studying knowledge creation and management. They propose an interesting model which they refer to as the "palm tree model". They see knowledge management as an instrument contributing to and enabling better decision making. They define the principal asset in any organisation as knowledge which has been made available for reuse and exploitation by other members of the organisation in order to add value. Once again, the focus is on the individual and the balance or alignment between the social and technical aspects of the systems studied.

> The seeds or origins of knowledge are tacit (or unstructured); as knowledge becomes more structured, it moves along a linear model until it eventually becomes more highly structured and thence explicit.

Al-Karaghouli, Fitzgerald and Alshawi focus on a system to improve the understanding of requirements in UK systems design. The authors examine the culture gap which exists between IT and business in many organisations. Systems developers often fall into the technical arena. Further analysis of this culture differential leads to the examination of the knowledge gap and the understanding gap between the customer and the software developer. The authors acknowledge that some organisations try to put in place "seamless teams" incorporating both cultures and try for co-location of interested parties as a solution when looking for good systems design. The work requires a clear and adequate understanding of requirements which constitutes a sociotechnical approach. The importance of the human or social side of the equation must not be underestimated. If adequate systems are to be developed which meet the needs of the organisation, it is necessary that the human-to-human communication is right. No amount of technology can solve the problem if the initial understanding of requirements is incorrect. Knowledge requirements systems that generate knowledge and understanding between the customer and the software developers are of vital importance. The aspect of the sociotechnical approach stressed by this paper is that a knowledge requirements system works by the customer and developer engaging in this human-to-human interaction process and there is no substitute for this. The authors conclude that their knowledge requirements system, whilst not being a methodology, is an approach that will lead to better understanding between developers and customers.

In the final chapter, Coakes, Sugden, Russell, Canilleli and Bradburn examine tacit knowledge in two different knowledge-intensive firms. They look at the results of both of these investigations and draw parallels and conclusions about the similarities and differences. They look at the role of technology in knowledge management and the lack of ability of companies to collect, store and harness the value of experiences of employees. This is a theme which has occurred in many of the chapters so far, particularly those by Scholtz and Phillips and Patrick, and for whom these are key issues. The question for knowledge management systems is how to make tacit knowledge explicit. A technological solution of an intranet is not believed by the authors to be a true knowledge sharing system in that it tends to house the artefacts of knowledge, the company documents, rather than knowledge per se. The authors argue that an intelligent system is required if it is to be truly a knowledge management system. As previously argued, they feel that tacit knowledge is firmly embedded in social networks and communities and that this type of knowledge cannot be automated. It is thought to be problematic trying to leverage knowledge through IT systems, given the non-automated nature of tacit knowledge. This tacit knowledge may become formalised over time after being shared amongst group members. The authors believe that the best way to share knowledge revolves not around a technical solution, but within the people who work for the organisation, i.e. a sociotechnical approach. The role of technology is therefore firmly relegated to that of supporting knowledge management by managing files and retrieving documents, i.e. dealing with explicit, not tacit knowledge. It may be necessary to instil a culture of knowledge sharing, otherwise the tacit knowledge will not be shared widely enough to enable it to be formalised. A system of regularly debriefing staff and mentoring those new to the organisation can be a better and more productive way of sharing knowledge than investing in IT systems. Again, the sociotechnical themes of the balance between the human/social and technical sides of the system is paramount.

> Knowledge resides within individuals and knowledge management provides a system to enable sharing and reuse of that knowledge.

The recurrent themes have been the role of the individual, the nature of knowledge, the difficulties in capturing knowledge, the need for knowledge sharing and reuse, the problems with leveraging knowledge to add value and the need to have a balanced approach or alignment between the various parts of the system. Several new models have been developed each of which adds something different to the total body of knowledge and all of which take a sociotechnical perspective. The chapters all offer a valid sociotechnical angle on the knowledge management field and fit well into the framework offered by the first chapter in the book. Further research may include those countries not represented by this book that may have equally valuable contributions to make to the field.

16.1 Concluding Thoughts

On the commencement of this project, the objective was to source a variety of global contributions, which would represent the rapidly emerging domain of knowledge management, viewed from a sociotechnical perspective. That the success in this regard has exceeded all our expectations as editors is due entirely to the exceptionally high quality of the submissions received, and for this we are indebted to all contributors.

To cover such a domain in one text is, of course, an impossible task. All that can be hoped is that the book is representative of the issues currently seen to be important. In this respect, whilst accepting that we have chosen to represent knowledge management as a highly sociotechnical area, perhaps at times to the detriment of alternative viewpoints, we feel content that, with the aid of our contributors, we have largely succeeded.

The final verdict, however, must rest with you, the readers, and we will be happy to receive any comments which you feel may help in furthering our understanding of the domain. At the very least, with your help, the next compilation of edited chapters on this subject, which we fully intend to produce, will be representative of current practices and theories.

Please forward any comments to the editors.

References

Abram Hawkes plc (1999) Knowledge Management for Customers and Markets. http://www.abramhawkes.plc.uk (accessed June 1999).

Ahrne, G. (1994) *Social Organizations. Interaction Inside, Outside and Between Organizations*. London: Sage.

Alfred, Lord Tennyson (1842) *Locksley Hall* l. 141.

Al-Karaghouli, W., AlShawi, S. and Fitzgerald, G. (2000) Negotiating and Understanding Information Systems Requirement: The Use of Set Diagram. *Requirements Engineering* 5: 93–102.

Al-Karaghouli, W., Elstob, M. and AlShawi, S. (1999) An OR Approach to Establishing Software Engineering Requirements. *OR 41, Operational Research Society Annual Conference*, 14–16 September, Edinburgh, UK.

Allee, V. (1997) *The Knowledge Evolution. Expanding Organizational Intelligence*. Boston, MA: Butterworth-Heinemann.

Anderson, D.R. Sweeney, D.J. and Williams, T.A. (1995) *Quantitative Methods for Business*, 6th edn. New York: West Publishing Company.

Angell, I. (1998) The knowledge scam (knowledge management). *Information Strategy (UK)* 3(6): 23–26.

Appelbaum, S.H. and Gallagher, J. (2000) The competitive advantage of organizational learning. *Journal of Workplace Learning: Employee Counselling Today*, 12(2): 40–56.

Applehams, W., Globe, A. and Laugero, G (1999) *Managing Knowledge: A Practical Web-Based Approach*. Harlow: Addison-Wesley Information Technology Series.

APQC (1996) *Knowledge Management: Consortium Benchmarking Study*. Houston: American Productivity & Quality Center.

Argyris, C. and Schön, D.A. (1996a) *Organizational Learning: A Theory of Action Perspective*. Reading, MA: Addison-Wesley.

Argyris, C. and Schön D.A. (1996b) *Organizational Learning II – Theory, Method, and Practice*. London: Addison-Wesley.

Avdic, A. (1999) Användare och utvecklare – om anveckling med kalkylprogram. PhD Dissertation, Linköping University, Linköping.

Axelrod, R. (1997) *The Complexity of Co-operation, Agent Base Models of Co-operation and Collaboration*. Princeton, NJ: Princeton University Press

Badaracco, J. (1991) *The Knowledge Link: How Firms Compete Through Strategic Alliances*. Boston, MA: Harvard Business School Press.

Barnes, B. (1974) *Scientific Knowledge and Sociological Theory*. London: Routledge and Kegan Paul.

Bauer, M.W. and Aarts, B. (2000) Corpus Construction: A Principle for Qualitative Data Collection. In: Bauer, M.W. and Gaskell, G. (eds) *Qualitative Researching with Text, Image and Sound*. London: Sage, Chap. 2.

Bellinger, G. (1999) Knowledge Management. http://www.wolfson.ox.ac.uk/~floridi/kmgmt.htm (accessed June 1999).

Bennett, R. and Gabriel, H. (1999) Organisational factors and knowledge management within large marketing departments: an empirical study. *Journal of Knowledge Management* 3(3): 212–225.

Berger, P.L. and Luckmann, T. (1967) *The Social Construction of Reality. A Treatise in the Sociology of Knowledge*. London: Penguin Books.

Bielaczyc, K. and Collins, A. (1999) Learning Communities in Classrooms: A Reconceptualization of Educational Practice. In: Reigeluth, C.M. (ed.) *Instructional Design Theories and Models: A New Paradigm of Instructional Theory*. Mahwah, NJ: Erlbaum, Lawrence Associates.

Bijker, W.E. (1995) *Of Bicycle, Bakelites, and Bulbs: Toward a Theory of Sociotechical Change*. Cambridge, MA: MIT Press.

Bijker, W.E., Hughes, T. and Pinch, T.J. (1987) *The Social Construction of Technological Systems: New Directions in the Sociology of History and Technology*. Cambridge, MA: MIT Press.

Billig, M. (1988) *Ideological Dilemmas*. London: Sage.

Binney, D. (2001) The Knowledge Management Spectrum – Understanding the KM Landscape. *Journal of Knowledge Management* 5(2): 33–42.

Bjerknes, G. and Brattenberg, T. (1995) User Participation and Democracy: A Discussion of Scandinavian research on System Development. *Scandinavian Journal of Information Systems* 7(1): 73–98.

Bjørn-Andersen, N. and Hedberg, B. (1977) Design af informationssystemer i et organisatoriskt perspektiv. In: Borum, F. (ed) *Edb, arbetsmiljö og demokrati*. Aaby-Tryk, Denmark: Nyt fra samfundsvidensaberne: 45–64.

Blackler, F. (1995) Knowledge, Knowledge Work and Organizations: An Overview and Interpretation. *Organization Studies* 16(6): 1021–1046.

Blau, P. (1977) *Inequality and Heterogeneity: A Primitive Theory of Social Structure*. New York, NY: Free Press.

Blumentitt, R. and Johnston, R. (1999) Towards a Strategy for Knowledge Management. *Technology Analysis & Strategic Management* 11(3): 287–300.

Boisot, M. and Griffiths, D. (1999) Possession is Nine Tenths of the Law: Managing a Firm's Knowledge Base in a Regime of Weak Appropriability. *International Journal of Technology Management* 17(6): 662–676.

Boland, R.J. and Tenkasi, R.V. (1995) Perspective Making and Perspective Taking in Communities of Knowing. *Organization Science* 6(4): 350–372.

Bostrom, R.P. and Heinen, J.S. (1977a) MIS Problems and Failures: A Socio-Technical Perspective. Part I: The Causes. *Management Information Systems Quarterly* 2: 17–32.

Bostrom, R.P. and Heinen, J.S. (1977b) MIS Problems and Failures: A Socio-Technical Perspective. Part II: The Application of Socio-Technical Theory. *Management Information Systems Quarterly* 1(4): 11–28.

Botkin, J. (1999) *Smart Business*. New York, NY: Free Press.

Boyce, M. (1995) Collective Centring and Collective Sense-making in the Stories and Storytelling of One Organization. *Organization Studies* 16(1): 107–137.

Brooking, A. (1998) *Corporate Memory: Strategies for Knowledge Management (Intellectual Capital Series)*. London: International Thomson Business Press.

Brown, J.S. (1988) Research that Reinvents the Corporation. In: *Harvard Business Review on Knowledge Management*. Boston, MA: Harvard Business School Press: 153–179.

Brown, J. and Duguid, P. (1991) Organizational Learning and Communities-of-Practice: Toward a Unified View of Working, Learning, and Innovation. *Organization Science* 2(1): 40–57.

Bukowitz, W.R. and Williams, R.L. (1999) *The Knowledge Management Fieldbook*. Harlow: Financial Times/Prentice-Hall/Pearson Education.

Bustard, D.W., Dobbin, T.J., *et al.* (1995) Integrating Soft Systems and Object Oriented Analysis. *Proceedings ICRE '95* Colorado Springs: IEEE Press.

Cameron, K. and Tschirhart, M. (1992) Postindustrial environments and organisational effectiveness in colleges and universities. *Journal of Higher Education* 63(1): 87–108.

Camilleri, J.-P. (2000) *Knowledge Management Initiative – A Case Study*. MSc in Information Management and Finance Project. London: Westminster Business School, University of Westminster.

Carey, J.M. (1990) Prototyping: Alternative Systems Development Methodology. Arizona State University. *Information and Software Technology* 32(2): 119–126.

Carr, C. (1996) *Choice, Change and Organisational Change*. New York, NY: American Management Association.

Cavell, S. (1999) Salespeople Buck the System: Survey Finds Software Fails to Take Account of Culture. *Computing* 25 February: 16.

Checkland, P. (1981) *Systems Thinking, Systems Practice*. Chichester: John Wiley and Sons.

Checkland, P. and Holwell, S. (1998) *Information, Systems, and Information Systems: Making Sense of the Field*. Chichester: John Wiley and Sons.

Checkland, P. and Scholes, J. (1990) *Soft Systems Methodology in Action*. Chichester: John Wiley and Sons.

Checkland, P. and Scholes, J. (1997) *Soft Systems Methodology in Action*. Chichester: John Wiley and Sons.

Cherns, A. (1976) The Principles of Sociotechnical Design. *Human Relations* 29(8): 783–792.

Cherns A. (1987) Principles of Sociotechnical Design Revisited. *Human Relations* 40(3): 153–162.

Christensen, C. (1997) Making Strategy: Learning by Doing. *Harvard Business Review* 75(6): 141–156.

Ciborra, C. and Suetens, N. (1996) Groupware for an Emerging Virtual Organisation. In: Ciborra, C. (ed.) *Groupware and Teamwork*. Chichester: John Wiley.

Clark, B. (1998) *Creating Entrepreneurial Universities. Organisational Pathways of transformation.* Oxford: Elsevier.

Coakes, E. (2000) Knowledge Management: A Sociotechnical Perspective. Keynote Paper at OR42, Swansea.

Coakes, E. and Sugden, G. (2000a) Knowledge Management in the University Sector: Some Empirical Results. In: Khosrowpour, M. (ed.) *Challenges of Information Technology Management in the 21st Century.* Hershey: Idea: 1066–1067.

Coakes, E. and Sugden, G. (2000b) *Knowledge Management in the University Sector: Some Empirical Results.* Working Paper, University of Westminster, June.

Coakes, E. and Sugden, G. (2000c) The Learning Organisation and Knowledge Management: Research in Progress. University of Westminster Working Papers CS 149.6/00.

Coakes, E., Willis, D. and Lloyd-Jones, R. (eds) (2000) *The New SocioTech: Gratfiti on the Long Wall.* London: Springer.

Colins, H.M. (1982) *Sociology of Scientific Knowledge: A Source Book.* Bath: Bath University Press.

Colins, H.M. (1983) The Sociology of Scientific Knowledge: Studies of Contemporary Science. *Annual Review of Sociology* 9: 265–285.

Collins, J. (2000) Knowledge Management Focus: Keeping Pace with Knowledge. *Information World Review* February: 23–24.

Cooper, C.L. and Mumford, E. (1979) *The Quality of Working Life in Western and Eastern Europe.* London: Associated Business Press.

Covey, S. (1989) *The 7 Habits of Highly Effective People: Powerful Lessons in Personal Change.* New York, NY: Simon & Schuster.

CSC (1999) *CSC Catalyst – A Business Change Methodology* Boston, MA: Computer Sciences Corporation.

Czarniawska, B. (1998) *A Narrative Approach to Organizational Studies.* Vol. 43. Thousand Oaks, CA: Sage.

Czarniawska, B. and Joerges, B. (1996) Travels of Ideas. In: Czarniawska, B. and Sevón, G. (eds) *Translating Organizational Change.* Vol. 56. Berlin: de Gruyter: 13–48.

Daniels, I., Axelsen, M., Tucek, G. and Sharma, R. (1999) Knowledge Management: Using Computer Technology. *Australian CPA (Australia)* 69(7): 24–27.

Davenport, T.H. (1996) Why Reengineering Failed: The Fad that Forgot People. *Fast Company*, Premier Issue: 70–74.

Davenport, T.H. (1997) Ten Principles of Knowledge Management and Four Case Studies. *Knowledge and Process Management* 4(3): 187–208.

Davenport, T.H. (2000) Attention: The Next Information frontier. In: Marchand, D. Davenport, T. and Dickson, T. (eds) *Mastering Information Management.* Harlow: Financial Times/Prentice-Hall: 46–49.

Davenport, T. and De Long, D. (1997) Building Knowledge Management Projects. Working Paper, Ernst & Young Center for Business Innovation.

Davenport, T.H. and Prusak, L. (1998a) *Working Knowledge – How Organisations Manage What They Know.* Boston, MA: Harvard Business School Press.

Davenport, T. and Prusak, L. (1998b) Working Knowledge: Hire People Who Can Create Knowledge. *Executive Excellence* 15(9): 10.

De Board, R. (1978) *The Psychoanalysis of Organisations: A Psychoanalytic Approach to Behaviour in Groups and Organisations.* London: Routledge.

De Geus, A. (1997) *The Living Company.* Boston, MA: Harvard Business School Press.

De Jager, M. (1999) The KMAT: Benchmarking Knowledge Management. *Library Management* 20(7): 367–372.

Demarest, M. (1997) Understanding Knowledge Management. *Long Range Planning* 30(3): 374–384.

Dogdson, M. (1993) Organizational Learning: A Review of Some Literatures. *Organization Studies* **14**(3): 375–394.

Drucker, P.F. (1988) *The Coming of the New Oganization. Harvard Business Review on Knowledge Management*. Boston, MA: Harvard Business School Press: 1–19.

Drucker, P.F. (1993) *Post-Capitalist Society*. Oxford: Butterworth Heinemann.

Duffy, M. (1993) London's Embarrassing Mistake. *Wall Street and Technology Journal*.

Earl, M.J. (2000) Every Business is an Information Business. In: Marchand, D. Davenport, T. and Dickson, T. (eds) *Mastering Information Management*. Harlow: Financial Times/Prentice-Hall: 16–22.

Eckhouse, J. (1999) Executive Reports: Get Creative with Knowledge Sharing. Information Week Online 8 February 1999. http://www.informationweek.com/720/sharing.htm (accessed July 2000).

Edvinsson, L. and Malone, M.S. (1997a) *Intellectual Capital. The Proven Way to Establish Your Company's Real Value by Measuring its Hidden Brainpower*. London: Piatkus.

Edvinsson, L. and Malone, M.S. (1997b) *Intellectual Capital: Realizing Your Company's True Value by Finding its Hidden Brainpower*. 1st edn. New York, NY: HarperBusiness.

Ehrlich, K. (1999) Design of Groupware Applications: A Work-Centred Design Approach. In: Beaudoin-Lafon, M. (ed) *Computer Supported Cooperative Work*. Chichester: Wiley & Sons.

Eijnatten, F.M. van (1993) *The Paradigm the Changed the Workplace*. Stockholm/Assen: Arbetslivscentrum/Van Gorcum.

Eldon, M. (1979) Three Generations of Work Democracy Experiments in Norway: Beyond Classical Socio-technical System Design. In: Cooper, C.L. and Mumford, E. (eds) *The Quality of Working Life in Western and Eastern Europe*. London: Associated Business Press, Chap. 11.

Evans, P. and Wurster, T. (2000) *Blown to Bits: How the New Economics of Information Transforms Strategy*, Boston: Harvard Business School Press.

Faraj, S. and Sproull, L. (2001) Coordinating expertise in software development teams. *Management Science* (in press).

Feltus, A. (1994) Exploding the Myths of Benchmarking. *Continuous Journey* April. http://www.apqc.org/free/articles/dispArticle.cfm?ProductID=646 (01-07-2001).

Fielden, J. (1996) Report on UCT's Administrative Systems and Services, Accepted by UCT Executive 21/5/96. Unpublished Report, University of Cape Town.

Flick, U. (1998) *An Introduction to Qualitative Research*. London: Sage: Chaps 7–8.

Flood, G. (2000) Are Users Satisfiable? *Computing* 10 February: 11.

Flynn, L. and Goldsmith, R. (1999) A Short, Reliable Measure of Subjective Knowledge. *Journal of Business Research* **46**(1): 57–66.

FOLDOC (2000) Free Online Dictionary of Computing. http://foldoc.doc.ic.ac.uk/foldoc/ (accessed July 2000).

Follett, M. Parker (1920) *The New State*. London: Longmans.

Follett, M. Parker (1924) *Creative Experience*. London: Longmans.

Frappaolo, C. (1999) What You Know, Shapes Where You Go. *Knowledge Management Journal* July/August.

Fulk, J. (1993) Social construction of communication technology. *Academy of Management Journal* **36**(5): 921–950.

Garud, R. (1997) On the Distinction Between Know How, Know Why and Know What. In: Shrivastava, P. Huff, A.S. and Dutton, J.E. (eds) *Advances in Strategic Management*. Vol. 14. Greenwich, CT: JAI Press: 81–101.

Garvin, D. (1993) Building a Learning Organisation. *Harvard Business Review* 71, July–August: 78.

Garvin, D.A. (1998) Building a Learning Organization. In: *Harvard Business Review on Knowledge Management*. Boston, MA: Harvard Business School Press: 47–79.

Geisler, E. (1999) Harnessing the Value of Experience in the Knowledge-Driven Firm. *Business Horizons (USA)* **42**(3): 18–27.

Giddens, A. (1984a) *The Constitution of Society. Outline of the Theory of Structuration*. Cambridge: Polity Press.

Giddens, A. (1984b) *The Constitution of Society*. Berkeley, CA: University of California Press.

Goldkuhl, G. (1996) Generic Business Frameworks and Action Modelling. In: Dignum, D. (ed.) *Communication Modelling – The Language Action Perspective. Proceedings of the 2nd International*

Workshop on Communication Modelling. Computer Science Reports, Eindhoven University of Technology.

Goldkuhl, G. (1998) The Six Phases of Business Processes – Business Communication and the Exchange of Value. Presented at *Beyond Convergence: The 12th Biennial ITS Conference* (ITS '98), Stockholm, Jönköping International Business School.

Goldkuhl, G. (1999) *The Grounding of Usable Knowledge: An Inquiry in the Epistemology of Action Knowledge.* Accepted to HSS99, Falun; also working paper 99:03 CMTO, Linköping University.

Goldkuhl, G. and Ågerfalk, P.J. (2000) Actability: A Way to Understand Information Systems Pragmatics. Accepted to the 3rd International Workshop on Organisational Semiotics, Staffordshire University.

Goldkuhl, G. and Nilsson, E. (2000) Ökad IT-användning – vad händer med organisationers och människors förmåga? In: Lennerlöf, L. (ed.) *Avveckla eller utveckla – en antologi om verksamhetskonsekvenser i magra organisationer, Rådet för* Stockholm: Arbetslivsforskning. (In Swedish.)

Goodrum, D., Dorsey, L. and Schwen, T. (1993) Designing and Building an Enriched Learning and Information Environment. *Educational Technology* 33(11): 10–20.

Granovetter, M. (1985) Economic Action and Social Structure: The Problem of Embeddedness. *American Journal of Sociology* 91: 481–510.

Grant, R. (1996) Prospering in a Dynamically-competitive Environment: Organizational Capability as Knowledge Integration. *Organization Science* 7(4): 375–387.

Grant, R.M. (1997) The Knowledge-based View of the Firm: Implications for Management Practice. *Long Range Planning* 30(3): 450–454.

Greco, J. (1999) Knowledge is Power. *Journal of Business Strategy* March/April 20(2): 19–22.

Griffin, J.D. (1998) Dealing with the Paradox of Culture in Management Theory. PhD Thesis, University of Hertfordshire.

Grint, K. and Woolgar, S. (1997) *The Machine at Work: Technology, Work and Organization.* Oxford: Polity Press.

Groom, B. (2000) Blair's e-Envoy to Oversee Strategy for IT. *Financial Times* 22 May: 4.

Guns, B. and Anandsen, K. (1996) *The Faster Learning Organization.* Johannesburg/London: Pfeiffer.

Guthrie, J. and Petty, R. (1999) Knowledge Management: The Information Revolution has Created the Need for a Codified System of Gathering and Controlling Knowledge. *Company Secretary* 9(1): 38–41.

Hansen, M.T. (1999) The Search-transfer Problem: The Role of Weak Ties in Sharing Knowledge Across Organization Subunits. *Administrative Science Quarterly* 44: 82–111.

Hansen, M.T., Nohria, N. and Tierney, T. (1999) What's your Strategy for Managing Knowledge? *Harvard Business Review* 77(2): 108–116.

Harlam, B. and Lodish, L. (1995) Modelling Consumers' Choices of Multiple Items. *Journal of Marketing Research* 32(4): 404–418.

Hildreth, P., Kimble, C. and Wright, P. (2000) Communities of Practice in the Distributed International Environment. *MCB Journal of Knowledge Management* 4(1): 13.

Hill, C. (1999) APQC Benchmarking Report – Benchmarking Benchmarking: Shared Learnings for Excellence. www.store.apqc.org

Hopper, M.D. (1990) Rattling SABRE – New Ways to Compete on Information. *Harvard Business Review* 68 (May–June): 118–125.

Howard, A. (1999) Viewpoint: As IT Increasingly Dominates the World, Developers Need a Touch More Humility. *Computing* 11 March: 38.

http://hsb/baylor.edu/ramsower/acis/papers/nosek2.htm (accessed 14 October 1996).

Huber, G. (1991) Organizational Learning: The Contributing Processes and the Literatures. *Organization Science* 2(1, February): 88–116.

Hutchins, E. (1995) *Cognition in the Wild.* Boston, MA: MIT Press.

Ishikawa, K. (1983) *Guide to Quality Control.* 11th Printing. Tokyo: Asian Productivity Organisation: 26–28.

Jacobs, R.W. (1994) *Real Time Strategic Change.* San Francisco, CA: Berrett-Koehler.

Janis, I.L. (1972) *Victims of Groupthink.* Boston, MA: Houghton-Mifflin.

Katsioloudes, M.I. (1996) Socio-technical Analysis: A Normative Model for Participatory Planning. *Human Systems Management* 15: 235–244.

Kavanagh, J. (1998) IT Departments Don't Learn the Art of Teamwork. *The Times* (Inter//face//) 2 December: 3.

Kazi, A.S., Hannus, M. and Charoenngam, C. (1999) An Exploration of Knowledge Management for Construction. In: Hannus, M., Salonen, M. and Kazi, A.S. (eds) *Concurrent Engineering in Construction: Challenges for the New Millennium.* Vol. 236. Helsinki: CIB: 247–256.

Kelly, L. (2000) Let Projects Fail Says Think Tank: The Government Needs to Learn From Its Mistakes. *Computing Public Sector Digest* January: 4.

Klavans, R. and Deeds, D. (1997) Competence Building in Biotechnology Start-ups: The Role of Scientific Discovery, Technical Development, and Absorptive Capacity. In: Sanchez, R. and Heene, A. (eds) *Strategic Learning and Knowledge Management.* Chichester: John Wiley.

Klein, L. Bayswater Institute. http://bprc.warwick.ac.uk/focus4.htm (21 December 1999).

Kleiner, A. and Roth, G. (1998) How to Make Experience Your Company's Best Teacher. In: *Harvard Business Review on Knowledge Management.* Boston, MA: Harvard Business School Press: 137–151.

Knowledge Based Businesses (KBB) (1999) Ernst & Young. http://www.ey.com/consulting/kbb/glossary.asp (accessed June 1999).

KNOWNET: Knowledge Network Project. http://www.know-net.org (accessed June 1999). http://cordis.lu/esprit/src/28928.htm (accessed July 2000).

Kogut, B. and Zander, U. (1996) What Do Firms Do? Coordination, Identity, and Learning. *Organization Science* 7(5): 502–518.

Kolb, D.A. (1984) *Experiential Learning: Experience as the Source of Learning and Development.* Englewood Cliffs, NJ: Prentice-Hall.

Kolb, D.A., Boyatzis, R. and Mainemelis, C. (1999) *Experiential Learning Theory: Previous Research and New Directions.* Working Paper WP 99–9. Cleveland, OH: Weatherhead School of Management, Case Western Reserve University.

Kotonya, G. and Sommerville, I. (1998) *Requirements Engineering: Processes and Techniques.* Chichester: John Wiley and Sons.

KPMG Management Consulting (1997) The Knowledge Journey: A Business Guide to Knowledge Systems. http: www.kpmg.co.uk 20 October 2000.

KPMG Management Consulting (1998) Knowledge Management Report. http: www.kpmg.co.uk 20 October 2000.

Krogh, G. (1998) Care in Knowledge Creation. *California Management Review* 40(3): 133–153.

Krogh, G., Ichijo, K. and Nonaka, I. (2000) *Enabling Knowledge Creation.* New York, NY: Oxford University Press.

Lam, A. (1997) Embedded Firms, Embedded Knowledge: Problems of Collaboration and Knowledge Transfer in Global Cooperative Ventures. *Organization Studies* 18(6): 973–996.

Lank, E. (1997) Leveraging Invisible Assets: The Human Factor. *Long Range Planning* 30(3): 406–412.

Larsen, H.H. (1979) Humanisation of the Work Environment in Denmark. In: Cooper, C.L. and Mumford, E. (eds) *The Quality of Working Life in Western and Eastern Europe.* London: Associated Business Press: Chap. 7.

Latour, B. (1987) *Science in Action: How to Follow Scientists and Engineers Through Society.* Milton Keynes: Open University Press.

Latour, B. (1992) Technology is Society made Durable. In: Law (ed.) *A Sociology of Monsters: Essays on Power, Technology and Domination.* London: Routledge and Kegan Paul: 196–233.

Laudon, K.C. and Laudon, J.P. (2000) *Management Information Systems: Organisation and Technology in the Networked Enterprise.* 6th edn (slides). Englewood Cliffs, NJ: Prentice-Hall.

Lave, J. and Wenger, E. (1990) *Situated Learning: Legitimate Peripheral Participation.* Palo Alto, CA: Institute for Research in Learning.

Lave, J. and Wenger, E. (1991) *Situated Learning: Legitimate Peripheral Participation.* Cambridge: Cambridge University Press.

Lawrence, P. and Lorsch, J. (1967) *Organisation and Environment: Managing Differentiation and Integration.* Boston, MA: Harvard University Press.

Leavitt, H.J. (1964) *Managerial Psychology: An Introduction to Individuals, Pairs, and Groups in Organizations.* Chicago, IL: University of Chicago Press.

Leavitt, H.J. (1970) Applied Organization Change in Industry. In: Vroom, V.H. and Deci, E.L. (eds) *Management and Motivation: Selected Readings.* Harmondsworth: Penguin.

Lee, D.M.S. (1994) Social Ties, Task-related Communication and First Job Performance of Young Engineers. *Journal of Engineering and Technology Management* 11(3): 203–208.

Lee, M.S., Trauth, E.M. and Farwell, D. (1995) Critical Skills and Knowledge Requirements of IS Professionals: A Joint Academic/Industry Investigation. *Management Information Systems Quarterly* September: 313–337.

Leidner, D.E. (1999) Information Technology and Organizational Culture. In: Galliers, R.D. Leidner, D.E. and Baker, B.S.H. (eds) *Strategic Information Management*. Oxford: Butterworth Heinemann: 523–550.

Lembke, S. and Wilson, M. (1998) Putting the "Team" into Teamwork: Alternative Theoretical Contributions for Contemporary Management Practice. *Human Relations* 51(7): 927–944.

Leonard, D. (1999) *Wellsprings of Knowledge – Building and Sustaining the Sources of Innovation*. Boston, MA: Harvard Business School Press.

Levine, F., Locke, C., Searls, D. and Weinberger, D. (2000) *The Cluetrain Manifesto*. London: Pearson.

Levine, J.M., Resnick, L.B. and Higgins, E.T. (1993) Social Foundation of Cognition. *Annual Review of Psychology* 44: 585–612.

Liang, D.W., Moreland, R. and Argote, L. (1995) Group Versus Individual Training and Group Performance: The Mediating Role of Transactive Memory. *Personality and Social Psychology Bulletin* 21(4): 384–393.

Liebenau, J. and Backhouse, J. (1990) *Understanding the Information*. New York: MacMillan.

Lipnack, J. and Stamps, J. (1997) *Virtual Teams. Reaching Across Space, Times, and Organizations with Technology*. New York, NY: John Wiley & Sons.

List, B. (1999) Managing Software Development and Maintenance. *OR/MS Today* February: 69.

Louis Harris International (1974) *Qualitative Research into Shopping Motivations*. London: Louis Harris International.

Louis, M.R. (1980) Surprise and Sense Making: What New-comers Experience in Entering Unfamiliar Organizational Settings. *Administrative Science Quarterly* 25: 226–251.

McAdam, R. and McCreedy, S. (1999) A critical review of knowledge management models. *Learning Organization* 6(3): 91–100.

McDermott, R. (1999) Why Information Technology Inspired but Cannot Deliver Knowledge Management. *California Management Review* 41(4): 103–117.

McGill, I. and Beaty, L. (1995) *Action Learning*. London: Kogan Page.

McLoughlin, I. (1999) *Creative Technological Change: The Shaping of Technology and Organisations*. London: Routledge.

Madhavan, R. and Grover, R. (1998) From the Embedded Knowledge to Embodied Knowledge: New Product Development as Knowledge Management. *Journal of Marketing* 62(4): 1–12.

Magalhães, R. (1998) Organisational Knowledge and Learning. In: Krogh, G. van, Roos, J. and Kleine, D. (eds) *Knowing in Firms: Understanding, Managing and Measuring Knowledge*. London: Sage: 87–122.

Mandl, H. and Reinmann-Rothmeier, G. (1999) Developing Learning Communities in Companies – A Pilot Study on Knowledge Management. Paper Presented at EARLI 1999 Symposium, Göteborg, Sweden, August.

March, J. (1991) Exploration and Exploitation in Organizational Learning. *Organizational Science*, 2(1): 71–87.

Matusik, S. and Hill, C. (1998) The Utilization of Contingent Work, Knowledge Creation, and Competitive Advantage. *Academy of Management Review* 23(4): 680–697.

Meriam-Webster online dictionary. http://www.m-w.com (accessed on July 2000).

Messinger, P. and Narasimhan, C. (1997) A Model of Retail Formats Based on Consumer's Economizing on Shopping Time. *Marketing Science* 16(1): 1–23.

Miller, G. (1968) *The Psychology of Communication*. London: Penguin Press.

Mirl, E. (1998) Management Change in a Socio-technical Environment. http://www.nemonline.org/mirl/ec/change.htm

Moorman, C. and Miner, A. (1997) The Impact of Organizational Memory on New Product Performance and Creativity. *Journal of Marketing Research* 34(1): 91–106.

Moreland, R.L. (1999) Transactive Memory: Learning Who Knows What in Work Groups and Organizations. In: Thompson, L.L., Levine, J.M. and Messick, D.M. (eds) *Shared Cognition in Organizations*. Vol. 3–31. Hillsdale, NJ: Lawrence Erlbaum Associates.

Moreland, R.L., Argote, L. and Krishnan, R. (1996) Socially Shared Cognition at Work: Transactive

Memory and Group Performance. In: Nye, J. and Brower, A. (eds) *What's Social about Social Cognition? Research on Socially Shared Cognition in Small Groups*. Thousand Oaks, CA: Sage.

Morgan, G. (1986) *Images of Organization*. Newbury Park, CA: Sage.

Mumford, E. (1983) *Designing Human Systems, The ETHICS Approach*. Manchester: Manchester Business School.

Mumford, E. (1984a) *Designing Human Systems for New Technology: The ETHICS Method*. Manchester: Manchester Business School.

Mumford, E. (1984b) Participation – From Aristotle to Today. In: Bemelmans, T. (ed.) *Beyond Productivity: Information Systems Development for Organizational Effectiveness*. Amsterdam: North Holland.

Mumford, E. (1985a) Defining System Requirements to Meet Business Needs: A Case Study Example. *Computer Journal* **28**(2): 97–104.

Mumford, E. (1995b) Book Review of Hammer, M. and Champy J. Reengineering the Corporation: A Manifesto for Business Revolution. *European Journal of Information Systems* **4**: 116–120.

Mumford, E. (1995c) *Effective Systems Design and Requirements Analysis – The ETHICS Approach*. London: MacMillan Press.

Mumford, E. (1996) Designing for Freedom in a Technical World. In: Orlikowski, W. Walsham, G. Jones, M. and DeGross, J. (eds) *Information Technology and Changes in Organisational Work*. London: Chapman and Hall.

Mumford, E. (1997) Assisting Work Restructuring in Complex and Volatile Situations. In: Neumann, J.E. and Kellner, K. (eds) *Developing Organisational Consultancy*. London: Routledge.

Mumford, E. and Weir, M. (1979) *Computer Systems in Work Design – The ETHICS Method*. London: Associated Business Press.

Murray, P.C. (1999) New Language for New Leverage: The Terminology of Knowledge Management. http://www.ktic.com/topic6 (accessed June 1999).

Nahapiet, J. and Ghoshal, S. (1998) Social Capital, Intellectual Capital, and the Organizational Advantage. *Academy of Management Review* **23**(2): 242–266.

Nelson, R.R. and Winter, S.G. (1982) *An Evolutionary Theory of Economic Change*. Cambridge, MA: Belknap Press.

Nonaka, I. (1991) The Knowledge-creating Company. *Harvard Business Review* **6**(8): 96–104.

Nonaka, I. (1998) The Knowledge-creating Company. In: *Harvard Business Review on Knowledge Management*. Boston, MA: Harvard Business School Press: 21–45.

Nonaka, I. and Konno, N. (1999) The Concept of 'Ba': Building a Foundation for Knowledge Creation. *California Management Review* **40**(3): 40–54.

Nonaka, I. and Takeuchi, H. (1995) *The Knowledge-creating Company*. Oxford: Oxford University Press.

Norman, D.A. (1998) *The Invisible Computer: Why Good Products can Fail, the Personal Computer is so Complex, and Information Appliances are the Answer*. Cambridge, MA: MIT Press.

Nosek, J.T. and Grillo, P. (1996) Expanding Organizational Transactive Memory Asynchronously: The Effect of Expertise. Nosek@cis.temple.edu.

Nurminen, M.I. (1987) In: Randall Whitaker (ed.) *Historical Background to CSCW and Groupware: Attention to Team-level Work Organisation (The Socio-Technical Tradition)*. http://www.informatik.umu.se/%7erwhit/SocioTechnical.html (13 May 2000).

Nurminen, M.I. (1988) *People or Computers: Three Ways of Looking at Information Systems*. Lund: Studentlitteratur.

Nuseibeh, B. (1996) Building Bridges: On the Development of Complex Software. *Computer Bulletin-BCS* **8**(4): 18–19.

O'Dell, C. and Grayson, C. (1998) *If Only We Knew What We Know*. New York, NY: Free Press.

O'Dell, C. and Grayson, C.J. (1999) If Only We Knew What We Know: Identification and Transfer of Internal Best Practices. *California Management Review* **40**(3): 154–174.

O'Dell, C., Wiig, K. and Odem, P. (1999) Benchmarking Unveils Emerging Knowledge Management Strategies. *Benchmarking: An International Journal* **6**(3): 202–211.

Orr, J. (1990) *Talking about Machines: An Ethnography of Modern Job*. New York, NY: Cornell University.

Pan, S.L. and Scarbrough, H. (1999) Knowledge Management in Practice: An Exploratory Case Study of Buckman Labs. *Technology Analysis and Strategic Management* **11**(3): 359–374.

Parsons, T. (1968) Social Systems. *Encyclopaedia of the Social Sciences* 15: 458–472.

Pasmore, W. and Sherwood (eds) (1978). *Sociotechical Systems: A Sourcebook*. La Jolla, CA: University Associates.

Pasmore, W.A. (1988) *Designing Effective Organisations: The Sociotechnical Systems Perspective*. New York, NY: John Wiley & Sons.

Pemberton, J.D. and Stonehouse, G.H. (2000) Organisational Learning and Knowledge Assets – An Essential Partnership. *Learning Organization* 7(4): 184–193.

Phillips, N. and Patrick, K. (2000) Knowledge Management Perspectives, Organisational Character and Cognitive Style. *Proceedings KMAC 2000*, 6–19 July, Operational Research Society.

Pinch, T. and Bijker, W. (1987) The Social of Facts and Artifacts: Or How the Sociology of Science and the Sociology of Technology might Benefit each Other. In: Bijker, W., Hughes, T. and Pinch, T. (eds) *The Social Construction of Technological Systems: New Directions in the Sociology of History and Technology* Cambridge, MA: MIT Press.

Pisano, G. (1994) Knowledge, Integration, and the Locus of Learning: An Empirical Analysis of Process Development. *Strategic Management Journal* 15 (Special Issue): 85–100.

Platts, M.J. and Yeung, M.B. (2000) Managing Learning and Tacit Knowledge. *Strategic Change (UK)* 9(6): 347–356.

Polanyi, M. (1962) *Personal Knowledge*. New York, NY: Anchor Day Books.

Polanyi, M. (1966) *The Tacit Dimension*. New York, NY: Doubleday.

Polanyi, M. (1983) *The Tacit Dimension*. Gloucester, MA: Peter Smith.

Powers, V.J. (1995) Sprint Corporation: Blending in Benchmarking with Quality. *Continuous Journey* 1995(Jan). http://www.apqc.org/free/articles/dispArticle.cfm?ProductID=650 (01-07-2001).

Prahalad, C.K. and Hamel, G. (1990) The Core Competence of the Corporation. *Harvard Business Review* 68(3, May–June): 79–91.

Preece, J. (1994) *Human–Computer Interaction*. Harlow: Addison-Wesley.

Price Waterhouse (1991, 1992) The Culture Gap. *Information Technology Review* 16–19.

Quinn, J.B., Anderson, P. and Finkelstein, S. (1998) Managing Professional Intellect: Making the Most of the Best. In: *Harvard Business Review on Knowledge Management*. Boston, MA: Harvard Business School Press: 181–205.

Quintas, P., Lefrere, P. and Jones, G. (1997) Knowledge Management: A Strategic Agenda. *Long Range Planning* 30(3): 385–392.

Ranger, S. (2000) IT Blunders Under the Microscope: CSSA to Investigate Why Public Sector IT Projects Fail. *Computing Public Sector Digest* January: 3.

Rayport, J.F. (2000) Information Resources: Don't Attract, Addict. In: Marchand, D. Davenport, T. and Dickson, T. (eds) *Mastering Information Management*. Harlow: Financial Times/Prentice-Hall: 42–45.

Resnick, L.B. and Williams Hall, M. (1998) Learning Organizations for Sustainable Education Reform. *Daedalus* 127(4): 89–118.

Riding, R. and Rayner, S. (1999) *Cognitive Style and Learning Strategies: Understanding Style Differences in Learning and Behaviour*. David Fulton.

RNSETT Website (1999) Commanders Statement. http://www.royal-navy.mod.uk/today/rnsett/index.htm

Roth, G. (1999) IT and the Challenge of Organisational Learning. *Financial Times Supplement. Innovation and the Learning Organisation* Part 10, 5 April.

Russell, S. (2000) *What Does it Mean to Manage Tacit Knowledge in an organisation?* MSc in Business Information Systems Project, Royal Holloway, University of London, School of Management and Department of Computer Science.

Sabbagh, D. (1999) User Behaviour is Key, Says Revenue: Difficulties in Forecasting Tax System. *Computing* 10 June: 18.

Sanghera, S. (1999) New Directions with Radar. *Financial Times* 21 April: 21.

Scarbrough, H., Swan, J. and Preston, J. (eds) (1999) *Knowledge Management: A Literature Review*. London: Institute of Personnel and Development.

Scholtz, V. (1999) An Examination of IT Resources, Competencies and Use in the Humanities Faculty, UCT, 1999. Unpublished report, University of Cape Town, October.

Schutz, A. (1962) *Collected Paper I: The Problem of Social Reality*. The Hague: Martinus Nijhoff.

Scott, J. (1991) *Social Network Analysis: A Handbook*. London: Sage.

Scott, R.W. (1995) *Institutions and Organizations.* Thousand Oaks, CA: Sage.

Scott, R.W. (1998) *Organizations: Ration, Natural and Open Systems.* 4th edn. Englewood Cliffs, NJ: Prentice-Hall.

Searle, J.R. (1998) *Mind, Language, and Society.* New York, NY: Basic Books.

Seemann, P. and Cohen, D. (1997) The Geography of Knowledge: From Knowledge Maps to Knowledge Atlas. *Knowledge and Process Management* 4(4): 247–260.

Senge, P.M (1990) *The Fifth Discipline: The Art and Practice of the Learning Organisation.* London: Century Business.

Senge, P.M., Kleiner, A., Roberts, C., Ross, R., Roth, G. and Smith, B. (1999) The Dance of Change – The Challenges of Sustaining Momentum in Learning Organizations – A Fifth Discipline Resource. 1st edn. New York, NY: Doubleday/Currency.

Shattock, M. (2000) March Report on Governance and Related Management Issues: Refocusing the Machinery to Match the University's Mission. Unpublished Report, University of Cape Town.

Sieloff, C.G. (1999) If Only HP Knows What HP Knows: The Roots of Knowledge Management at Hewlett-Packard. *Journal of Knowledge Management* 3(1): 47–53.

Simon, H.A. (1991) Bounded Rationality and Organizational Learning. *Organization Science* 2(1): 125–134.

Skyrme, D.J. (1997) From Information to Knowledge Management: Are You Prepared? *Information Age* 1(20): 16–18.

Skyrme, D. (1998) *Measuring the Value of Knowledge: Metrics for the Knowledge-based Business.* London: Business Intelligence. UK.

Skyrme, D. and Amidon, D. (1997) *Creating the Knowledge-based business.* London: Business Intelligence.

Slaughter, S. and Leslie, L. (1997) *Academic Capitalism. Politics, Policies and the Entrepreneurial University.* Baltimore, MD: Johns Hopkins University Press.

Smith, M. (1991) *Software Prototyping – Adaptation, Practice and Management.* London: McGraw-Hill.

Sommerville, I. (1992) *Software Engineering.* Reading, MA: Addison-Wesley.

Spender, J.-C. (1996) Making Knowledge the Basis of a Dynamic Theory of the Firm. *Strategic Management Journal,* Winter Special Issue 17: 45–62.

Spender, J.-C. (1998) The Dynamics of Individual and Organizational Knowledge. In: Eden, C. and Spender, J.-C. (eds) *Managerial and Organizational Cognition.* London: Sage: 56–73.

Stamps, D. (1997) Communities of Practice. *Training* February: 34–42.

Starbuck, W. (1992a) Learning by Knowledge Intensive Firms. In: Prusak, L. (ed.) *Knowledge in Organisations.* Oxford: Butterworth-Heinemann: 147–175.

Starbuck, W. (1992b) Learning by Knowledge-intensive Firms. *Journal of Management Studies* 29(6): 713–740.

Stonehouse, G.H. and Pemberton, J.D. (1999) Learning and Knowledge Management in the Intelligent Organisation. *Participation and Empowerment: An International Journal* 7(5): 131–140.

Sturt, T. (2000) These Craz-e Days: Can the Right ejargon Turn You into a Guru? *Computing* 10 February: 80.

Svieby, K. (1997) *The New Organisational Wealth: Managing and Measuring Knowledge-based Assets.* San Francisco, CA: Berrett Koehler.

Swan, J. (1999) Introduction. In: Scarbrough, J. and Swan, J. (eds) *Case Studies in Knowledge Management.* London: Institute of Personnel and Development: 1–12.

Taylor, D. (1998) Knowledge Management – Hot Button or Hot Air? *Computer Weekly* 2 July: 26.

Teece, D.J. (1998) Capturing Value from Knowledge Assets. *California Management Review* 40(3): 55–79.

Teece, D., Pisano, G. and Shuen, A. (1997) Dynamic Capabilities and Strategic Management. *Strategic Management Journal* 18(7): 509–533.

Tenkasi, R. and Boland, R., Jr (1996) Exploring Knowledge Diversity in Knowledge Intensive Firms: A New Role for Information Systems. *Journal of Organizational Change Management* 9(1): 79–91.

Tissen, R., Andriessen, D. and Deprez, F.L. (1998) *Value-based Knowledge Management: Creating the 21st Century Company: Knowledge Intensive, People Rich.* The Netherlands: Addison Wesley Longman.

Tiwana, A. (1998) What Truly Comprises a Knowledge Management Technology? E-mail to ISWORLD@LISTSERV.HEANET.I.E 2 December.

Trist, E.L. and Bamford, K.W. (1951) Some Social and Psychological Consequences of the Longwall Method of Coal-getting. *Human Relations* 4(1): 6–24, 37–38.

Tsoukas, H. (1996) The Firm as a Distributed Knowledge System: A Constructionist Approach. *Strategic Management Journal* 17: 11–25.

Walsh, J.P. (1995) Managerial and Organizational Cognition: Notes from a Trip down Memory Lane. *Organization Science* 6: 280–321.

Weerakkody, V. and Hinton C.M. (1999) Exploiting Information Systems and Technology Through Business Process Improvement. *Knowledge and Process Management* 6(1): 17–23.

Weick, K. (1995) *Sensemaking in Organizations*. Newbury Park, CA: Sage.

Weick, K.E. and Roberts, K.H. (1993) Collective Mind in Organizations: Heedful Interrelating on Flight Decks. *Administrative Science Quarterly* 38: 357–381.

Weizenbaum, J. (1976) Computer Power and Human Reason. San Fransisco, CA: Freeman.

Wenger, E. (1998) *Communities of Practice: Learning, Meaning, and Identity*. Cambridge: Cambridge University Press.

Wenger, E. (1999) Communities of Practice: The Key to Knowledge Strategy. Unpublished Manuscript, North San Juan, CA.

Wiig, K. (1995) *Knowledge Management Methods – Practical Approaches to Managing Knowledge*. Vol. 3. Arlington, TX: Schema Press.

Wiig, K. (1997) Knowledge Management: Where Did it Come From and Where Did it Go? *Expert Systems With Applications* 13(1): 1–14.

Wiig, K., Hoog, R. de and Spek, R. van der (1997) Supporting Knowledge Management: A Selection of Methods and Techniques. *Expert Systems With Applications* 13(1): 15–27.

Index

Action learning 2, 106, 108, 109
Agent-based model 67,69,70, 73,74,76,201

Best practice 21,63,82,98,101,102,103,109,115, 119, 140, 147, 160,164,
Business culture 171
Business processes 32, 94, 95, 96, 97, 99, 101, 102, 121, 122, 123, 124, 125, 126, 127, 129, 130, 142, 150, 155, 160, 169, 181, 202

Codification 21, 32, 134
Cognitive style 68, 73
Community of practice 105, 107, 108, 109, 113, 116, 117, 202
Congruence 2, 7, 13, 40, 41, 199
Content knowledge 62, 63
Core processes 121, 122, 124, 125, 126
CRE *see* Customer Requirements Engineering
Cultural norms 197
Customer requirements engineering 174

Decision making 41, 44, 77, 100, 102, 153, 154, 155, 159, 186, 204
Distributed knowledge system 53

Electronic discussion forum 83
Embedded knowledge 186
Evaluation 8, 31, 111, 200
Experiential learning 58
Expert networks 45
Explicit knowledge 1, 21, 32, 45, 77, 80, 83, 84, 148, 155, 156, 157, 161, 163, 164, 165, 166, 167, 186, 187, 193, 194, 204

Group formation 68, 76
Groups 25, 27, 43, 54, 59, 63, 67, 68, 72, 73, 74, 75, 76, 79, 80, 86, 94, 95, 102, 107, 109, 116, 118, 133, 143, 171, 186, 191, 197, 200, 201

Human factors 108

Individual knowledge 39, 54, 77, 78, 79, 83, 87
Information flow 113
Information systems 1, 2, 10, 38, 52, 67, 80, 94, 95, 96, 102, 121, 122, 123, 129, 130, 135, 149, 170, 187
Institutionalised knowledge 34, 37, 38, 38, 40, 41

KMS *see* Knowledge Management System
Knowledge acquisition 86, 101, 121, 122
Knowledge architecture 150, 203
Knowledge audit 146, 149, 150, 203
Knowledge brokers 97, 98, 99, 103, 202
Knowledge capture 154, 161, 173
Knowledge community 107
Knowledge conversion 32, 148, 157, 158
Knowledge creation 24, 52, 105, 147, 153, 166, 167, 200
Knowledge enablers 153, 160, 164, 166
Knowledge gap 171, 174, 204
Knowledge management 1, 2, 3, 4, 6, 10, 11, 12, 14, 17, 18, 19
Knowledge Management Spectrum 18, 19, 20, 22, 23, 24, 25, 27, 28, 199
Knowledge management strategy 18, 62, 78, 82, 139, 141, 142, 145
Knowledge maps 86
Knowledge processes 47, 153, 160, 164
Knowledge profiling 146, 147
Knowledge Requirement System 170, 173, 174, 177, 178
Knowledge reuse 123, 134, 160, 203
Knowledge sharing 3, 37, 57, 80, 82, 83, 85, 86, 88, 94, 96, 97, 100, 102, 103, 106, 107, 108, 109, 110, 111, 112, 113, 119, 120, 142, 158, 161, 191, 197, 203, 205
Knowledge storage 80, 166
Knowledge transfer 1, 45, 73, 77, 79, 82, 84, 85, 86, 88, 108
Knowledge worker 21, 43, 46, 48, 49, 143, 144, 146, 147, 156, 159, 163, 164, 165, 166, 167, 188
Knowledge-based culture 81, 83, 85, 88, 89
Knowledge-centric 2, 77, 78, 80, 81, 82, 84, 85, 88
Knowledge-intensive 185
KRS *see* Knowledge Requirement System

Learning styles 59, 60

Management science 179
Migratory knowledge 186
Modes of learning 68

Organisational ability 30, 33, 34, 36, 37, 38, 41
Organisational change 14, 40, 170, 199
Organisational knowledge 11, 40, 77, 79, 94, 100, 101, 102, 103, 141, 193, 194, 201

Out of Print Titles

Dan Diaper and Colston Sanger
CSCW in Practice
3-540-19784-2

Steve Easterbrook (ed.)
CSCW: Cooperation or Conflict?
3-540-19755-9

John H. Connolly and Ernest A. Edmonds (eds)
CSCW and Artificial Intelligence
3-540-19816-4

Mike Sharples (ed.)
Computer Supported Collaborative Writing
3-540-19782-6

Duska Rosenberg and Chris Hutchison (eds)
Design Issues in CSCW
3-540-19810-5

Peter Thomas (ed.)
CSCW Requirements and Evaluation
3-540-19963-2

John H. Connolly and Lyn Pemberton (eds)
Linguistic Concepts and Methods in CSCW
3-540-19984-5

Alan Dix and Russell Beale (eds)
Remote Cooperation
3-540-76035-0

Stefan Kirn and Gregory O'Hare (eds)
Cooperative Knowledge Processing
3-540-19951-9